Making the Most of Retirement

FOR

DUMMIES®

Making the Most of Retirement

FOR DUMMIES®

by Julienne Garland

WILEY

Wiley Publishing Australia Pty Ltd

Making the Most of Retirement For Dummies®

published by
Wiley Publishing Australia Pty Ltd
42 McDougall Street
Milton Qld 4064
www.dummies.com

Copyright © 2009 Wiley Publishing Australia Pty Ltd

The moral rights of the author have been asserted.

National Library of Australia
Cataloguing-in-Publication data

Author:	Garland, Julienne.
Title:	Making the Most of Retirement For Dummies / Julienne Garland.
ISBN:	978 0 7314 0939 6 (pbk.)
Notes:	Includes index.
Subjects:	Retirement — Planning.
Dewey Number:	646.79

Cover images: © Uppercut Images (front) and © Digital Vision (back)

Printed in China by
Printplus Limited

10 9 8 7 6 5 4 3 2 1

About the Author

Julienne (Julie) Garland worked as an adult educator until she retired and began to enjoy her new life as a frustrated golfer, grandma, traveller and writer.

Her role as an educator saw her working in neighbourhood houses and other adult education centres, TAFE colleges, migrant education centres, universities and industry. She helped establish writing and publishing groups for beginning writers, and wrote curricula and communication skills manuals for TAFE.

Much of Julie's work involved helping people whose worlds had changed because of retirement, redundancy, marital break-up, migration and other circumstances, and who were struggling to find a new path to follow. Julie encouraged them to explore and embrace these changes.

Being involved in the community and with her family has taught Julie the importance of creating and maintaining social connections as part of a healthy and balanced lifestyle.

Julie has a Bachelor of Arts degree, a Diploma of Education and a Postgraduate Diploma of Education. She is currently studying for her Masters of Creative Media at RMIT University, and contributes articles and stories to books, magazines and newspapers.

Dedication

I dedicate this book to all those who've retired and to all those who are about to retire. Enjoy your new life!

I also dedicate this book to my husband, Bob, my children, David, Kathryn, Rob and James, and my granddaughter, Mikayla.

Acknowledgements

Many people helped make this book possible. Firstly, I want to thank all the people I've taught over the years and all the retirees I've met. You've taught me more than you realise.

I also want to thank the team at Wiley, especially my acquisitions editor, Charlotte Duff, who suggested the book and encouraged me to write it, and Louise Kubecki. And special thanks to my editor, Caroline Hunter, who worked so hard and edited so seamlessly, and who promptly answered my many questions.

Thank you to all the people who so generously shared their stories, particularly Leonie Ball, Francis Ellis, Andrea Fay, Michael Lewis and Margaret Small. And my gratitude to Trish Power, who reviewed the financial aspects of the book and whose own books make the topic of superannuation so clear.

Finally, a special thank you to my family who've supported me all the way, especially my husband, Bob, and to my parents, Michael (deceased) and Mollie Kolody, who shared their life stories with me and showed me how to really live my retirement.

Publisher's Acknowledgements

We're proud of this book; please send us your comments through our Dummies online registration form located at www.dummies.com/register/.

Some of the people who helped bring this book to market include the following:

Acquisitions, Editorial and Media Development

Project Editor: Caroline Hunter, Burrumundi Pty Ltd

Acquisitions Editor: Charlotte Duff

Technical Reviewer: Trish Power

Editorial Manager: Gabrielle Packman

Production

Layout and Graphics: Wiley Composition Services, Wiley Art Studio

Cartoons: Glenn Lumsden

Proofreader: Pamela Dunne

Indexer: Don Jordan, Antipodes Indexing

Contents at a Glance

Table of Contents

Introduction

. . . .

Retirement can be like an exciting voyage to an unknown country. You pack up your previous life and set sail for new shores. You see some interesting sights and meet a lot of new people along the way. You even have the opportunity to totally reinvent yourself if you so wish.

Most retirement planning focuses on the financial aspects of retirement. Although I agree that you need to get this aspect of your life in order, there's more to life than money. *Making the Most of Retirement For Dummies* provides you with an overall plan for living the next 20 to 30 years with as much verve and enjoyment as possible.

About This Book

In *Making the Most of Retirement For Dummies* I explore how to take control of your finances by working out how much money you really need in retirement and by understanding your super and the government age pension. After you have this knowledge under your belt, you can begin to explore the diversity of opportunities open to you in your retirement.

Your health and wellbeing are vitally important at this stage of your life. If you haven't looked after yourself well, follow my tips for getting into shape so you can get the most out of your life. You also find a lot of ideas to prevent boredom and stagnation — the enemies of health and wellbeing — including travelling, taking up study, returning to work, volunteering and hobbies.

Relationships change with retirement. You may suddenly be sharing the same space 24/7 with a partner you haven't seen for at least eight hours every day for the past 30 years, or you may be confronted with an empty house. I provide suggestions on how to negotiate the chores at home and connect with the wider world.

Foolish Assumptions

Because you've picked this book off the shelf I imagine you're either thinking about your retirement or have already retired and are keen to start making plans to enjoy this stage of your life. I've also assumed that you're Internet savvy. If you're not, you can find out how to surf the Internet at your local neighbourhood house or branch of the University of the Third Age (see Chapter 13 for more details).

How To Use This Book

You can read this book from cover to cover or turn to the table of contents and jump in wherever you like. You can read each chapter on its own or follow the cross-references to other chapters. Each chapter contains handy hints on how to achieve the result you want. It also gives you useful references to helpful Internet sites.

The sidebars contained in this book are stories from real retirees' lives. They're used to illustrate a point and aren't essential reading to the text, but they may strike a chord with you.

How This Book Is Organised

When you retire you can reinvent your life to take on whatever shape you want. Sometimes the choices are simply too overwhelming — or you may find it all a bit mystifying. This book is organised in six parts to take you through an overall plan of your retirement. The following is a summary of each part.

Part I: Getting Ready to Retire: The Next 20 or 30 Years

In this part, I take you through some ideas for embarking on this new phase of your life, covering everything from financial management to day-to-day living. I also suggest some exercises you can do to help you understand how you spend your time now and to work out what you'd like to do in the future.

Part II: Money Matters

This part addresses the important topic of money. The state of your finances now plays a big part in how you're able to live in your retirement. I give you some ideas on how to budget for your future needs, outlining how much money you need to fund a modest or comfortable retirement. I explain superannuation and offer some tips on how to grow your super faster. I also explain the government age pension, benefits and allowances. Finally, I outline the advantages of making a will and what's involved in appointing a power of attorney.

Part III: Living Well in Retirement

To make the most of your retirement and enjoy it to the full you need to stay fit and healthy. In this part, I outline the essential medical checks you need to undergo regularly and explore various exercise regimens like water aerobics and dance. I explain the Medicare system and help you to work out whether you also need private health insurance. I detail the assistance available if you find yourself having to look after an elderly parent or relative. I also outline the advantages and disadvantages of moving house in your retirement, whether you're looking for a sea change or tree change, or are considering downsizing to an apartment.

Part IV: Using Your Time Wisely

In this part, I provide loads of information and ideas for occupying your body and mind in retirement. If you have the travel bug, check out the tips and information on short breaks at home, round-Australia trips and abroad. You find handy hints for those who want to return to work or study or get involved in volunteering. If you want to turn your hobby into a small business, this part points you in the right direction.

Part V: Relationships Now and in the Future

Your relationships undergo a change when you retire, especially if you move away from your old neighbourhood. But keeping connected with others is essential to maintaining your mental and physical wellbeing. In this part, I give you some ideas for (re)connecting with family and friends and expanding your circle of friends. I also provide some hints and tips for beginning this new phase of life with your partner.

Part VI: The Part of Tens

In this part I explore 10 secrets to a happy and healthy retirement. I also include the 10 most useful government Web sites for checking your superannuation and pension entitlements, as well as health and travel information.

Icons Used in This Book

This icon marks important information you need to remember to help you with your retirement planning.

These handy hints are useful for getting the most out of your retirement, whether it's sorting out your finances or organising your travel.

This icon introduces true stories of people living in retirement. Read about how other retirees have handled living their retirement dream.

Sometimes, you need to get extra advice from experts such as lawyers, financial advisers or healthcare specialists. Look out for this icon.

This icon flags handy Web sites you can visit for further advice, information and reading.

Part I

Getting Ready to Retire: The Next 20 or 30 Years

Glenn Lumsden

In this part ...

*N*ot quite sure what retirement holds for you? Retirement gives you an opportunity to follow your dreams. Now is the time to think about how you want to live the next 20 to 30 years. In this part I give you some ideas for embarking on this new phase of your life. I explore some of the exciting adventures and changes retirement can bring. I also provide some pointers to help you analyse your wants and needs and to decide in which direction you'd like to take your new life.

Chapter 1

Life After Work

*W*hether you approach retirement willingly or with trepidation — or indeed are forced into it — you should hopefully have a good 20 to 30 years to devote to this stage of your life.

Your first few months as a retiree will no doubt be one long holiday, but sustaining such a lifestyle is difficult long term. Good as it sounds to simply lie on the beach, sipping champagne and munching on lobster, you'll tire of it eventually — no, really, you will! Like many others, you'll want a more structured and fulfilling lifestyle.

In this chapter I take you through the different aspects of retirement, from making the decision to retire to sorting out how to occupy your time. You find information on money matters, plus how to keep mentally and physically fit and healthy.

Deciding When to Retire

Retirement means different things to different people. You may set yourself a clear date for retirement and work steadily towards it with anticipation and a good map. Or perhaps the idea creeps slowly up on you: You may find it hard to let go of your working life and have no idea what you'll do for the next 20 or 30 years. Or, like many others these days, retirement may be thrust upon you.

Getting ready

For most people, retirement means the end of paid work. As you plan for your retirement, you may compare your imaginary retired life with your working life. The importance that work plays in your life will have an impact on your decision to retire. If you think letting go of your career may be difficult, you may find it helpful to understand exactly what work means to you. You may work to

- ✔ **Enjoy the social benefits.** Maintaining relationships and feeling useful help keep you well and happy. Social isolation can lead to both mental and physical ill health.

- ✔ **Give your life structure.** Although you may not acknowledge it, like many people you may enjoy the discipline of getting up each day and getting ready for work.

  In retirement, some people continue with the habit of getting up at a certain time and leaving the house early, perhaps for breakfast or a coffee or to buy the newspaper. My mother, who's in her 90s, is adamant that lying in bed makes you old. She's up at 7.30 every morning and enjoys a life full of friends, crosswords and bridge.

- ✔ **Identify who you are.** Perhaps you're used to identifying yourself in terms of your work. You may feel that your success or failure as a person is based on how you perform at work, rather than how you perform in other areas of your life.

- ✔ **Keep your mind active.** As the adage goes, if you don't use it, you'll lose it. Do you enjoy the mental stimulation that work brings? People who read regularly, solve crossword puzzles, play cards or visit museums are less likely to experience mental decline. Keeping your mind active by doing new things, like studying a new language, is important.

- ✔ **Pay the bills.** This one's obvious — unless you're one of the lucky few who were born wealthy or have won the Lotto. Even very wealthy people like to work at least part-time or perhaps in a voluntary capacity.

If you can't imagine letting go of work because of any of these reasons, you can ease yourself into retirement by reducing your working hours before you finally retire. You can also begin to take on some activities outside of work like a hobby or course of study.

If you *have* to retire, use your understanding of what work means to you to map out what to do in your retirement. For example, you can help keep your sense of self intact by taking on community work, perhaps mentoring others. Chapter 15 has more on volunteering.

Brian faces retirement — reluctantly

Brian had dedicated himself to his work since the age of 17. He'd enjoyed a successful career and wasn't looking forward to retirement: He'd tried it once and lasted only two months before returning to work. However, at 63 Brian developed health problems, and his wife, Gwen, urged him to stop work to look after his health. Brian relented.

For the first few months he was kept busy with medical appointments. Then he and Gwen took a long-planned trip to Europe. When they returned home Gwen settled back into running the house and pursuing her other activities, and Brian settled in front of the television. However, he soon realised that he needed to be more active — and Gwen had begun dark mutterings about couch potatoes and when would it be her turn to retire from cooking.

Brian took some positive action and bought a simple cook book, determined to learn to cook some evening meals. Although his first few meals each took many hours to prepare, he got more adept.

Missing company, he also took some golf lessons and joined a club. He enjoyed the exercise and competitive spirit among the players, but his back and knees complained if he played more than two or three days a week.

One day over lunch some of the other players were discussing a project they were involved in — making toys for disadvantaged children. Brian was invited to join them. He went along and found working with his hands very calming.

Not long after this, Brian's first grandchild was born. Now, what with cooking, golf, making toys and spending time with his grandchild, Brian wonders how he ever had time to work.

Getting to know yourself

Changing from full speed to full stop may not be easy. One day you have a full work diary, the next a blank page. Adjusting to a new lifestyle takes time. If you can begin that process *before* you retire, you'll find facing the next 20 to 30 years much easier to deal with.

As you contemplate your retirement, think about how to fill all those spaces that work takes up. Unless you find your own activities to enjoy, you'll have no reason to get out of bed in the morning, no reason to change out of your pyjamas. And married or single, you'll still need to make your own social connections.

No longer can you hide behind your business suit or workers overalls. You have to work out a new persona to face the world.

In Chapter 2, I provide exercises and pointers to help you decide who you are and what you want out of retirement.

Managing Your Money During Retirement

One of the first things you need to sort out when planning your retirement is exactly where you stand from a monetary point of view. The state of your finances *before* you retire plays a big part in how you'll be able to live your life *after* you retire. You need to know how much money you have now and how much you need for a comfortable retirement.

Assessing how much money you need

Early in your retirement you're more likely to spend up big on items like travel, renovating your house or moving house, and buying a new car.

As you age the perceived wisdom says you're less likely to want to travel, but I know several octogenarians who still enjoy their annual overseas trip — usually business class. The amount of money you have to play with will dictate how often — and where — you can travel.

Chapter 3 helps you to calculate how much money you need for your retirement. It covers everything you need to consider, including what sort of lifestyle you'd like to have in your retirement, what costs you need to factor in and how to set a budget.

Knowing how superannuation works

Like most Australians, your retirement savings are probably tied up in *superannuation* (or super). Make sure that you know how your particular super fund works and exactly how much money you have in your fund. By understanding the ins and outs of super and getting some sound financial advice where required, you can take control of your super and make the most of your retirement dollars.

Chapter 4 takes you through the different types of super funds, and explains how and when you can access your money.

You don't have to cash out your superannuation at any stage. You can leave your money in your super fund and turn it into an income stream through an allocated pension. After the age of 60 your income from this source won't be taxed.

If you've got small amounts of super floating around in various funds, you may find that you're better off rolling them all over into the one fund. However, first you need to check whether you'll be up for any fees or lose any benefits. Talk to your super fund or financial adviser for more information.

If you've 'lost' or forgotten about some of your super, you can search for it on the ATO's Superannuation Web site at `www.ato.gov.au/super` using the 'SuperSeeker' facility.

You can top up your super by taking advantage of the government's co-contribution scheme and by making use of spouse contributions. If you're over 65, you can continue contributing to super until you're 75, as long as you work 40 hours in a continuous 30-day period. See Chapter 4 for more information.

If you haven't yet retired, you can take advantage of various strategies to top up your savings, such as salary sacrificing. In addition, the government has recognised that you may prefer to ease yourself into retirement rather than suddenly stop working. It is actively encouraging retirees to keep working, even on a part-time basis, by setting up arrangements such as the transition-to-retirement pension (TRIP) scheme. This scheme is also a very tax-effective way to build up your super.

Chapter 4 has more advice on how you can benefit from these schemes.

Sourcing a government pension

If you don't have much in the way of assets or retirement funds, you should be eligible for a government age pension. To qualify you need to meet certain age, income, assets and residency tests. Your primary home is not included in the assets test, but if you sell your home the money from the sale will be included. If you receive a pension from overseas, you must declare this and your Australian pension payments will be adjusted accordingly.

If you're not eligible for the age pension, you may qualify for a Commonwealth Seniors Health Card. This card entitles you to discounts on your utilities bills, rates and many medicines.

Chapter 5 covers the ins and outs of the government age pension and how to make the most of concession cards.

Safeguarding your assets through your will and estate planning

You can join the Spending-the-Kids'-Inheritance (or SKI-ing) movement and blow all the money you have in your retirement — or you can leave some behind to help the next generation. Even if you spend all your savings, you'll probably still have a few assets, such as a house or caravan and a car. To make sure that these are distributed the way you want them to be, you must make a will. Your will doesn't have to be an elaborate item, but it needs to be valid. Chapter 6 explains how to make a valid will and discusses the options regarding capital gains tax and not being able to bequeath your super in your will.

While you're well and alert you tend not to worry about powers of financial and medical attorney, but this is exactly the time to be making provisions for the future. Chapter 6 examines these issues in detail.

Looking After Your Health, Fitness and Emotional Wellbeing

As well as sorting out your money, you need to take stock of your health so that you can live well and enjoy your retirement. This means not only taking care of your body, but also making sure that you're happy with your living arrangements.

Keeping well — and fit

Begin looking after yourself by having all the appropriate health checks. Ensure your heart is fit and strong, your blood pressure is within the normal range and your cholesterol level is on target. Chapter 7 outlines the medical checks you should undergo on a regular basis.

Talk to your doctor about any health concerns that you may have. For example, you may have a family history of a certain disease, such as osteoporosis, or may think you're at risk of developing conditions such as Type 2 diabetes.

Your doctor can also advise you on starting an appropriate diet and exercise plan. The adage 'use it, or lose it' certainly applies to your body. You need to keep active! What exercise should you do? The best exercise is one that you enjoy: Exercise does *not* have to be a torture session in the gym. Pilates, yoga and Tai Chi all give you a sense of wellbeing. You can turn your exercise session into a social event by joining a walking or cycling club or taking up ballroom dancing. You find a full rundown of exercise options in Chapter 7.

Insuring your health

The Medicare system provides Australians with a great healthcare scheme. It ensures that you have access to free or low-cost medical and hospital care and basic eye examinations anywhere in Australia. For the full range of benefits offered by the Medicare system, see Chapter 8.

Unfortunately, Medicare won't cover you for every medical situation. For example, alternative and auxiliary treatments such as podiatry and physiotherapy are not covered, nor are some medicines. In addition, it's becoming increasingly difficult to find doctors who bulk-bill (meaning Medicare picks up the tab), especially on short notice. If you think you may need to take out private health cover, see Chapter 8, which outlines the pluses and minuses of the private healthcare system.

Caring for the elderly and the sick

Over the next few years you may find yourself having to look after an elderly relative. If you make the decision to place your relative in an aged-care home, you need to contact an aged-care assessor. The assessor assesses your relative's health and ability to care for himself or herself. This assessment is essential, because without it you cannot place anyone in an aged-care residential home — even for temporary respite care. Chapter 9 has more detailed information about the aged-care system.

In addition, your partner — or you — may become ill and need extra assistance. In such situations the government encourages you to stay in your own home, if possible, by providing you with care through your local council and by subsidising private care providers. You can find out more about how this works in Chapter 9.

Changing houses

Retirement is a time of assessing where and how you want to live. If you've raised a family, you may want to downsize to a smaller house or apartment — not that this may deter your offspring from coming home to live with you. As rents and housing costs continue to increase, more grown-up children are returning to their parents' previously empty nests. You may find your downsized home bulging at the seams!

If you decide to downsize, remember that moving from a suburban house with a garden into an apartment — especially one that's high rise — can be quite a culture shock. You probably have to contend with more traffic, and you certainly have limited parking space, so when family and friends visit they may have trouble parking. On the plus side, you won't have to mow the lawn, worry about the drought's effects on your garden or listen to the neighbour's children banging their basketball repeatedly against the garage wall.

You may want to move near your children, especially if you have grandchildren. Or you may like to undergo a tree change or a sea change. The trend of moving to the country or seaside is a growing one. Some embrace it wholeheartedly, while others keep a foot in town by holding onto a unit. Chapter 10 discusses the issues involved in changing house.

Alternatively, you may like the extra security provided by retirement village living. If you buy into a retirement village, you have the added benefit of a social life as well as 24-hour medical care. When you think of retirement villages, don't think of little old men and women huddled under their shawls drinking tea. Retirement villages have swimming pools, bowling greens, cinemas, social centres and high-class restaurants. What's more, you can go off travelling without having to worry about who's looking after your property while you're away. Chapter 10 has more on village life.

Using Your Time to Enjoy Yourself

Retirement should be all about doing what you want to do and enjoying yourself. Plan to accomplish some of the things you've always wanted to do: Travel to Nepal, finish your studies, return to work if you want to, volunteer to save the whales or get going with your hobby again.

Pat makes a list

After Pat retired from teaching, she began to reflect on how little time she'd had to spend on herself. When she wasn't teaching a group of rambunctious youngsters, she was organising her family, cleaning the house or tearing around the supermarket.

She decided that it was high time she did all the things she hadn't had time for over the last 30 years. She sat down with a notepad and listed every idea that came into her head. As the list grew her ideas got bolder and bolder.

Perhaps she wouldn't actually visit a space station, but she could trek in Nepal or climb a mountain — it needn't be Everest. She picked her favourite idea first and began to investigate how fit she had to be to go trekking. She engaged a personal trainer and started with some short hikes. Nearly two years later she boarded a plane to Nepal. Trekking in the Himalayas: Tick!

Next on Pat's wish list were learning to swim and volunteering at a local community centre. She set to researching her options at once.

Travelling

One of your first major retirement plans is likely to be some form of trip. Retirement is a great time to travel, whether for long overseas expeditions, complete circumnavigations of Australia or just short trips around your own neighbourhood. The options are endless. You can take a world tour or pack up and hit the road with your 4WD and caravan. You can travel simply to see the sights or you can do some volunteer work or study along the way. Instead of staying in hotels you can rent a villa in Tuscany or an apartment in Paris. And if all that choice isn't enough, in the not-too-distant future Richard Branson plans to offer trips into outer space!

To turn your dreams into reality, you need to work out your finances and decide what you can afford in the way of accommodation etc. Check out Chapter 11 for advice on setting your travel budget and investigating the many travel options available to you in your retirement.

If you'd like to join the Grey Nomad trail, you need to decide whether you want to travel in a car, a 4WD/caravan combo or a mobile home. You may also need to learn how to drive the beast or tow a caravan. If you want to sell your house and take to the road permanently, you have to consider how this may affect your pension — after you sell your home, the money you receive from the sale becomes an asset liable to the means test.

Chapter 12 has loads of information on preparing for your big trip. You discover what to pack, how to avoid dangers on the road, some great spots to camp — and even how you can find work along the way.

Exercising your mind

Keeping your mind active in retirement is important. Returning to study is a great way to challenge yourself mentally, whether you take a short course on local history at a neighbourhood house or a full-time degree at university. Studying again may also help if you miss the mental challenges you faced at work.

You don't need any previous formal education for many of the courses on offer, and you can always get your skills up to speed if you need to with a bridging course. Here are some study options you may like to consider:

- ✓ Enrol in a short course that will set you up with an interesting hobby. Neighbourhood houses and the University of the Third Age (U3A) provide opportunities to study in a friendly and relaxed atmosphere.

- ✓ Study for a certificate or diploma at TAFE. If you like, you can use the course to help you qualify for university study.

- ✓ Study online with the Open Universities scheme. You can study at your own pace and you don't have to sit the assessments at the end of the course.

- ✓ Take a single degree subject at university and participate without having to do the assessments. This is a great way of investigating in-depth a subject that interests you.

To find out more about your study options, including courses on offer, entry requirements, fees and scholarships, as well as tips for mature-age students, see Chapter 13.

Returning to work

You may decide to return to work after experiencing retirement for a year or two. Your reasons may be financial, or perhaps you want some extra mental and social stimulation. If you know that you'll be returning to work at some time in your retirement, it's important to lay the groundwork before you retire: You can quickly feel out of touch with the workplace when you retire.

Perhaps you'd like to completely change your working life? After years in an office you may want to begin a career in the fresh air. Conversely, you may like to put your trade skills to good use by taking on a training role. You find more on these topics in Chapter 14.

If you're over 55 and still working, but want to ease into retirement, you can take advantage of the government's transition-to-retirement pension (TRIP) scheme. This allows you to draw down on your superannuation and salary sacrifice your work earnings. See Chapter 4 for details.

Volunteering

You gain as much from volunteering as you give to it. When you make the commitment to volunteer, a whole world of opportunities opens up to you. You can volunteer close to home, working with babies in hospitals, animals in zoos and everything in between. Or you can travel abroad and work in orphanages and schools, learning new languages along the way.

You may have to undergo a police check and a Working With Children check before you're accepted as a volunteer.

Chapter 15 explains the ins and outs of volunteering.

Taking up a hobby

Sometimes you take on a hobby, and sometimes the hobby takes you on. Whichever way around it is, if you want to get far away from the world of work, find a hobby. Woodworking, cheese making, gardening, genealogy — you can turn anything into a hobby, even collecting the colour blue.

Hobbies are also a great means of socialising. You find clubs, swap meets and trips centred around particular hobbies. You may even decide to turn your hobby into a small business.

Where to begin? For some ideas and suggestions about hobbies, see Chapter 16.

Looking After Your Relationships

When you leave work, not only do you give up your profession, but also you often lose contact with friends and colleagues. You may find yourself spending your days alone, or with only your partner for company.

Taking it home

If you're the primary breadwinner in your relationship, when you retire and are at home full-time you may find yourself in your partner's work space. It's probably *not* a good idea to tell your partner how to run the house — he or she will have developed routines and interests over the years, and will have to get used to sharing the house with you. Chapter 17 has some ideas and pointers for beginning this new phase of your relationship.

Expanding your social circle

You have time to forge deeper relationships with your family after you retire. If you have grandchildren, spend time with them. Don't underestimate how important you are in your grandchildren's lives. You can also spend more time with your own parents if they're still alive. You'll no doubt hear many interesting family stories as your parents reminisce. Perhaps you can organise a big family get-together. You may be surprised how easily you slot back into childhood relationships with siblings and cousins.

Although it can be hard to make friends later in life, don't forget that many others are in the same boat as you. If you actively take part in a community group like the University of the Third Age, you find that you're quickly welcomed into the group. You may even extend your friendships by meeting each other for lunches and outings.

And don't ignore the animal community as a source of companionship. You can volunteer to work with animals at your local animal shelter or join one of the vast number of animal volunteer groups working overseas.

Chapter 18 has more ideas for growing your relationships.

Chapter 2

Taking Stock

*R*etirement is an opportunity for you to follow your dreams if you haven't already been able to do so. After working for 30 years or more, you may have buried yourself under the wants and needs of others. Now you need to think about how you want to live for the *next* 20 to 30 years. If you take the time to analyse your needs, you're in a good position to set your retirement goals and maximise your future enjoyment.

In this chapter, I provide some tips for exploring what may be important to you. I also give you some ideas for getting started on your new life.

Knowing What's Important To You

When you're preparing to change careers, you assess your life's direction and goals. If you're attending a job interview, to maximise your chance of success, you take the time to prepare an audit of your skills and experience.

Similarly, to maximise your success in your retirement — in other words, to live a happy and enjoyable life — you need to take the time now to think about who you really want to be after you retire your work persona.

Forget the person who wakes up, puts on work clothes and rushes headlong into a hectic working day — you're leaving those days behind. Now is the time to think about you. Maybe you have a daredevil buried under your suit, or a person with a mission to bring comfort to others.

Listing who you are now

To begin the process of working out how you want to live your life in retirement, take a few minutes to complete the following exercise:

1. **Take a piece of paper and a pen and make a list of all the roles you have now.** As well as writing down your profession — such as accountant, IT consultant, plumber or teacher — break down your professional and personal life into its components. Don't take more than five minutes, and *don't* analyse what you write. Write what you *actually do*, not what you want to do.

   Here are some examples to start you off:

   - Analyser
   - Carer
   - Chauffeur
   - Counsellor
   - Gardener
   - Mentor
   - Negotiator
   - Parent
   - Traveller

2. **Look at the list. Underline the roles you want to take with you into your new life and cross out those you want to leave behind.** You can keep your old roles or you can change them completely.

If you want to completely change your lifestyle, see the exercises in the following section 'Figuring out who you want to be'. If you have some vague ideas floating around in your head, these exercises help you to give them substance.

Chapter 2: Taking Stock 21

Figuring out who you want to be

Your list may include some roles that you want to keep in your retirement. Here are some ideas for expanding the roles you may already have:

- ✔ **Carer:** If you have a caring nature and like to feel useful, you can find many ways in which you can satisfy this need. You can care for orphans in India or cuddle sick babies in a maternity hospital nearer to home. Or you may prefer to help out the animal kingdom — for example working with orphaned orang-utans. For more information on volunteering see Chapter 15.

- ✔ **Gardener:** If you love gardening, in retirement you have plenty of time to do more of it. If you don't have a big garden of your own, check whether your local council runs a community garden scheme that you can join, or offer to help out someone who's unable to care for his or her own garden. Or, for a complete change of lifestyle, you could grow your gardening hobby into a business: See Chapter 16 for more information.

- ✔ **Mentor:** If you're involved in mentoring children or adults, you don't need to stop when you retire. You may even be able to take on more or varied projects now that you have the time. You can mentor young people in school situations or use your skills and knowledge in the business world. See Chapter 15 for more information on mentoring roles in the community

- ✔ **Traveller:** Have you whizzed round the world on business trips? Would you like to extend your knowledge and enjoyment of different countries — or, indeed, your own backyard? Chapter 11 helps you to make the most of your travel plans.

The following two exercises should start you thinking about retirement and what you want to get out of it. Grab yourself a cup of coffee or glass of wine, find a quiet place and have a go at them.

Exercise 1: Brainstorm a to-do list for retirement

Brainstorming: Sounds a little bit '70s hippy, huh? But you may be amazed at what pops out of your subconscious when you give it free rein. Brainstorming is a good way to bypass your natural censor and get to the real you. Follow these steps:

1. **Jot down all the things you want to do on a piece of paper.**

   Include all the things you dreamt about or thought about as you were growing up. You don't have to write in straight lines or columns. Just jot down everything that comes into your head anywhere on the page. Try not to think too much at this stage of the exercise.

I did this exercise when I turned 40 and over the next few years had some amazing adventures and met some great people. I went horse riding again — something I used to love when I was 10 but thought I was too old for at 40. I also began bushwalking, which has taken me to breathtakingly beautiful places and tested my endurance.

2. **Analyse your page of random words and put them into groups.**

   You may use headings such as travel, adventure and study.

3. **Choose two main items to use as a starting point for setting your retirement goals.**

   For example, if one item is 'find adventure', make a list of all the adventurous things you want to do. Then choose two of these and make doing them a goal (see the section 'Setting Retirement Goals' later in the chapter).

4. **Do some research to find out whether your goals are achievable.**

   For example, if one of your goals involves walking the Swiss Alps, are you physically capable of actually doing this, and can you afford the travel costs? What will it take to acquire the necessary level of fitness, and how long will it take you to get in shape? How much will the trip cost?

It may be possible to combine two or three of your goals. For example, you can combine travel and adventure, travel and study or travel and hobbies. Some adult education facilities offer study tours on different subjects. You can combine photographic studies with a visit to the Easter Islands. Or what about a gastronomic tour of France or Vietnam? Chapter 11 has more travel ideas.

Exercise 2: Imagine a day in the life

This section lets you indulge in some daydreaming. Imagine you've been retired for six months. How do you see your day? Check out these alternatives.

- ✔ **Scenario 1:** Get up after a leisurely lie in. Read the papers and do the crossword, then take a stroll to the local cafe for a coffee. Head back home to watch Foxtel until lunchtime. Lunch over, have a nap. Stroll to the shops to find something for dinner. Have a pre-dinner drink or two, then after dinner watch television until bedtime.

- ✔ **Scenario 2:** Get up and jog to the gym for a three-hour workout, before enjoying the steam room and spa. Head home for an early lunch, then go to the beach cafe for a drink or two with friends. Back home, potter around the garden until dinner time. Have an early night, ready to start early again in the morning.

✔ **Scenario 3:** Get up and join the aqua aerobics class. After breakfast, head down to the community centre to do some woodwork or painting with friends. Have lunch with your partner and spend the afternoon with your grandchildren. After dinner, enjoy more time with your partner or family, perhaps playing cards or going to the movies.

✔ **Scenario 4:** Get up, open the caravan door and breathe in the desert air. Cook breakfast, explore the area and catch up with fellow travellers before heading off to your next destination.

Now write your own scenario, and remember that however you perceive your retirement is right for you.

Exploring Your Values

Your values — principles and standards — shape your life and the decisions you make. Your values are forged early in life by your family, school, friends and religion. Most people take their values for granted and don't want to challenge them.

By operating within your value system you feel comfortable, and if your values are the same as those of the people around you, you feel safe and included. And after all, you don't usually have the time to sit down and reflect on the values that have shaped you and consider how they can contribute to your happiness and wellbeing.

However, at certain times in your life, particularly during periods of change, you may question your values. These times include the following:

✔ Leaving school and starting university

✔ Losing your job

✔ Reaching the big 4-oh!

✔ Starting your retirement

✔ Suffering the loss of a loved one

✔ Tackling a health issue

At such times some people decide to take on an entirely new value system: They may change religion, take on another culture, volunteer to help others or take on an ecologically sustainable lifestyle.

By reflecting on your values you can work out what motivates you. If your value system tells you that helping others is good, and your job has centred on personal attainment, you may decide to change tack and contribute to the community in your retirement. Or, if your job's been all about giving, you may decide that when you retire you're going to do something just for you.

One of the most important benefits of reassessing your values at this time is to understand what's important to you and not to change your lifestyle to fit into a perceived retirement persona. For example, if you value helping others, ultimately you won't feel satisfied if you embark on a lifestyle where you don't do this in some form or another.

What makes you tick?

Take a few minutes to think about what *really* makes you tick. Then, on a piece of paper write down as many things as you can think of. Here are some examples:

- ✔ Being organised
- ✔ Belonging to a church community
- ✔ Campaigning for your beliefs
- ✔ Caring for animals
- ✔ Eating well and working out
- ✔ Enjoying your garden
- ✔ Having fun
- ✔ Helping others
- ✔ Keeping busy
- ✔ Looking after the environment
- ✔ Making sure your house is a haven for family and friends
- ✔ Meeting new people
- ✔ Passing on your skills, knowledge and beliefs to others
- ✔ Spending time with your family
- ✔ Studying new things

Next, go through your list and identify your top *six* items. Take time to reflect on them and think about how you can incorporate them into your retirement plans. For example, if one of your priorities is

- ✔ Enjoying your garden, think carefully before selling up and buying a caravan or mobile home to live in.

- ✔ Helping others, you can become a volunteer. See Chapter 15 for more ideas and information.

- ✔ Keeping busy, have plenty of projects lined up *before* you retire. You'll find numerous ideas in Chapter 16.

- ✔ Keeping fit and healthy, make time each day to exercise: See Chapter 7.

- ✔ Passing on your ideas and values to the next generation, think about mentoring, volunteering to work with children or setting up a legacy through your will. Chapter 6 has information on wills and estate planning, and Chapter 15 looks at volunteer roles.

- ✔ Spending time with your family, think hard before you move away from them to another state. The climate may be better interstate, but you may be lonely, especially if you or your partner becomes ill. Refer to Chapter 10 for more on the pros and cons of moving house.

The most important part of an exercise such as this is making time for yourself to discover what's important to you. You may like to do this by

- ✔ Meditating on the subject during your daily exercise routine

- ✔ Talking about the issues with family and friends

- ✔ Unwinding at a spa or health resort to help clear your mind and avoid interruptions

Values questionnaires

To help you to define your values, you may like to undertake one of the many values questionnaires on the Web. Most are designed for work or school situations, but you may find some of them useful to help you to identify your values and incorporate them into your retirement planning.

For example, at the Legenis Web site at `www.legenis.com` you can find a discussion of the relevance of values in your future planning.

Tracking How You Spend Your Time Now

By working out exactly how you spend your time now, you can see what's missing in your life and where you need to make some changes. Start by keeping a time diary for a short period, say, a week, and figure out how you'd like to spend your time.

The more you plan before you retire, the more rewarding you'll find your retirement.

Keeping a time diary

If you're currently working full-time, you may find it interesting to keep a time diary to examine how you actually spend your time. Many people find their days work out like this:

- Get up
- Exercise (if you're organised)
- Go to work
- Shop for ingredients for the evening's meal on the way home from work
- Have a drink and prepare the evening meal
- Watch television
- Go to bed
- Get up and repeat all this the next day

Weekends are devoted to recovering from the working week and getting ready for the next week, with some relaxation time thrown in.

Even if you've already retired, you may still find it useful to keep a time diary. Either way, the diary-keeping exercise helps you to identify changes you want to make in your life.

What you find when you keep a time diary may shock you. One of my students found that his only exercise was walking between his house and car each morning and evening. Another found that the only time she had to herself during the day was a brief amount of time in the shower in the morning.

A time diary isn't like a work diary. You don't need to account for every hour or half hour. Follow this process:

1. **Get hold of an exercise book or notepad, and for seven pages (one page each for Monday–Sunday) rule off each page into the following column headings:**

   ✔ Time

   ✔ Activity

   ✔ Companion

2. **Divide each Time column into the following chunks:**

   ✔ Early morning

   ✔ Morning

   ✔ Lunchtime

   ✔ Early afternoon

   ✔ Late afternoon

   ✔ Evening

   This step gives you an idea of what activities you do before you go to work and after you come home.

3. **Carry your diary around with you and note down major activities as you complete them.** Note how much time you spend on each activity and your companion (if any). At this stage all you need do is write down the activities — don't analyse them just yet. Record how much time you spend on the following:

   ✔ Being by yourself

   ✔ Enjoying your hobby

   ✔ Exercising

   ✔ Socialising with people outside work

   ✔ Talking to your partner or spouse

If your partner agrees, you can log his or her activities as well — or better still, work together. Your retirement impacts both you and your partner — and in fact on all those close to you.

Give particular attention to activities that don't involve paid work.

Check out Table 2-1 for an example of a time diary for one working day.

Table 2-1	Keeping A Time Diary for One Day	
Time	*Activity*	*Companion*
Early morning	Run, 30 mins	None
	Breakfast, 20 mins	Partner
	Getting ready for work, 30 mins	None
	Driving to work, 15 mins	None
Morning	Work	
	Meeting, 30 mins	Colleagues
Lunchtime	Lunch, 30 mins	None
Early afternoon	Meeting, 1 hr	Colleagues
Late afternoon	Driving home, shopping on the way, 45 mins	None
Evening	Preparing and eating dinner, 1 hr	Partner
	Reading newspaper, 45 mins	Alone
	Watching television, 2 hrs	Partner

When you've completed your diary for seven days, take the time to analyse the results. Look at where you spend the majority of your time and ask yourself how much value these activities really add to your life. How much time do you spend

- ✔ Catching up with family?
- ✔ Exercising?
- ✔ Enjoying quality time with your partner?
- ✔ Having fun with friends and family?
- ✔ Laughing?

Your busy working lives may mean that you and your partner simply pass each other every day like ships in the night. Stop and smell the coffee — preferably with the person you love.

Now that you can see exactly how you spend your time and what's missing in your life, you can plan to make some changes. Check out the following section for more information.

Planning your time in retirement

In retirement you may find that you get up later in the morning, dawdle over breakfast, read the papers, have a coffee, do some shopping, eat lunch and potter in the shed or garden all afternoon. Or you may be up at 5.30 am so that you can hit the golf course at 7.00 am. Whatever happens when you retire, you can be sure that the rhythm of your days will change.

How would you like to spend your days? For example:

- ✔ Do you want to spend more time doing an activity that you enjoy with like-minded people? For more information on staying in touch and widening your circle of friends, check out Chapter 18.
- ✔ Have you sacrificed family life for your career and now want to spend more time with your loved ones? You find more information on reconnecting with your family in Chapter 18.
- ✔ Would you like to get fit? Chapter 7 has more ideas for introducing exercise into your daily life.

Setting Retirement Goals

People spend their time in retirement in all sorts of different ways. Your retirement is unique to you. The important thing is to enjoy the time you have. You don't have to run around frantically filling every minute, but you benefit if you do a little preparation and think about what you feel is important and find interesting.

If you're not prepared for retirement, you may spend the first few months — or even years — wandering around in a haze. You're no longer defined by your job, but haven't yet found something to fill the void retirement has created.

However, now that you have a broad idea of what makes you tick, you can set some goals, at least for your first year of retirement.

Your retirement goals don't have to be believable — or have measurable outcomes: You're not setting *work goals*. Your retirement goals can be outrageously different from anything you've ever done before. If you don't fully achieve a goal, no-one suffers.

The many faces of retirement

John, Joe and Diane all worked in a large corporation. For 35 years, five days a week, each of them got out of bed in the morning, had breakfast, put in a long day at the office, had dinner and slumped back into bed. Then they all retired.

John threw himself into his retirement, doing everything he'd missed out on during his working life. He hardly has enough time in his days to fit in golf, home renovations, cycling, travelling and grandparenting.

Joe dedicated his retirement to helping others. He's on the board of a charity, teaches computing to seniors and is a runner at the local football club. He's made a new circle of friends through his charity work.

Diane moved to northern New South Wales when she retired. She'd always dreamt of spending her life on or near the water. She describes the first few months of her retirement as getting up in the morning and going down to the beach to make sure that the waves were still coming in and there were still the same number of grains of sand on the beach. After three months she found a new job in the city, leased her beach house and rented a city flat. Retirement will have to wait.

To begin with, your goals may simply be ideas at the back of your mind. Perhaps something has been niggling away at you for years. Now's the time to put your thoughts into action.

Here are a few do's and don'ts of goal setting:

- ✔ *Do* take a chance at doing something different.

- ✔ *Do* put your ideas down on paper. Write down some concrete steps you need to take to make your idea a reality.

- ✔ *Do* include your partner in your plans. You'll need your partner's support along the way.

- ✔ *Don't* let your ideas remain abstract thoughts for too long — you can't go on forever.

- ✔ *Don't* worry if a goal seems out of character for you, and your family and friends are urging you not to be silly. I'm not exhorting you to do anything injurious to your health, but after all, you are a grown-up.

Being Proactive

Work often provides more than a job: It can also give you a sense of achievement, feelings of self-worth and social contacts. When you retire you can lose these important benefits. Experts agree that social isolation is bad for your mental and physical health, so keeping in contact with others and achieving some goals are important for your wellbeing.

Follow these tips for becoming proactive about your new lifestyle and getting started on a healthy and active retirement.

Engaging a life coach

A life coach can help you make changes in your life. He or she can assist you in setting goals and achieving those goals, provide a listening post and give you feedback.

The quality of life coaches varies enormously, as do their qualifications. The most important thing to look for in a life coach is compatibility with you. You must be able to trust and respect your coach, and your coach needs to be able to inspire and guide you. Before you commit to a coach, make sure that she has suitable qualifications — for example, training in psychology, career counselling or some other field related to dealing with people. Ask about the coach's previous work experience and ask what sort of clients she usually deals with. If you want someone to help you with fitness, make sure the coach is qualified in exercise science or rehabilitation. Ask for a free introductory session and use it to assess the coach's suitability and compatibility. Your chosen coach should be able to understand what you're aiming for.

You can find a selection of life coaches on the Web. To find one near you, type 'hiring a life coach' into your search engine.

Joining a neighbourhood house

Neighbourhood houses are volunteer-run community-based organisations that offer numerous programs and activities such as bridge, yoga classes and games nights. Most classes and activities cost only a small amount.

To find your nearest neighbourhood house, go to your local council Web site or visit the National Link of Neighbourhood Houses and Community Learning Centres Web site at www.nationallink.asn.au. Chapter 13 has more details on neighbourhood houses and the courses and activities they offer.

Neighbourhood houses

Mollie and Michael worked for many years in Singapore, where they had an interesting circle of international and local friends. When they retired they decided to return to Australia, settling in Melbourne. They needed to find a way to make new friends, so they investigated their local neighbourhood house.

Mollie played bridge and Michael gave science lectures. In addition, they both took up office roles at their local house. This new community provided Mollie and Michael with mental activities to look forward to, as well as sustaining friendships.

Investigating retirement activities

You don't have to be isolated. When your life has been so structured, it may be difficult at first to break into a new group, but soon you'll find that there are many others like you, looking for company and mental stimulation. Plus you'll discover that your contribution is valued by other members of the group.

Check out these Web sites for information on retirement activities to get you out and about meeting new people:

- ✔ Council on the Ageing (COTA) at www.cota.org.au
- ✔ Life Planning Association of Australia at www.life.org.au

Networking

Does the word 'networking' conjure up visions of interconnected computers — or maybe producers schmoozing the room to get backing for their films? In the retirement world, *networking* means creating links between you and others so that you can enjoy yourself. Sounds much more interesting, doesn't it?

Networking usually involves you joining a club or two — something that you're interested in and where you can meet people with similar interests to yours.

If you're thinking of returning to some sort of work after retirement, consider joining a club such as Lions, Probus or Rotary, where you can build relationships with your local professional community. Even if you don't want to take on any work after retirement, joining one of these clubs enables you to devote time to helping build a more solid community.

Both Rotary and Lions require a bigger commitment than joining a small volunteer group where you may be required to give only a few hours of your time now and then. Rotary and Lions are highly organised groups that raise large amounts of money for charity. You may be required to attend a certain number of meetings each year to retain your membership. However, these clubs are excellent for networking with a view to maintaining some links to the workforce.

Ideally, you should start networking before you leave full-time work, so you have both social and business contacts when you retire.

Lions

Lions began in Australia in 1947. The club draws members from all parts of the community. To join Lions you must be over 18 years of age and of good moral character and reputation. Lions has strong links to the Australian community as well as on the international scene. The club emphasises making friends, serving the community and learning leadership skills. Members can either provide service or raise money for the community.

Go to www.lionsclubs.org.au for more information on Lions.

Probus

Probus was created as a forum for retirees and semi-retirees to get together, keep active, expand their interests and make new friends. Membership is open to anyone of good character. The structure of the clubs is simple and the cost of involvement is minimal. Members attend monthly meetings and can take part in a variety of outings.

Visit www.probus.com.au for more information or to find a Probus club near you.

Rotary

Rotary gives you an opportunity to join a group of professional people in a local and international capacity. As a member of Rotary, you become involved in community and other humanitarian projects. Rotary has 32,000 autonomous clubs around the world. To become a member you must be invited to join. Most often, this involves being sponsored to a meeting by a Rotarian. In order to join Rotary you must hold or have held a professional or propriety job, and be prepared to attend a certain number of meetings and community projects each year. You also need to live or work in the locality of the club.

Visit www.rotary.org.au for more information on Rotary.

Volunteering to help young people

Nothing keeps you young like staying in touch with young people and participating in some of the things they do. 'But I'm still young', I hear you say. Yes, you and I both believe we're still young, but really, it's easy to get set in your ways. You may develop habits like listening to the same radio station — you know what happens to the radio or CD when your children or grandchildren get in the car.

Working with children can be one of the most rewarding events of your life. You may work hard much of the time, but when you see a child grasp a new concept or conquer a demon, you're paid back a hundredfold.

The first thing you have to accept when you volunteer for any role that involves interacting with children is that you're required to undergo a police check and/or Working With Children check. A police check searches the criminal records database for criminal convictions or charges yet to be heard. The searches don't usually go beyond the past 10 years and don't include childhood convictions. Unlike the police check, a Working With Children check takes spent convictions into account, including any convictions and findings of guilt from when you were under 18. You can read more about these checks in Chapter 15.

Here are some ways to get involved with the younger generation:

✔ Help out at a grass-roots level and show children 'the ropes'. For example, you can

- Become a Guide or Scout leader

- Help organise sporting events

- Help out with youth programs at your local church

- Offer your services as a tutor at your local community centre

- Step in as a sporting team manager or coach

- Volunteer for reading help at your local school

> ✔ Share your skills or talents with children. Stephanie Alexander, for example, is passionate about promoting healthy eating habits to children. Her Kitchen Garden Program at Collingwood College sees many children spending time each week working in the vegetable garden they helped design and build, and preparing meals with their produce in the kitchen. The program has now expanded Australia-wide.

For more on getting involved with your community through volunteering, go to Chapter 15.

Grumpy old men and women

Perhaps you can't wait to fall into the role of the grumpy old man or the grumpy old woman, annoyed that the world is changing around you. Do you remember when:

✔ You lay in the sun all day on the beach covered in coconut oil for that smooth brown tan?

✔ You played backyard cricket or rode your bike around the streets?

✔ You took your saucepan to the Chinese takeaway and it was filled up with pretty much whatever was cooked for that day? Usually rice and cabbage featured heavily.

✔ Your mum made ice-cream instead of buying it? Or, if it was bought, it came in a cardboard packet and tasted like cardboard?

Unfortunately, for better or worse, those days are gone. Now you can eat all your food from packets. Disposable containers clog up our waterways. And lying in the sun gives you skin cancer. Here are some antidotes to take when you feel an attack of the grumps coming on:

✔ Ask your grandchildren to tell you a story.

✔ Have a conversation with a child.

✔ Laugh.

✔ Listen to the Top 5 hits (music, that is).

✔ Learn something a fifth grader would know.

✔ Open your mind to new ideas. Be aware of the zeitgeist.

✔ Play a computer game — watch out, though, you may get hooked.

✔ Volunteer to help out at a basketball or netball tournament at your old school or your grandchildren's school.

✔ Watch cartoons.

Studying — again

The Department of Health and Ageing (www.health.gov.au) urges you to keep your mind healthy by keeping it active. Minds need a workout, just as muscles do. You can keep your mind healthy by doing crosswords or Sudokus or by studying something new. And studying with a diverse group of people, including the younger generation, is even better for your mental stimulation.

If you go back to study, you meet people just like yourself, as well as people very different from you. You discover more about yourself and others, and your horizons are widened by the people you meet. During your classroom discussions and tutorials, you find that your contributions and ideas are valued by the other students. You also get the opportunity to hear and value their ideas. Be open to learning from your fellow students as well as your tutor. And make the most of your studies by joining in after-class coffee sessions and social activities.

Many people feel intimidated by the thought of going back to school, but universities, TAFE colleges and Community Adult Education centres offer numerous opportunities for mature-age students. See Chapter 13 for all you need to know about returning to study in your retirement.

Returning to paid work

Not everyone looks forward to retirement. Some people are forced to retire through retrenchment, while others retire from a long-term job but don't intend to retire completely from paid work. Perhaps you've tried retirement and found it difficult to relax in your new lifestyle? Or maybe you just can't afford to retire full-time and need to find a way to earn an income. Chapter 14 examines how you can return to the paid workforce.

Part II
Money Matters

Glenn Lumsden

'Mum, Dad, I didn't want you wasting my inheritance on expensive overseas travel, so I bought you a decade's worth of Getaway DVDs instead.'

In this part ...

The state of your finances now plays a big part in how you're able to live in your retirement. In this part, I give you a basic idea how much money you need to put aside to support yourself for the next 20+ years. I help you to take control of your super and make the most of your retirement dollars, including offering some tips on how to grow your super faster. I also explain the government's age pension scheme and other income streams you may need to rely on in your retirement. Finally, I show you how to safely pass on your legacy via your will and estate planning.

Chapter 3

Accounting for the Future

*F*orecasting your future needs is a difficult task, mainly because you don't know how long you'll live. However, you can make a few assumptions about the future.

You can also decide what sort of lifestyle you want to have in your retirement years. For example, if you choose to downsize your house and car and take short trips rather than long holidays, your retirement dollars will go much further than if you keep up your pre-retirement lifestyle.

In this chapter, I discuss how to set a budget for your retirement, as well as how to make the most of Seniors Cards and other money-saving devices.

Calculating How Much Money You Really Need

Statistically speaking, most Australians can expect to live to 80 or more, although on average women live five years longer than men. So, if you're 55 now, for example, you need to budget your money for roughly another 25 years if you're male or 30 years if you're female.

Most people assume that they'll spend less in their retirement than they spend when they're working. You've paid off your mortgage, raised your children and don't have to buy expensive work clothes or spend money on daily commuting. So you should have fewer outgoings, right?

Finding out your lifespan forecast

Check out the life expectancy trends on the Australian Bureau of Statistics Web site at www.abs.gov.au or use one of the Web sites that help you to estimate your date of departure from planet earth. Type 'lifespan' into your search engine or try Dr Perls' life expectancy calculator at http:// calculator.livingto100.com/ calculator. To use this calculator you have to answer a series of questions on your health and lifestyle habits, but in return, as well as your lifespan forecast, you get lots of advice on how to improve your chances of living longer.

Well yes, but on the other hand, you'll still want to enjoy eating out, children have a habit of returning home in hard times, and you may need to contribute towards supporting your grandchildren — or you may just want to spoil them. What's more, you can keep travelling until a very old age — and this is only going to get more expensive as the cost of fuel rises.

To have a comfortable, although by no means luxurious, lifestyle in retirement, the Association of Superannuation Funds of Australia (ASFA) calculates that a couple needs an income stream of about $50,561 per year and a single needs about $37,829 per year. This covers the basic necessities plus eating out once a week and the occasional overseas trip.

On the ASFA's Web site at www.superannuation.asn.au/RS/default.aspx you can view the Westpac–ASFA Retirement Standard, which has budgets for modest and comfortable retirement living for Australians. These ASFA income estimates are after tax, so if you retire early or don't have your money in super you'll have to factor in tax as well.

The ASFA's Web site also has a detailed budget breakdown for comfortable and modest retirement living based on the most recent quarter. The budgets give a detailed breakdown of weekly expenses for a comfortable couple and a modest couple, and a comfortable single and a modest single. For the September 2008 quarter, the suggested weekly and annual budgets are as follows:

	Weekly budget	*Annual budget**
Comfortable couple	$969.67	$50,561
Modest couple	$526.51	$27,454
Comfortable single	$725.49	$37,829
Modest single	$376.21	$19,617

Weekly amounts multiplied by 52, with another day's allowance added due to 2008 being a leap year.

By examining the budgets, you can see where the differences in expenditure lie between the comfortable and modest retirees. This information should give you ideas for your own budget and indicate where you can make savings.

Setting Your Retirement Budget

Before you retire you should think about what source of income you have to live on in your retirement and whether this is enough for your needs. To do this, you need to set a budget to cover your predicted lifestyle.

Usually, you spend more money in the early years of your retirement than you will later on. The reason for this is that early in your retirement you may want to pay off your mortgage, renovate your house, buy a new car and travel extensively.

As you age you may begin to think about downsizing your house and property to make more funds available, or you may consider moving into a retirement village. You probably still want to travel and may even have your grandchildren's education costs to think about.

Further into retirement, like most people you may be more content to explore your own surroundings rather than continue with overseas trips. You may also move into an aged-care facility. And your entertainment and travel costs will probably dwindle — although I've just read a story about Mary Taylor who at 90 was still enjoying driving around Australia.

Knowing which costs to factor in

Here are some of the costs you need to factor into your retirement budget, starting with perhaps the largest: Your mortgage repayments or rental payments.

House and garden

The most basic housing costs you need to consider are rental or mortgage payments. These payments may account for the largest part of your annual budget. If you own your home outright, of course, you won't have these costs.

You also need to factor in:

- House and contents insurance
- Maintenance and cleaning costs
- Parking permits (if you live in the city or inner suburbs)
- Rates
- Replacement appliances and furniture
- Utility costs such as electricity, gas and water

Unfortunately, when one appliance dies, the rest usually follow. At some stage you have to replace big-ticket items like your clothes dryer, dishwasher, fridge, freezer, hot-water service, television and washing machine, so you need to factor these costs somewhere in your budget.

Consider how you can cut down on your electricity and water usage and save money in the long term. For example, find out about double-glazing your windows and insulating your roof to retain heat. Installing rainwater tanks will save water — and your garden. And although installing solar panels for heating and electricity is expensive initially, you may be eligible for a government subsidy, and over time the panels will reduce your utility bills and pay for themselves.

Look also at drought-proofing your garden. Some initial outlay now saves money on water — and the need to replace dead plants later on.

If you're entitled to a Pensioner Concession Card, you should receive a discount on your rates and utility bills. See the section 'Taking Advantage of the Concessions Available' later in the chapter for more information.

Early in retirement is a good time to get your property in top condition, so you may need to factor in some renovation costs initially. For instance:

- Do any patching and painting jobs.
- Make sure the kitchen and bathrooms are in good condition.
- Organise your garden to make it easy to look after. For example, you can place your flower and vegetable patches in raised beds so you don't have to bend down so far to maintain them, and you can change the lawn area to a low-maintenance Australian native garden and do away with the lawnmower.

Gardening is a personal thing. If gardening is your hobby, you may want to keep what you have. But if you want to travel or take up a different hobby, you may consider moving to a house with a smaller garden or an apartment with no garden.

Some people have two homes: their main residence in the city, and a holiday home at the beach or in the bush. You may need to make the hard decision of which home to keep. See Chapter 10 for help with making this decision.

Food

Depending on how much you've saved for your retirement, you may not be able to budget the same amount for food each week as you did when you were working. Of course, if your children have flown the nest, your food costs will be lower now. If you have to tighten your belt to make ends meet, you can do a number of things to make this enjoyable:

- ✔ **Invest in a cooking course.** As well as providing you with a fun hobby, the knowledge you gain will help you to understand the nutrient value of the food you eat. A cooking course is a particularly good idea if you're not used to thinking about what'll be on your plate until 7.00 at night, when takeaway chicken and chips seems like a good idea.

- ✔ **Try cheaper cuts of meat like lamb shanks and gravy beef.** These cuts need extra cooking time but are tastier than regular cuts. You can also include beans and pulses in your stew pots. These options are healthy, nutritious and inexpensive.

- ✔ **Turn shopping into an enjoyable activity by browsing through fresh food markets rather than whizzing around the supermarket.** Farmers' markets have wonderful fresh seasonal produce, but they can put a bit of a hole in your pocket if you succumb to too many treats. However, since they're usually held only once a month in most districts, a few indulgences won't hurt. Also, many stallholders sell off their produce very cheaply at the end of the day's trading.

If you like to eat out at restaurants and cafes but need to watch your budget, eating out at lunchtime is cheaper — and more decadent — than going out for an evening meal.

Car and fuel

Car owners need to factor in the costs of running and maintaining their car, as well as the costs of fuel, registration, insurance and CTP insurance.

Fuel prices are unlikely to go down in the future, whether because of the scarcity of oil or climate change strategies. If you're planning to go on some long road trips, you need to factor this increase into your budget.

If you're eligible for a Pensioner Concession Card, you should be entitled to a discount on your vehicle registration.

Many people buy a new car at the start of their retirement, expecting the car to see them out, but if you have 20 to 30 years of retirement ahead of you, you should probably budget for at least one other new car during this time.

Some retirees need to downsize, and that may involve changing to a smaller car or, for a two-car family, selling one car. Obviously, where you live has a bearing on this decision. If you live close to public transport, having only one car may not be a problem. But if you live away from public transport, selling one car may mean a loss of independence for one partner.

When you reach the age of 60 and have retired from full-time work, you're eligible for a Seniors Card, which entitles you to discount travel on public transport as well as some free country rail travel. If you have a disability, you can apply for taxi vouchers.

Clothing

How much you spend on clothing is dictated by your tastes, lifestyle and budget. If you want to save money on clothing you can

- Enrol in a commercial or TAFE course on sewing and/or clothing design and make your own clothes.
- Go op-shopping for cast-off bargains.
- Shop at Direct Factory Outlet centres and warehouses. Find your local outlets in your telephone directory.
- Take up knitting. You can make beautiful designer garments for a fraction of the cost you pay in the shops.

Entertainment

Entertainment is an important aspect of living well and enjoying your retirement. You can still dine out, go to the movies and enjoy reading your favourite newspapers and magazines. Here are a few things you can do to make enjoying your favourite activities less costly:

- Attend performances at your local theatre, rather than at ritzy theatres in town. By doing this you'll not only save money, but you also support your local community and meet your neighbours. You can even get involved in the local theatre troupe if you want to.

- ✔ Pre-book your theatre tickets for the following year: You get better seats *and* save money.

- ✔ Revive the art of the dinner party. Make it a communal affair and ask your friends to bring a dish to share.

- ✔ Take advantage of discount days at your local cinema or take out annual membership at your favourite cinema. Membership often costs about $20 a year and entitles you to discounts and other advantages.

- ✔ Take out a subscription to your favourite magazines and newspapers. Subscribers usually receive good discounts. Or read the magazines and newspapers at the local library — for free.

- ✔ Use your Seniors Card to get discounted admission at most cinemas, theatres, museums and exhibitions.

Health and wellbeing

Australians have their basic medical costs covered by the federal government's Medicare system. The government also operates the *Pharmaceutical Benefits Scheme (PBS)*, which ensures that a range of necessary prescription medicines are available at affordable prices to Australian residents. Visit the Medicare Web site at www.medicareaustralia.gov.au or see Chapter 8 for more information.

If you don't wish to use the public health system and prefer private healthcare, you need to take out private health insurance. Chapter 8 has more information on private health insurance providers, including what they cover and what they don't cover. The Australian government offers a 30 per cent private health insurance rebate: Visit www.medicareaustralia.gov.au or see your financial adviser for more information.

As well as any private health insurance premiums, you also need to factor in the cost of dental check-ups, optical and hearing consultations, medical consultations, ambulance cover, auxiliary care such as physiotherapy and chiropractic, and pharmaceuticals. Have at least one thorough medical check-up each year: See Chapter 7 for a list of basic health screens you should have regularly.

The latest health catchcry is 'Move it or lose it'. To stay fit and healthy you need some form of regular exercise, so don't forget to budget an amount for gym or swimming pool membership, personal training costs or other sporting club membership fees. Chapter 7 has numerous tips on how to stay healthy. You also need to keep your brain ticking over, so factor in the costs of study or bridge club membership as well.

Travel

Most retirees plan to travel at some point in their retirement, but just how much money do you need to set aside? Travelling can be as expensive as you want to make it. If you're going to do the Grey Nomad thing in style and buy a big 4WD and caravan or a motor home, you need to set aside a couple of hundred thousand dollars. Of course, you can travel for less. Chapter 12 has ideas on how to budget for your trip around Australia.

Make a travel wish list, do some research and decide just how much money you're able to set aside for travel. You may decide to do one big trip and then settle for smaller trips closer to home. Or you may opt for a series of five- or six-week trips to different countries. See Chapter 11 for advice on planning your trips, as well as tips on how to reduce your travel costs.

Hobbies

If you watch collecting shows on television, you know just how much money some people are prepared to devote to their hobbies. When your hobby brings you enjoyment, you'll find a way to raise the required funds, whether through swap meets or selling your surplus. Chapter 16 has numerous hints on financing your hobby.

Pets

For your pet, at a minimum you need to factor in amounts to cover food and shelter, annual medical check-ups and vaccinations. In addition, many pets require flea and tick treatments, and special shampoos, and some need to be professionally groomed. And don't forget the occasional treats and toys.

If you're planning to travel and can't take your pet with you, you may also need to factor in boarding costs, unless you have a very obliging friend or relative.

As your pet ages, the veterinary bills will mount. You may also find that your pet has to change to a special (read 'expensive') diet.

Drawing up your budget

Put together a table listing all your *weekly* expenses. Include *everything* you can think of. Use this table as a guide.

Item	Weekly expense
Birthday presents and other gifts	
Books, magazines and newspapers	
Car running costs	
Cleaning products	
Clothing and footwear	
Donations	
Electricity	
Entertainment	
Food and alcohol	
Fuel	
Garden supplies	
Gas	
Gym membership	
Hobbies	
Insurance: health, house and contents, and car	
Internet access	
Medical consultations	
Mortgage repayments or rent payments	
Pets: food, vet fees, treatments	
Pharmaceuticals	
Postage	
Rates	
Telephone (landline and mobile)	
Vehicle running costs	
Water	
Other	

Total this amount and multiply it by 52 to find your *annual* budget for running costs. After you know how much money you need to live on per year, you can add in any extra expenses such as home renovations and travel. From this you can work out how much income you need to generate from your savings and any pensions and allowances.

If you find that you have a shortfall between the amount of money you need to live on and the amount of income you can generate from your savings and pension, you have several options:

✔ If you're still working, you can top up your superannuation before you retire. I explain how to do this in Chapter 4.

✔ If you're no longer working, you can find a part-time job or perhaps make some money from your hobby. Chapter 14 has some hints for job hunting in retirement and Chapter 16 outlines how to turn your hobby into a business.

Your financial adviser can explain how to manage your savings and spending so that you may be eligible for an age pension or part age pension.

Taking Advantage of the Concessions Available

You may be eligible for concession cards such as the Pensioner Concession Card, Seniors Card and Commonwealth Seniors Health Card. These cards offer savings on household, medical and travel expenses.

Pensioner Concession Card

To qualify for the age pension, you must meet certain requirements (see Chapter 5). If you qualify for an age pension (even a partial payment), you also qualify for a Pensioner Concession Card. This card offers a number of concessions to make your retirement income stretch further.

The main benefit of the card is that it gives you discounts on medicines under the PBS and on your medical bills. The card can save you thousands of dollars in medical and pharmaceutical fees each year.

In addition, you may be entitled to receive concessions from state and local government authorities on items such as utility bills and council rates. The concessions vary from state to state. See Chapter 5 for more information.

Seniors Card

All Australians who turn 60 and comply with the work requirements in their state are eligible for a Seniors Card. This card is a reward for your contribution to your local community.

To receive a Seniors Card, you don't need to meet any income or pension limit requirements. The exact conditions of eligibility vary between the states and territories, but the most common conditions are

- You must be retired or not working full-time.
- You must be an Australian citizen, or the holder of a permanent visa.
- You must have lived in your state or territory for a certain number of years.

Some of the main benefits a Seniors Card offers are

- Discount travel on public transport
- Discounts from various supermarkets and wine merchants
- Discount entry at movie theatres, exhibitions and shows
- Discounts at a wide range of other businesses (the exact details vary by state)
- The opportunity to take part in Seniors Week each year, where you can watch free film screenings, try new hobbies and join seniors networks

Although the Seniors Card is an Australia-wide initiative, each state and territory offers the card to its citizens in conjunction with local businesses. Thus, each state and territory offers slightly different benefits to card holders. For example, your state may also offer one or more free country rail trips each year.

Unfortunately, your Seniors Card won't arrive automatically through the post when you turn 60. You have to lodge an application form via your home state or territory. The card is free.

Apply for your card online at www.seniorscard.com.au (click on your home state or territory). Alternatively, you can apply in your home state or territory as follows:

- **Australian Capital Territory:** Apply at ACT government shop fronts, public libraries, Dickson Motor Vehicle Registry and COTAS (Hughes Community Centre, Wisdom Street, Hughes).

- **New South Wales:** Pick up an application form at ANZ bank branches, DADHC regional offices, Legislative Assembly Members' electoral offices, NSW government Access Centres, NSW local council offices, NSW Office of Fair Trading centres, participating council libraries and public trustees offices.

- **Northern Territory:** Apply through your local Post Office, TIO office, motor vehicle registry or community care centre, or call the Office of Senior Territorians on 1800 777 704.

- **Queensland:** Call Smart Service Queensland on 13 13 04. You must have proof-of-age documents or a declaration signed by a Justice of the Peace.

- **South Australia:** Call the Seniors Unit on 1800 819 961.

- **Tasmania:** Download an application form from www.dpac.tas.gov.au/.

- **Victoria:** Download an application form from www.seniorscard.vic.gov.au or pick up a form from your local Post Office.

- **Western Australia:** Download an application form from www.seniorscard.wa.gov.au/index.htm or pick up a form at most major banks. You need to sign a statutory declaration as to your age and identity.

In most cases your application form must be signed by someone who can take sworn declarations, such as a Justice of the Peace, a police officer, a pharmacist, a doctor, a solicitor, a local council officer or a member of Parliament. Rules differ slightly between the states and territories.

You need some form of identification, such as your birth certificate, passport, Australian citizenship papers or driver's licence. Some states and territories require you to show three such pieces of evidence to the Justice of the Peace or other authorised person signing your application form.

Depending on where you live, your application should be processed in about three weeks.

Commonwealth Seniors Health Card

If you're not eligible for the age pension, you'll be pleased to know that you may still qualify for a Commonwealth Seniors Health Card. This card helps you to pay for medical expenses. For example, the card saves you money on pharmaceuticals purchased through the PBS. The cost of PBS prescriptions increases with inflation on 1 January each year, but using the year 2008 as an example, you'd pay $5.00 for a prescription rather than $31.30.

In addition, the government gives doctors an incentive to bulk-bill Commonwealth Seniors Health Card holders. Not all doctors take up this offer, so you need to check with your own doctor.

You may also be eligible for both a Telephone Allowance and a Seniors Concession Allowance. The Telephone Allowance is a small non-taxable payment every three months to help with the costs of your telephone bill, and the Seniors Concession Allowance is a non-taxable payment every six months to help you with regular bills such as rates and utilities bills.

The Seniors Health Card isn't available to everyone. To receive the card you must be an Australian citizen of pensionable age and you must pass an income test. As of 2008, to be eligible to receive the card your annual adjusted taxable income must be less than $50,000 for a single or $80,000 for a couple. If you're separated from your partner due to ill health — for instance, one of you is in a nursing home — your combined income must be less than $100,000.

Go to the Centrelink Web site at www.centrelink.gov.au and search under 'Seniors Health Card' for more detailed information.

Chapter 4

Understanding Superannuation

The federal government introduced the compulsory *superannuation* system in 1992 as a way to ensure that Australians have enough money to live on when they retire and so are less reliant on the age pension. The government *age pension* is a fortnightly payment for those people who can't afford to fully support themselves in their retirement: For more details see Chapter 5. However, many retirees would like a more comfortable lifestyle than they can have living on the age pension alone, and some retirees won't qualify for the age pension, so they use superannuation as a way to save for their retirement.

Amazingly, although billions of dollars are tied up in superannuation, many Australians have no idea how much money they actually have in super — nor how much super they need to have before they can retire.

Superannuation may sound complex, but by understanding a few basics and getting some sound advice, you can take control of your super and make the most of your retirement dollars.

In this chapter I explain some of the basics and point you to places where you can get more information. Knowledge is power — especially when it comes to understanding how your money is working for you.

The information provided in this chapter is of a general nature and you need to seek independent advice specific to your circumstances.

You can find detailed information about superannuation from these great resources:

- The Australian Taxation Office (ATO) Superannuation Web site at www.ato.gov.au/super
- The books *Superannuation For Dummies*, Second Edition, *Superannuation: Planning Your Retirement For Dummies*, and *Superannuation: Choosing a Fund for Dummies*, all by Trish Power (Wiley Publishing Australia Pty Ltd)

Knowing How Super Works

If you're aged between 18 and 70 and earn at least $450 per month before tax working for an employer full-time, part-time or on a casual basis, your employer must pay the equivalent of 9 per cent of your salary into your superannuation fund or retirement savings account. This is called the *superannuation guarantee*. The funds paid are called *employer contributions*.

If you earn less than this amount but are on an award rate, your employer may still have to contribute to your superannuation: Check this out with your union.

If you're self-employed you aren't obliged to pay your own superannuation and have a choice about how to invest your super. Refer to the section 'Making contributions if you're self-employed' later in the chapter.

Have a look at the handy glossary on the ATO's Superannuation Web site if you're not familiar with superannuation terminology.

Who's looking after your super?

Although the government can't guarantee that your super will make a lot of money — or that it won't decrease in value, as happened to many funds in the crash of 2008 — it does make sure that your fund is run properly. Three government agencies regulate and enforce the laws that protect you and your super:

- The *Australian Prudential Regulation Authority* (APRA) regulates how all super funds (except self-managed funds) are run.

✔ The *Australian Securities & Investments Commission* regulates and licenses all super funds (except self-managed super funds) and makes sure that they're run efficiently and honestly.

✔ The *Australian Taxation Office* regulates all self-managed funds, as well as keeping an eye on employer contributions, co-contributions and other tax rules.

Understanding the benefits of super

By investing in a superannuation fund your money compounds over time, so when you retire you should have a decent nest egg. You'll also get tax benefits. To put it very simply:

✔ Any concessional contributions your employer makes on your behalf and any salary sacrifice contributions you make to your super fund attract only a 15 per cent tax levy.

✔ Money earned through investments in your super fund is taxed at 15 per cent. Money invested outside super attracts normal tax rates, which can be as high as 45 per cent (plus the Medicare levy of 1.5 per cent).

In addition, when you turn 60 and take your money out of your super fund, either as a lump sum or via an allocated pension, you won't have to pay any tax on it. (This is a general rule. If you belong to an untaxed super fund, you'll be taxed at a marginal rate of 15 per cent.)

Keep tabs on how much has been paid into your super fund by checking your annual member statement, which you'll receive from the fund. This statement also details any co-contributions or other payments you've made into the fund.

To ensure that all employer contributions and your salary sacrifice contributions are taxed at the rate of 15 per cent, you must supply your tax file number (TFN) to your super fund. If you don't supply your TFN, then after-tax contributions can't be accepted by the super fund, and before-tax contributions are taxed at the top marginal rate (including the Medicare levy) of 46.5 per cent. Visit the ATO's Web site at www.ato.gov.au for more details.

Calculating your retirement needs

The big question is, how much money do you need to have in your super fund to lead a comfortable life in your retirement?

To answer this question, follow these steps:

1. **Work out how much money you need to live the retirement lifestyle you want.** According to the Association of Superannuation Funds of Australia (ASFA), to have a *comfortable* retirement a couple needs about $50,561 per year and a single about $37,829, and for a *modest* retirement a couple needs about $27,454 per year and a single $19,617. 'Comfortable' covers the basic necessities plus eating out three times a week and domestic travel plus the occasional overseas trip, whereas 'modest' means no expensive overseas trips, eating out at low-budget restaurants no more than once a week and buying your clothes from chain stores, not boutiques.

See the ASFA's Web site at www.superannuation.asn.au/RS/default.aspx to view more budgets for retirement living for Australians.

2. **Calculate out how much superannuation savings you need to fund that lifestyle.** One of the easiest ways to do this is by using an online superannuation calculator.

For example, according to one online calculator, if you plan to retire at 65 and want to have a comfortable lifestyle in your retirement, you'll need to have a superannuation fund of about $710,000 to give you and your partner a retirement income of $50,000 per year. For this calculation you need to own your own home and make no big purchases when you retire.

Unfortunately, you can only live until 84 before your money runs out. However, this calculation assumes that your spending remains at the same level throughout your retirement. In reality, you probably spend more money in the first five or so years of retirement than you do in later years, so hopefully you can afford to live a bit longer.

Here are just some of the many superannuation calculators you can find on the Web:

- AMP: www.amp.com.au
- Bridges: www.bridgesweb.com.au
- Colonial First State: www.colonialfirststate.com.au
- FIDO (Australian Securities & Investments Commission): www.asic.gov.au/fido (this site also covers how much money you'll need for your retirement)
- Vanguard: www.vanguard.com.au

You may like to try more than one to see whether the results differ.

Online superannuation calculators are guides only and you need to seek independent financial advice.

Think you may not have sufficient funds in your super for your retirement years? See the section 'Growing Your Super Fund' later in the chapter for tips on how to grow your super faster.

Choosing Your Fund

Under the latest superannuation rules most people can now choose which superannuation fund they wish to invest in. Visit www.fido.gov.au to find out whether you're eligible to choose your super fund.

Being able to choose your fund is especially useful if you change employer. You can roll over your funds into the fund your new employer favours or you can ask your new employer to pay into the fund of your choice. For more information on rolling over any funds, see the section 'Finding lost super and consolidating your accounts' later in the chapter.

Whichever fund you choose, it must be a *complying* super fund — that is, one that meets certain government rules and regulatory requirements. Ask your super fund about this or check out the ATO's Superannuation Web site.

When you're opening a new super fund, read all the instructions on the form carefully and supply all proof-of-identity documents required, or you'll have to submit the form again.

The ATO lists the main types of superannuation schemes available as:

- Corporate super funds
- Industry super funds
- Public offer funds
- Public sector funds
- Retail funds
- Retirement savings accounts
- Self-managed super funds
- Small APRA funds

Industry super funds and retail funds can be public offer funds too. Generally, you can't choose a corporate super fund unless you're employed by the company, and the same usually applies to public sector funds.

Talk to your financial adviser if you're not sure which type of fund is best for you.

Industry super funds

Some workers are subject to agreements or awards which means that their super contributions are paid into an *industry super fund*. Many industry super funds are now public offer funds, meaning that the funds can accept members who don't necessarily work for a particular employer in a particular industry. If you're able to choose your own fund, you can choose to contribute to an industry super fund.

Check out the Industry SuperFunds Web site at www.industrysuper.com for more information. The site details the benefits of joining an industry super fund, the various industry super funds available and how to choose a fund, as well as having helpful links to SuperRatings, the Australian Securities & Investments Commission and the ATO.

Retail funds

Retail funds are super funds that are run by financial institutions such as banks and financial planning groups — for example, Asgard, AMP and Colonial First State. The superannuation industry has traditionally viewed retail funds as offering more features, such as greater investment choice, than industry or corporate super funds.

Retirement savings accounts

Retirement savings accounts (RSAs) are offered by banks, credit unions, life insurance companies, building societies and prescribed financial providers. They aren't super funds, but they operate under similar rules. Your employer can pay into your RSA as it would into a superannuation fund: contributions are tax deductible and satisfy the superannuation guarantee obligations. You can find comprehensive information about RSAs on the ATO's Superannuation Web site.

Self-managed super funds

You can choose to set up your own superannuation fund called a *self-managed super fund* (SMSF). The main advantage of such a fund is that you have the ability to control your own investments. You and up to three other people can be trustees of the fund: The trustees control the fund. As a trustee, you can choose to seek advice from a financial adviser, but by law the trustees must make all the investment decisions.

You generally can't use your self-managed super fund to buy golf membership, homes for family members or an expensive cellar of wine. Any investment that is made by your super fund must benefit the fund, *not* the trustees' personal business affairs.

When you set up a self-managed super fund, you need to meet a number of conditions. For example, you must

- ✔ **Appoint an approved auditor each year to audit your fund.** The auditor must meet certain standards of registration and qualifications.
- ✔ **Lodge a tax return each year.** You can engage a tax accountant to do this for you.
- ✔ **Maintain accurate accounting records.** This can be done by a qualified accountant.

All trustees must comply with the rules and regulations as set out on the ATO's Superannuation Web site. From the site you can download a very easy-to-follow pamphlet, 'Roles and responsibilities of SMSF trustees'.

The trustees of a self-managed super fund are ultimately responsible for the fund. Trustees must keep their fund's affairs separate from their personal business affairs. They mustn't withdraw money from their fund until the fund members reach preservation age or retire permanently from the workforce. If trustees don't meet their responsibilities, they can be disqualified from acting as trustees of a superannuation fund and the fund can be made non-complying, meaning that investments are taxed at the penalty rate of 45 per cent instead of 15 per cent.

Making Super Contributions

You can contribute to your super fund in two ways:

- ✔ Your compulsory employer contributions
- ✔ Your voluntary contributions

Compulsory employer contributions

The contributions your employer makes to your super fund are called the superannuation guarantee. Your employer must pay the equivalent of 9 per cent of your salary into your super fund on a quarterly basis.

Voluntary contributions

If you wish to top up your super so that you have more money in retirement, and you're under 65, you can make personal contributions to your complying super fund whether you're in the workforce or not. In some cases you may be able to claim a tax deduction where you receive no employer superannuation contributions. If you're between 65 and 75 you can make contributions if you've worked 40 hours in a continuous 30-day period in the financial year in which you plan to make a super contribution.

Your voluntary contributions take the form of concessional, or pre-tax, contributions and non-concessional, or after-tax, contributions:

- ✔ *Concessional contributions* are those contributions made into your fund from your pre-tax income. You can contribute only $50,000 before tax per year to your fund. Currently, after you turn 50, there's a limit of $100,000 before tax on such contributions, but this limit will revert to $50,000 from 1 July 2012.

- ✔ *Non-concessional contributions* (formerly known as undeducted contributions) are personal contributions to your super from your after-tax income. These contributions are deducted from your pay after tax has been taken out and you don't receive a tax deduction for making them. You can contribute up to $150,000 per year to your super fund (or you can contribute $450,000 averaged over three years if you're under 65 and contribute more than $150,000 in the first year).

If you make concessional or non-concessional contributions, you may be able to take advantage of the federal government's Super Co-contribution Scheme. You can read more about this in the section 'Super Co-contribution Scheme' later in the chapter.

Making contributions if you're self-employed

Self-employed people aren't obliged to pay their own superannuation, so if you're self-employed, statistically you're less likely to have money invested in a super fund. As a result, the government has tried to make superannuation more attractive to you.

For instance, if you're self-employed or *substantially self-employed*, you can generally claim a full tax deduction for any payments you make into super until you're 75. *Substantially self-employed* means you earn less than 10 per cent of your annual assessable income from an employer. The ATO's Web site explains the specific requirements for claiming a tax deduction as a self-employed person.

You can also top up your super by making concessional and non-concessional contributions (see the section 'Voluntary contributions' above). You may also be able to take advantage of the federal government's Super Co-contribution Scheme. If you earn less than $60,342 per year (for the 2008/2009 financial year) and make a personal after-tax contribution to your super fund, you may be eligible for the government's co-contribution, whereby for every $1 you put in, the government will put in up to $1.50, to a maximum of $1,500 per year. To work out what you're earning, add up your income (including fringe benefits) and subtract your business expenses. For more information about the Super Co-contribution Scheme and your eligibility if you're self-employed, go to the ATO's Superannuation Web site.

The rules discussed here came into effect from 1 July 2007. If you're researching information on the Web, make sure you're visiting up-to-date sites or go to the ATO's Superannuation Web site for more information.

If you're self-employed but are hired as a contractor principally for your labour, whether physical or artistic, your employer may have to pay your superannuation benefits. You can find out more about this on the ATO's Superannuation Web site under the heading 'Super for contractors'.

Growing Your Super Fund

If you're nearing retirement age and don't think you have enough money in your super fund, don't panic — you can grow your super account in a number of ways. Check out the ideas in this section.

These strategies are especially important for women, who may have less super than men if they've taken career breaks to raise their children.

Up to the age of 65 your employer makes contributions on your behalf and you can contribute to your super whenever you like. If you're between 65 and 70 your employer makes contributions on your behalf and you can contribute yourself if you've worked 40 hours in a continuous 30-day period in the financial year in which you plan to make a super contribution. After you turn 70 your employer isn't required to make contributions on your behalf but you can still take advantage of salary sacrifice opportunities. Consult the ATO for more specific information on contributing to super after you turn 70.

The advantage of putting more funds into super is that when you reach 60 and retire your income from your super fund will be tax-free.

You can put extra money into super by direct debit, BPAY, Internet banking or cheque, depending on the payment procedures applicable to your fund.

Ask your financial adviser how to time contributions of large amounts of money to your super fund for the best possible tax benefits.

Super Co-contribution Scheme

The federal government's *Super Co-contribution Scheme* is targeted at low-income earners. Basically, under the scheme for every after-tax dollar you voluntarily contribute to your superannuation fund the government gives you up to an extra $1.50 tax-free to put into your super fund, up to a maximum of $1,500 per year.

Of course, rules apply. If you earn up to $30,342 per year (for the 2008/2009 financial year), you're eligible for the full $1.50 government co-contribution for every $1 you put in. The government's co-contributions decrease as your income increases and phase out if you earn more than $60,342 (for the 2008/2009 financial year).

So, if you're a low-income earner (earning up to $30,342) and make an additional after-tax contribution of $20 per week over the course of the year (that's $1,000 per year) you're eligible for an *extra* $1,500 which the government pays into your super fund.

Salary sacrificing

You can choose to make *extra* contributions to your super fund from your pre-tax income to top up your super. This is known as *salary sacrificing*. With salary sacrificing, not only do you add to your super account, but you also don't pay as much tax on your income. This is because the amount you sacrifice into super is concessionally taxed at a rate of 15 per cent and your remaining salary is lower, so you don't pay as much tax on that. The amount that can be taxed concessionally is limited per year.

To view a table demonstrating the amount of tax you can save by salary sacrificing go to the ATO's Superannuation Web site and click on 'Individuals Superannuation Essentials' under 'For Superannuation'. Then select 'Growing and Consolidating Super' and click on 'Salary Sacrificing Super'.

You may also be eligible for the mature-age worker tax offset, which rewards mature-age workers for staying in the workplace with a tax offset of $500.

Currently, the maximum amount that can be salary sacrificed is $50,000 if you're 49 or under and $100,000 if you're 50 or over. You have to get going if you wish to take this path because from 2012 this maximum amount will be reduced to $50,000. This concessional cap covers all your concessional super contributions for the year, including additional employer super guarantee payments. Contributions that exceed the capped amount are taxed at 45 per cent plus the 1.5 per cent Medicare levy.

You may not want to salary sacrifice your entire income, because the first $6,000 of your taxable income is free from tax.

Make sure you negotiate salary sacrificing carefully with your employer, or you could find that your salary sacrificing decreases your compulsory employer super contributions. For more information, talk to your financial adviser or see the ATO's Superannuation Web site.

Taking a TRIP to retirement

If you've reached your preservation age (the minimum legal age at which you can retire and be eligible for superannuation benefits) and are still working, you can start a *transition-to-retirement pension (TRIP)*. This enables you to salary sacrifice part or all of your income to build up your super and then draw down a pension from your super fund. You can enjoy the tax advantages associated with income streams such as a 15 per cent rebate on your pension income if you're under the age of 60, or tax-free income if you're 60 or over.

TRIPping a tax benefit

If you choose to start a transition-to-retirement pension (TRIP), depending on the strategies you use you can reduce the amount of tax you pay while boosting your super benefit.

For example, an individual with a $1 million super balance and earning $100,000 a year can save more than $25,000 per year in taxes by starting a transition-to-retirement pension, while still receiving the same level of after-tax income and boosting her super benefit. *Note:* You don't need $1 million in super to slash your tax bill.

To avoid tripping up on your TRIP, work through this scenario with your financial adviser.

The money used to pay the TRIP is in *pension phase*, which means that any earnings on those pension assets are tax-free. This is a very tax-effective way to build up your super.

You can take a TRIP without salary sacrificing if you want to access your super early, but this won't help you to increase your super.

TRIPs have a number of associated conditions, so seek sound financial advice before taking this option.

Finding lost super and consolidating your accounts

Like many Australians, if you've held a number of jobs over the years you probably have small amounts of super in several different funds. In addition, you may have forgotten about some of your super funds if they were set up some years ago.

To search for lost super funds go to the ATO's Superannuation Web site and use the 'SuperSeeker' facility.

To consolidate or roll over your funds you can download the 'Portability form' (otherwise known as the 'Request to transfer whole balance of superannuation benefits between funds' form) from the ATO's Superannuation Web site, or you can ask your super fund for the form. Note:

- ✔ If you use the ATO's 'Portability form', you must transfer *all* of your super balance, not part of it.
- ✔ You must use a separate form for each fund you wish to roll over.

You can make periodic transfers from your super fund, provided you leave a minimum of $5,000 in the account.

By rolling over all your different funds into the one fund you should save on multiple administration fees.

However, first you need to check whether in so doing you'll be up for any fees (such as termination fees) or lose any benefits, particularly insurance benefits. Read the small print.

Be careful also about changing funds because your fund hasn't performed well over the past year. It may not be cost-effective to change funds: You may lose insurance benefits or have to pay an exit fee.

Seek sound financial advice before you make any changes.

Contributing to your spouse's super

If your spouse has a low income, you can contribute to his or her super fund. You can claim a tax offset of 18 per cent for up to $3,000 worth of contributions to a complying super fund or RSA on your spouse's behalf. Your spouse is someone who lives with you as your husband or wife — you don't have to be married to your spouse.

If your spouse earns less than $10,800 per year, you can make an after-tax contribution of $3,000 to his or her super fund. This may qualify you for a tax rebate of $450.

Similarly, if you're the one with a low income, your spouse can contribute to your super fund as outlined here.

Taking Money Out of Super

Before 9 May 2006 you had to cash in your super when you reached 65, unless you satisfied a work test. Now you don't have to take your benefits out of super: they can stay there indefinitely. However, if you do want to cash in your super, you have to wait until you reach 65, or your preservation age and retire. Your *preservation age* is the minimum legal age at which you can retire and be eligible for superannuation benefits. If you were born before 1960, your preservation age is 55.

Saved by the bell

Paula Davies is a freelance artist and teacher who longs for retirement. Teaching was Paula's life for more than 30 years, but after several clashes with problematic staff and the ongoing challenges of bureaucracy, Paula found herself spending more and more time on her part-time work as an artist.

At first, Paula wasn't terribly concerned about her super. She had some invested for her in a teacher's industry fund, but paid little attention to it. However, as her troubles at work mounted and her retirement age grew closer, she became more interested in her super.

'My first priority was to renovate my home to suit my soon-to-be freelance life, and then pay off my mortgage', Paula says. Paula invested much of her time and money in building a detached studio next to her home. 'I can use the space for my own art, or to teach workshops, or even as a gallery space.'

Paula rolled over her existing super into a more suitable fund. 'I didn't realise that I had a choice. I just thought I had to do as I was told, but I went to see a financial planner who suggested I look at alternative funds to the one that I was in. Now I feel like my money is working harder for me, and I'm much more likely to have a nice little nest egg ready for when I finally quit.'

Even though retirement is still a couple of years away, Paula is glad she's planning now with an ongoing career as a freelancer in mind. 'I don't want to teach any more, but I won't ever stop being an artist. This way I can be freelance, without worrying about not having any money. It's the best of both worlds.'

Accessing your super fund early

If you're under 65 or haven't reached your preservation age and retired, you may be able to take money out of your super account, but you have to meet a *condition of release* before you can access the money. This means you have to have turned 65, retired permanently, become permanently incapacitated or satisfied another condition of release. You can find out more about the conditions of release on the ATO's Web site. An exception to this rule is if you decide to begin a transition-to-retirement pension.

You can also apply for early release of your money on compassionate grounds. If you're suffering a terminal illness or facing extreme financial hardship, you may be able to access your super. You need to apply to the Australian Prudential Regulation Authority to access your super benefits early on compassionate grounds. You can find out more on APRA's Web site at www.apra.gov.au.

The ATO has issued a warning about illegal schemes to access your superannuation early. Both the instigators and the users of any such schemes face fines and worse. See the ATO's Web site to download a brochure on the topic.

Turning your super into an income stream

When you retire, you'll probably want to set up an income stream using your super, so that you receive a regular living allowance. You can do this in several ways:

✔ Set up a standard account-based pension from your super fund, which provides you with an income stream from your super savings.

✔ Purchase an annuity or other form of lifetime income stream.

✔ Withdraw all your money from your super account in one lump sum and invest it in non-super assets. You can then set up your own income stream subject to marginal tax rates.

The Department of Families, Housing, Community Services and Indigenous Affairs has a downloadable booklet on its Web site at www.fahcsia.gov.au detailing the pros and cons of different income streams.

You don't have to confine yourself to just one type of income stream in retirement. You can combine different pensions — just be aware of the fees charged.

Standard account-based pensions

A *standard account-based pension* enables you to roll over your super money into an account held in your name in your super fund. It's an account-based income stream that grows as your investment grows and decreases as you withdraw money.

A standard account-based pension can run for your lifetime and transfer to your spouse after you die. You can will it to your beneficiaries. You can access your capital at any time, including as lump sums.

Standard account-based pensions have a number of tax benefits:

✔ A 15 per cent rebate is available on the taxable amount of the pension income received for individuals under age 60.

✔ All pension payments are tax-free for those aged 60 and over.

✔ No tax applies on investment earnings from pension assets.

However, several regulations apply. For example:

- An account-based pension isn't exempt from the assets test for social security benefits.
- You can take your payments monthly, quarterly, six-monthly or annually.
- You must take a minimum payment from your account each year in accordance with payment factors set by the federal government.

Your pension can run out. Its life depends on a number of factors, including:

- How much money you have in your super account
- How many lump-sum withdrawals you make
- How much you pay in fees and charges
- How well your investments perform

Try using an online calculator to get an estimated projection of your account-based pension benefit.

If you've turned 60 and retired, you don't have to set up an account-based pension to access your super. You can simply make lump-sum withdrawals when you need to.

Annuities

An *annuity* is a regular payment of income for a specified period that you purchase with a lump sum. It provides you with a guaranteed minimum income. You don't have to worry about market fluctuations: Your payment is guaranteed for the agreed term. You can purchase an annuity or lifetime income stream from a product provider such as a life insurance company or funds manager. You can't commence a lifetime income stream within your self-managed super fund, although such income streams exist in older self-managed super funds.

A lifetime annuity:

- Can't be cashed out in a lump sum. You can't get extra money for a big purchase if you need it.
- Has locked-in payments at the beginning of the year. Payments can't be varied over the course of the year.
- Run for a fixed term based either on your life or life expectancy or your spouse's life or life expectancy (if your spouse is a beneficiary and is expected to live longer than you).

In most cases, if you die prematurely, you can't pass on your money unless it goes to your spouse or dependent child, who will receive only a percentage of the income.

Willing Your Super

You may think your superannuation fund is an asset that you own and thus you can bequeath it to whomever you like. Unfortunately, this isn't quite the way it works.

You need to make very certain that you have a valid nomination regarding your super. You must renew this nomination every three years, although some self-managed super funds allow you to make a perpetual nomination.

If you've stipulated the beneficiary of your superannuation fund, when you die the payment can go directly to your beneficiary rather than through your estate.

Your non-dependent heirs (adult children) will generally have to pay a tax on this money, but if you leave your super to your spouse he or she won't have to pay tax on it.

Find more on this topic in Chapter 6 and on the ATO's Web site.

Chapter 5

The Age Pension

· ·

In This Chapter

▶ Working out your entitlements

▶ Assessing your eligibility for the pension

▶ Completing your application

▶ Identifying what benefits you'll receive

▶ Accessing a pension if you've lived overseas

▶ Knowing what pension to apply for if you're a veteran

· ·

*L*ike many Australians, most, if not all, of your income in retirement will probably be made up of pensions. People who can't fully support themselves in their retirement may qualify for the federal government's age pension. The *age pension* is a taxpayer-funded basic retirement income, paid fortnightly.

In this chapter, I outline who's eligible to receive the age pension, how you apply for the age pension and the benefits you'll receive.

Understanding the Age Pension

A government age pension gives you a small income stream in your retirement. You can apply for the age pension when you reach the qualifying age. The qualifying age is different for men and women, and to be eligible for the pension you also need to meet the income and assets tests — see the section 'Qualifying for the Age Pension'.

Make sure that you seek financial advice if you have a source of income, so that you can maximise your opportunity to get a full or part age pension income or a Pensioner Concession Card. This card is worthwhile, especially if you have lots of medical and pharmaceutical bills.

The Pension Bonus Scheme rewards you if you continue in paid work after your pensionable age and defer claiming the age pension or service pension. You can find more about this scheme in Chapter 14.

Centrelink is the federal government agency responsible for administering Australia's social security system. Contact Centrelink for more detailed information about the age pension.

- ✔ Call 13 23 00
- ✔ Go to www.centrelink.gov.au
- ✔ Visit your local Centrelink office

Qualifying for the Age Pension

Not everyone qualifies for the age pension. To be eligible to receive the age pension you need to meet certain age, income, assets and residency tests:

- ✔ **Age requirements.** Men must be over 65. For women, the qualifying age depends on their date of birth and rises on a sliding scale. For example, for women born before 30 June 1944 the qualifying age is 63, and for women born after 1 January 1949 the qualifying age is 65.

- ✔ **Income and assets requirements.** To qualify for the full age pension your income and assets must be valued below a certain amount. You may be able to get a part pension if they're valued over this amount. The qualifying assets test was relaxed in 2008. Full details of these tests are available on Centrelink's Web site.

- ✔ **Residency requirements.** You must be an Australian resident and in the country on the day you lodge your application for the pension. Check out Centrelink's Web site for the full meaning of the term 'resident'. In addition, you must meet the 10-year permanent residence requirement unless you meet certain criteria, as outlined on Centrelink's Web site.

Before you can receive the age pension you must provide a full list of your income and assets. The rate of payment you receive is calculated under both the income and assets tests. The test that results in the lower rate (or nil rate) is the one that applies.

If you're legally blind you don't need to meet any income or assets tests to qualify for the age pension.

Meeting the assets test

For the purpose of the age pension, assets include just about anything you own, although *not* your family home or any permanent fixtures in your home such as wall heaters and fitted carpets. Here are some examples of assets:

- ✔ Any money you have, whether in a bank account or another form such as shares, insurance policies and loans you've made to anyone, including family
- ✔ Cars, boats and caravans
- ✔ Collections
- ✔ Holiday homes and rental properties
- ✔ Household contents and personal effects
- ✔ Most income streams
- ✔ Superannuation and roll-over funds

The following are some of the items that are *exempt* from the assets test:

- ✔ All the land included on the title of the house if you own a rural property (but you must have a 20-year attachment to the land and be making productive use of the land)
- ✔ Burial plots, prepaid funeral plans and funeral bonds valued at no more than $10,250 in total as of November 2008 — for more information see Centrelink's Web site
- ✔ Income derived from renting out your house after you've moved into an aged-care facility if the rent is used to pay an accommodation bond by periodic instalments (a carer's allowance isn't income tested)
- ✔ Medals of valour if they aren't part of a collection
- ✔ Your caravan or boat if it's your home

If you have a lot of assets and not much income, you may not qualify for the age pension unless under special circumstances whereby it's impossible for you to sell your assets. Contact Centrelink for more information.

Assets are calculated on two levels: homeowners and non-homeowners.

Homeowners

The following qualifying thresholds apply:

- ✔ **Couples.** If your combined assets are worth up to $243,500 you may qualify for the *full* age pension, and if they're worth more than $243,500 but less than $873,500, you may qualify for a *part* pension. If you're separated due to illness, the figure for qualifying for a part pension increases to $1,001,000.

  Note: If you have more than $243,500 worth of assets, your age pension will reduce by $1.50 per fortnight for every $1,000 you have above this limit.

- ✔ **Singles.** If your assets are worth up to $171,750, you may qualify for the *full* age pension, and if they're worth more than $171.750 but less than $550,500, you may qualify for a *part* pension.

  Note: If you have more than $171,750 worth of assets, your age pension will reduce by $1.50 per fortnight for every $1,000 you have above this limit.

Non-homeowners

The following qualifying thresholds apply:

- ✔ **Couples.** If your combined assets are worth up to $368,000, you may qualify for the *full* age pension, and if they're worth more than $368,000 but less than $998,000 you may qualify for a *part* pension. If you're separated due to illness, the figure for qualifying for a part pension increases to $1,125,000.

  Note: If you have more than $368,000 worth of assets, your age pension will reduce by $1.50 per fortnight for every $1,000 you have above this limit.

- ✔ **Singles.** If your assets are worth up to $296,250 you may qualify for the *full* age pension, and if they're worth more than $296,250 but less than $675,000 you may qualify for a *part* pension.

  Note: If you have more than $296,250 worth of assets, your age pension will reduce by $1.50 per fortnight for every $1,000 you have above this limit.

Check the qualifying thresholds each year on Centrelink's Web site, because the upper thresholds are indexed quarterly in line with adjustments to the age pension and the lower threshold is indexed annually.

Make sure that you get advice specific to your circumstances, especially with regard to superannuation assets and income. Talk to your financial adviser.

Meeting the income test

Income means pretty much any money, gifts, goods or services that you receive. Your income can be derived from sources such as:

- ✔ Allocated or term pensions or annuities
- ✔ Farm or business income
- ✔ Overseas pensions or other monies
- ✔ Rent from property or boarders
- ✔ Superannuation
- ✔ Work

You can work or have other income and still qualify for the age pension:

- ✔ Couples can have a combined income of $240 per week and still qualify for the full pension (the amount is the same if partners are separated due to illness)
- ✔ Singles can have an income of $138 per week and still qualify for the full pension

However, after your income exceeds the qualifying amount the pension reduces by 20 cents in the dollar each for couples and 40 cents in the dollar for singles. Check these thresholds for updates on Centrelink's Web site.

Accessing the Age Pension

When you reach pensionable age, you need to take certain steps to gain access to the age pension; you don't receive the payments automatically. You have to apply to Centrelink to receive them. This includes filling in forms and supplying proof-of-identity and financial information to Centrelink. It may take six to eight weeks before you begin to receive your income and other benefits, so start the ball rolling as soon as you can.

If you want the age pension to apply from the earliest possible date, you or your representative need to notify Centrelink that you intend to apply for the age pension. You must then return your application form within 14 days or your pension payments may not begin until the date the form is returned.

You must supply Centrelink with the required approved proof-of-identity documents, including

- ✔ Australian visa
- ✔ Birth certificate
- ✔ Citizenship certificate
- ✔ Current Australian passport

For a full list of documents that can provide proof of identity, go to Centrelink's Web site and download the 'Proving your identity to Centrelink' form.

You must also allow Centrelink access to all your financial information. You need to supply

- ✔ Bank statements
- ✔ Financial statements
- ✔ Lists of shares you hold
- ✔ Tax returns

Understanding Your Benefits

The benefits supplied by Centrelink to age pension recipients consist of fortnightly payments and/or discounts in the form of a Pensioner Concession Card, as well as a Pharmaceutical Allowance, Utilities Allowance and Telephone Allowance. You may also be eligible to receive Rent Assistance if you are paying rent, subject to certain conditions.

Fortnightly payments

As of September 2008, for the full age pension, singles receive fortnightly payments of $562.10 and couples receive fortnightly payments of $469.50 each.

If you're eligible, you may also receive a loan under the Pension Loans Scheme. Those eligible for the scheme receive a loan against their assets, charged at compound interest rates.

Pensioner Concession Card

As an age pension recipient you also qualify for a Pensioner Concession Card. The main benefits of the card include

- ✔ Discount medicines under the Pharmaceutical Benefits Scheme (PBS) and discounted medical care
- ✔ Discounts from participating supermarkets, cinemas and other places offering concessions

Using the card can save you thousands of dollars in medical and pharmaceutical fees each year.

In addition, you may be entitled to receive concessions from state and local government authorities. For example, you may be able to receive

- ✔ Discounts on council rates, energy bills, telephone expenses and motor registration
- ✔ Reduced fares on public transport

These concessions vary from state to state. Go to www.australia.gov.au for more information on the benefits and payments in your state.

Pharmaceutical Allowance

You'll also receive a Pharmaceutical Allowance, which is included in your pension, if you're eligible. This is a small fortnightly payment to help with the costs of buying medicine. You don't need to apply separately to receive this allowance: You receive it automatically with your pension if you're eligible. However, you can apply to receive your allowance in advance. After you've paid for 58 prescriptions through the PBS in a calendar year, any further PBS prescriptions you need filled are free for the rest of the year.

Telephone and Utilities Allowances

The *Telephone Allowance* is paid to eligible pensioners and Commonwealth Seniors Health Card holders to help them to pay their telephone bills. You may get an increased payment if you subscribe to a home Internet service.

The *Utilities Allowance* is a payment that helps age pensioners with the costs of energy, rates, water and sewerage bills. This payment is not subject to an income assets test.

You don't have to apply for either of these allowances: Your eligibility is assessed automatically by Centrelink when you claim your Centrelink payment or Seniors Health Card.

The Telephone and Utilities Allowances come with a set of obligations. For example, if you receive the Telephone Allowance you must tell Centrelink if you cease to be a telephone and/or home Internet subscriber. And, as with all monies received under the age pension, you must advise Centrelink if your financial situation changes. Visit Centrelink's Web site for more information.

Rent Assistance

As part of the age pension you may be entitled to Rent Assistance if you don't own your own home and are renting privately. To view the full eligibility criteria, go to Centrelink's Web site.

You don't need to lodge a separate claim for Rent Assistance, but you do need to provide Centrelink with proof that you pay rent and complete a Rent Certificate.

The maximum rate for Rent Assistance is as follows:

- ✔ **Couples.** $103.80 if your rent is above $298.00 per fortnight. You receive no payment if your rent is below $159.60 per fortnight.
- ✔ **Singles.** $110.20 if your rent is above $244.93 per fortnight. You receive no payment if your rent is below $98.00 per fortnight.

When you're living in a retirement village

You may be entitled to Rent Assistance if you live in a retirement village. This is determined by the amount you contribute on entry to the village. The amount of assistance you receive is based on your weekly accommodation payments. You need to provide Centrelink with your purchase contract or entry agreement so that Centrelink can decide whether you're eligible for Rent Assistance.

When you're travelling around in your Winnebago

If you own your own home and rent it out while you're away travelling, the rental income you receive is counted as income and your pension will be reduced accordingly. You aren't entitled to Rent Assistance for the first 12 months you're travelling. After that, if you're still renting out your own home it's counted as an asset and will affect your pension accordingly, but you may be entitled to Rent Assistance.

If you don't own your home and are paying rent on your principal home while you're travelling, you're entitled to Rent Assistance. If you leave your principal home permanently and take to the road you may still get Rent Assistance, but you need to notify Centrelink of every change of principal dwelling, whether it's a motel, caravan or tent.

Travelling overseas

You can travel overseas for up to 26 weeks and keep your fortnightly payments and Pensioner Concession Card. If you're going to be away from Australia for longer than this, your pension may be reduced. However long you're going to be away, you must notify Centrelink of your travel dates before you go and confirm how your benefits may be affected.

Some entitlements may change, so it's important that you notify Centrelink of your travel arrangements and check that you don't need to reapply for your Pensioner Concession Card when you return to Australia.

Gifting

When you receive the age pension, you're limited in how much money you can give away each year. This is called *gifting*. You can gift no more than $10,000 per year or $30,000 over five years. Any amounts you gift above this are counted as assets.

The rules on gifting apply for five years *before* you start to receive the age pension. This prevents people giving away their money so that they can qualify for the full age pension or part age pension. However, you can spend your money in other ways, such as renovating your home, travelling overseas and purchasing funeral bonds.

Receiving a Pension if You've Lived Overseas

Many countries, of which Australia is one, see the age pension as being derived from your financial contributions and believe it should be portable. Australia has reciprocal social security agreements with a number of countries, including: Austria, Belgium, Canada, Chile, Croatia, Cyprus, Denmark, Germany, Greece, Italy, Ireland, Malta, New Zealand, Portugal, Spain, Slovenia, Switzerland, the Netherlands and the US. These are known as *agreement countries*. Australia is finalising its negotiations with Finland and Poland. If you've lived in both Australia and an agreement country you may be able to receive at least part of an Australian age pension under the scheme.

If you've lived and worked in another country or are the widow or widower of someone who has lived and worked in another country or served in the army of another country, Centrelink may require you to apply for an age pension from that country as well as receiving your Australian age pension. You must advise Centrelink of the outcome of this application and your Australian age pension will be reduced accordingly.

If you're from the UK, you can retain your UK pension scheme (see the section 'Retaining your UK pension' later in the chapter).

Benefiting from reciprocal social security agreements

If you live in Australia now but have lived in another country for a creditable amount of time (for example, you worked in or served in the military of another country), before you can claim the age pension in Australia you must first try to get a pension from your other country of residence. If the country is an agreement country, you can obtain the forms to claim this pension from Centrelink. If it is a non-agreement country, you need to obtain a claim form from that country's social security department. Centrelink can help you with this.

In addition, if you live in Australia but don't have enough years of residency to meet the requirements for the age pension, you may be able to use the years you were resident in an agreement country to count towards your Australian residency status. Each country will pay you a part pension. Contact Centrelink for help and more information.

Retaining your UK pension

Australia no longer has a reciprocal social security agreement with the UK. If you were receiving benefits under the agreement before it ended on 1 March 2000, you'll continue to receive those benefits.

You can transfer your UK pension funds to an Australian superannuation fund. A number of companies listed on the Web can help you to do this for a fee. Alternatively, if you want to find your own information go to Her Majesty's Revenue and Customs (HMRC) Web site at www.hmrc.gov.uk.

If you want to transfer your UK pension funds to an Australian super fund, here are some things you need to know:

✔ Not all UK pensions can be transferred. Check the rules of your UK pension fund to see whether your funds can be transferred. For example, UK state pensions cannot be transferred.

✔ You may pay little or no tax if you transfer your money within six months of becoming an Australian resident. After that time, you could lose up to 55 per cent of your pension in UK tax. Some benefits are subject to 15 per cent contributions tax if they were not fully vested in the member at the time of transfer.

✔ You must abide by the caps of the Australian super fund. This means that you can transfer only $450,000 averaged over three years if you're under 65.

✔ Your pension must be transferred to a fund approved by the HMRC as a Qualified Recognised Overseas Pension Scheme. You can find a list of these funds on the HMRC's Web site. If you don't transfer your money to an approved fund, you'll be taxed at 55 per cent in the UK.

Receiving the Service Pension

Veterans may be paid a service pension by the Department of Veterans' Affairs (DVA). This pension provides regular income (paid fortnightly) for people with limited means and is paid to veterans and to their eligible partners, widows and widowers. The service pension is paid five years earlier than the regular age pension in recognition of the effects of war.

When you become eligible for an age pension, you cannot receive *both* the age pension and a service pension.

If you'd prefer to receive your age pension through the DVA, you can transfer your payments from Centrelink using form DO664 ('Claim for transfer of payment of Centrelink age pension to DVA') available from your nearest DVA office. Your partner may also receive an age pension paid through the DVA.

To find out more about the service pension, visit the very user-friendly DVA Web site at www.dva.gov.au.

Chapter 6

Will Making and Estate Planning

*O*nce upon a time, unless you were extremely wealthy, bequeathing your property was very straightforward. You divided up what you had and left it to your children. Nowadays most people have added complications to consider, such as children from different marriages, blended families and superannuation.

You probably didn't expect your parents to provide for you beyond the grave. If they managed to survive the depression years and the war intact, and gave you a happy home environment, good food and an education, you probably felt your parents had fulfilled their duties.

Nowadays, however, while most children believe their parents should enjoy their retirement and the money they worked for, many children also believe they have the right to an inheritance. Due to soaring property costs many young adults cannot afford a family home, so they hope for an inheritance to help them move into the property market down the track.

Baby Boomers are retiring earlier than their parents and grandparents. At the same time, life expectancy has increased. *SKI-ing*, a fun acronym for 'spending the kids inheritance', has now snowballed into a sort of rite of passage to retirement. Retirees no longer imagine spending their retirement years dedicated to a quiet life of knitting, playing bowls and cooking the Sunday roast. Most expect to travel, socialise, and keep mind and body fit and active.

However you decide to dispose of your property — assuming you have anything left after you've SKI-ed through your retirement — you need to make a will.

In this chapter, I explain how to make a valid will and discuss the financial effect your will can have on your heirs. I also outline what you need to know about nominating an executor and granting power of attorney.

Although you can make a valid will yourself, you need to ensure that you understand all the points of law involved in will making and estate planning. This chapter offers a general overview of wills and estate plannings. As these are complex subjects, you should seek qualified professional advice before proceeding further.

You can also find more detailed information on this subject by reading *Australian Wills and Estates For Dummies* by Graham Cooke (Wiley Publishing Australia Pty Ltd).

Making a Will

A *will* is a very important document: It lets other people know what you want to do with your assets when you die. You can download a will-making kit from the Web or buy one at the local newsagency or post office. You can ask a solicitor or the Public Trustee in your state or territory to draw up a will for you. You can even write your will on the back of an envelope. But you *must* make sure that your will is *valid*.

Ensuring that your will is valid

For your will to be valid, it must be

- ✔ **In writing:** It doesn't matter if it's handwritten, printed or typed. It can't be made on an audiocassette or DVD.

- ✔ **Signed by you:** Although you need only sign the end of the document, you may prefer to sign every page, just in case the pages become separated.

- ✔ **Witnessed by two adults in your presence:** The witnesses must be present at the same time and both must witness your signing the will. The witnesses should not be beneficiaries or spouses of beneficiaries.

Your will can be challenged even if it fulfils these criteria. For instance, if it can be argued that you weren't of sound mind or that you left everything to the lost dogs home and disinherited your children, your will can be challenged. If you don't make proper provision for your spouse and children, including your ex-nuptial children, they can take proceedings against your will under the Family Provision Act in your state or territory.

Engaging the Public Trustee to make your will

Each state and territory has a Public Trustee, established by an Act of Parliament. The role of the Public Trustee is to act as an independent and impartial executor, administrator and trustee. This includes making wills, acting as executor in deceased estates, managing trusts and providing attorney services.

The Public Trustee can make a will for you, usually for a fee. Fees and charges differ between states. For example, the Public Trustee of Queensland makes your will free of charge if you appoint it as your executor, whereas the State Trustee of Victoria charges by the hour to make your will, but reduces the fee if you appoint it as your executor.

If you die without a will (*intestate*), the Public Trustee can administer your estate. This doesn't mean your estate will go to the government — but it will be administered according to a set government formula.

If you have no-one to administer your estate, or if appointing an executor from within your family will create family tension, the Public Trustee can execute your will for you. You may also prefer the Public Trustee to take on this role to save your family or friends the trouble. Again, a fee will be charged, on a sliding scale. In some states the Public Trustee publishes these fees on its Web site, whereas in others the fee is calculated based on the real value of the estate and/or the amount of work required to administer the estate.

Find the Public Trustee in your state or territory as follows:

- ✔ **Australian Capital Territory:** Public Advocate of the ACT at www.publicadvocate.act.gov.au

- ✔ **New South Wales:** The Public Trustee of New South Wales at www.pt.nsw.gov.au

- ✔ **Northern Territory:** Office of the Public Trustee Northern Territory at www.nt.gov.au/justice/pubtrust

- **Queensland:** The Public Trustee of Queensland at `www.pt.qld.gov.au`
- **South Australia:** The Public Trustee South Australia at `www.public trustee.sa.on.net`
- **Tasmania:** The Public Trustee for Tasmania at `www.publictrustee.tas.gov.au`
- **Victoria:** State Trustees of Victoria at `www.statetrustees.com.au`
- **Western Australia:** The Public Trustee for Western Australia at `www.justice.wa.gov.au`

Keeping your will up to date

Your will *must* be up to date. Usually you should review it every three to five years. If you get married or remarried, your will is automatically revoked. When your life circumstances change, it's a good idea to update your will (or make a new one). For instance, you should update your will if you:

- Experience the death of a beneficiary
- Find a new partner or re-partner
- Get divorced or separate
- Have a child or grandchild
- Lose your executor through death or other circumstances
- Marry or remarry
- Undergo a change in financial circumstances

Using your will to express your wishes

Make a list of the items you wish to distribute to certain people. You may like to discuss this with your beneficiaries first, to avoid any conflict later. For example, you may want to leave your Royal Albert dinner set to your daughter-in-law or your complete set of *Secret Seven* books to your grandchild. Don't leave it up to your executor to make such decisions, especially if you haven't discussed your wishes with him or her beforehand.

You can either include the list in your will (in which case it will automatically be legally binding) or you can store the list with your will. But don't attach the list with a paper clip. Any marks left on your will from paper clips or staples can indicate that the will has been changed (and thus it may be invalid). If you need to re-staple the pages or make any amendments, print out a new copy of your whole will and get your signature witnessed again.

Be wary of favouring one child over the other(s), because this can lead to expensive court fights where everyone loses.

You can use your will to give bequests to charities or to people who're important to you outside your family. You can also use your will to wield power beyond the grave. For example, you may want to stipulate that your heirs can't use the capital of their inheritance until they reach a certain age.

If you're a tenant in common with another party, you can will your part of the property to another person. However, if you're a joint owner of a property, you can't will your part of the property to another party — your part automatically goes to the other joint owner(s) on your death.

Willing Your Super

You can't bequeath your superannuation in your will. Your superannuation must go to the person(s) you nominated as a beneficiary to your superannuation fund. You don't own the account balance in your super fund and therefore this isn't counted as an asset in terms of bequeathing it to your descendants. However, you can nominate *your estate* as the beneficiary of your superannuation. If you do this, your superannuation will be distributed as per the terms of your will.

Bear in mind that if you nominate your estate as the beneficiary of your superannuation but you haven't made a will, your super fund will be distributed according to government intestacy laws.

If you leave your superannuation separate from your will, the money can be distributed more quickly to your nominated beneficiaries because they don't have to wait until your whole estate has been settled to receive the money.

Nominating a beneficiary

When you start your super fund you're asked to nominate a beneficiary or beneficiaries. Your ideas about who this should be usually change over the life of your fund. For example, when you marry you may wish to nominate your spouse as a beneficiary, but this may change if you remarry. If you die without having any dependants, the super trustees usually pay out to your next of kin.

To be *valid*, your nominated beneficiary must be

- Someone financially dependent on you or in an interdependent relationship with you — this can be a same-sex partner
- Your child/children
- Your legal personal representative (the executor of your estate)
- Your spouse, legally married or de facto, but not a same-sex partner

If you nominate a friend, uncle or some other person who is *not* a valid beneficiary, your nomination won't be legally binding. If this happens, your super will be distributed by the trustees of your super fund according to what they perceive to be the best interests of your descendants and according to superannuation law.

Making a binding or non-binding nomination

You can nominate your beneficiary/beneficiaries in a *binding* or *non-binding* nomination.

- A *binding nomination* lasts for three years and is legally binding as long as it is valid at the time of your death. To be valid it must comply with superannuation law. That is, it must nominate a spouse or de facto, adult or infant children, a person who's financially dependent on you, a person who's in an interdependent relationship with you or the executor of your will, and it must be witnessed by two adults. The trustees of your super fund *must* comply with a binding nomination. If your circumstances change but you don't have time to change your nomination before you die, the person you nominated will get your money.
- A *non-binding nomination* acts only as a guide to the trustees of your super fund as to how to distribute your super. The fund must still be guided by superannuation law regarding your dependants.

Some super funds don't give you the option of making a binding nomination. Instead they have preferential nominations, which are non-binding.

If you have a self-managed super fund, you can make non-lapsing death nominations, which can last indefinitely. The trustees must then distribute your superannuation according to your nomination.

Nominating an Executor

The executor of a deceased estate has certain duties to carry out. Consult your preferred executor about taking on the role before you nominate that person in your will, to make sure that he or she agrees to act in this capacity. Ideally, the person you choose should have some knowledge of the legal responsibilities involved and be familiar with accounting and taxation matters.

The role of executor can be difficult and time-consuming, and your chosen person will have to be able to cope with this role as well as his or her grief.

Acting as executor

Your executor is responsible for paying funeral and other expenses and debts, paying taxes and distributing your estate to the beneficiaries according to the terms of your will. He or she will be paid for any administrative expenses incurred but doesn't receive payment for the role. However, if required an application can be made to the Supreme Court for some payment.

The executor must carry out the following duties:

1. **Organise the funeral, if necessary.**

2. **Locate the will.**

3. **List and value all the assets and monies of the estate and keep them secure.**

4. **Apply for a grant of probate at the Probate Office in your state or territory (a filing fee is involved).**

   This step gives the executor the authority to deal with the assets and liabilities of your estate. If all assets are jointly owned and one owner dies, the executor probably doesn't have to apply for probate.

5. **Pay the funeral expenses.**

6. **Pay himself or herself for any administrative expenses relating to the estate.**

7. **Pay any other debts and taxes.**

   This step includes contacting the ATO for advice on tax owing on the estate and completing the deceased's tax return, if necessary.

8. **Publish a notice requiring anyone with a claim against the estate to provide particulars of the claim within a certain period.**

9. **Distribute the estate to the beneficiaries.**

Provide the beneficiaries with a list of assets that were sold and debts and expenses paid.

If any beneficiaries are under 18 or have a mental disability, the executor must keep the monies owing to these beneficiaries in trust until they can take it on themselves. The executor may have to manage this money for a long time, investing the money and distributing it as necessary.

If your executor finds the role too daunting, he or she can contract a solicitor or the Public Trustee for help.

Renouncing the role

If your chosen person no longer wishes to take on the role of executor, he or she can sign a *renunciation*. This form can be downloaded from the Web site of your state's Supreme Court. The form should be lodged at the address given on the Web site. Your executor can hand over the role to another person, a solicitor or the Public Trustee.

Minimising the Payment of Death Taxes

Death duties no longer apply in Australia, but capital gains tax may have to be paid and a tax applies when your super fund is wound up. If superannuation death benefits are paid to your non-dependent adult children or other types of non-dependants, under the tax laws tax is payable on the taxable component of the super benefit.

Capital gains tax doesn't have to be paid on a deceased estate if the estate is willed directly to

✔ The beneficiaries

✔ The executor, who then passes the estate on to the beneficiaries

However, capital gains tax has to be paid if a deceased estate is

✔ Transferred from the executor to an entity who isn't a beneficiary

✔ Willed to

  • A tax-advantaged entity

  • A non-resident

By making your will straightforward and leaving your estate to your beneficiaries, you shouldn't have to worry about capital gains tax. The problem arises when one of your beneficiaries wants to pass on some of that estate to a non-beneficiary.

For example, if you die and leave your property to your spouse only, he or she won't have to pay capital gains tax on that property. However, if your spouse then passes all or some of that property onto your children, your spouse may have to pay capital gains tax on the property and your children may have to pay stamp duty. You can ease this situation by setting up a living or testamentary trust. See the section 'Setting up a trust' below for more information on trusts.

The rules around capital gains tax can be complex, so check out the ATO's Web site at www.ato.gov.au or talk to your solicitor.

Planning to Distribute Your Estate

Because of capital gains tax and other taxes, as well as the high rate of divorce, many Australians are setting up trusts to safeguard their assets. A *trust* is basically an agreement or a promise whereby a person is entrusted to hold and manage money, assets or property on behalf of another person. It's a way of passing your assets onto others when you're alive or after your death. You may think only the wealthy have trusts, but anyone can set up a trust.

Setting up a trust

Several types of trust exist. For example, *living trusts* take effect when you're alive and *testamentary trusts* take effect after your death. When you set up a trust your assets go into that trust. You and your beneficiaries don't own the assets: The assets are owned by the trust and are managed and distributed by the trustee/trustees. When you die and leave your estate to your trust, your trustee/trustees will distribute your assets as they see fit.

You need to carefully consider who to appoint as your trustee/trustees. Trustees must understand legal issues and accounting. Unqualified trustees can make poor investment decisions or use your trust fund inappropriately. If you're unsure who to appoint as trustee, the Public Trustee offers a professional trust administration service.

You must seek legal advice to set up a trust, so talk to your solicitor.

Safeguarding your children's inheritance

Any person over the age of 18 who's a beneficiary of your superannuation fund will be paid in a lump sum. Before the new super rules came into play in 2007, you could set up a pension for your adult children so that their inheritance could be given to them over a period of time. This prevented them from blowing it all on a silver Porsche or a yellow Lamborghini. Although you can no longer set up a pension for them, by setting up a trust you can have some control over the spending habits of your non-dependent adult offspring.

Passing on more than just money

Estate planning can be about more than just money. You may wish to pass on your values and beliefs as well as your financial support to your family and even to the wider community. The Legenis Web site at www.legenis. com has more information on building a powerful legacy while you're alive and how to go about leaving more than just money when you pass away.

Granting Power of Attorney

If you want to give someone the power to make financial and legal decisions on your behalf, you can grant that person *general power of attorney* (financial) or *enduring power of attorney* (financial). General power of attorney ceases to have effect if you lose your mental capacity to make decisions, while enduring power of attorney continues to be valid even after you become mentally incapacitated. By granting someone power of attorney, you allow that person to act on your behalf. In most states, this doesn't cover your medical or welfare needs, so you may also need to grant power of attorney (medical).

You can grant someone general power of attorney for a limited time and to carry out specific tasks. For example, you may want to appoint someone to look after your finances while you're travelling overseas or while you're in hospital. Or you can grant someone enduring power of attorney if you want that person to continue to act on your behalf after you become mentally incapacitated. Your power of attorney ceases on your death. The responsibility of acting on your behalf then passes to your executor.

Financial power of attorney

In order to grant someone power of attorney over your financial and legal affairs, you must be 18 years of age or older and be mentally competent. In addition, the power of attorney must be

- ✔ Authorised by the donor (you)
- ✔ Understood and accepted by the attorney (whomever you choose to carry out your wishes)
- ✔ Witnessed by two people, one of whom must be authorised to witness statutory declarations (for example, a Justice of the Peace)

If you wish to buy and sell real estate, the power of attorney must also be registered with the Office of Titles in your state or territory.

You can ask your solicitor to draw up the power of attorney or you can download a form from the Web. You can also obtain a form from larger newsagencies, law stationers, lawyers and the Office of the Public Advocate in your state or territory.

Medical power of attorney

By granting someone medical power of attorney, you enable your attorney to make decisions about your medical treatment after you become incapacitated. This may be required for a short time — for example, if you're in a coma — or indefinitely. To grant a power of attorney (medical) you must abide by the rules as set out in the section 'Financial power of attorney'.

Your attorney can refuse medical treatment on your behalf, such as:

- ✔ Blood transfusions
- ✔ Cancer treatment
- ✔ Life support

However, your attorney can't refuse

- ✔ Emergency life-saving treatment
- ✔ Palliative care

If you suffer a heart attack and an ambulance is called, your attorney can't refuse you resuscitation but he or she can refuse treatment that will support or sustain your life. In addition, your attorney can't grant permission for you to participate in medical experimentation or organ donation.

The medical staff will want to see a refusal of treatment certificate signed by your attorney. Your attorney can revoke this certificate at any time, even verbally.

Revoking power of attorney

To revoke your power of attorney, inform your attorney in writing that you wish to cancel the power of attorney. You should also inform your solicitor of your decision and, for power of attorney (financial), any financial institutions you deal with. You must be of sound mind to revoke your power of attorney.

Your power of attorney is revoked automatically in the following instances:

- If your attorney dies or becomes bankrupt
- On the ruling of a court or tribunal
- When you become mentally incapacitated (unless you have an enduring power of attorney)
- When you die

Enduring guardianship

By granting someone *enduring guardianship*, you enable your chosen guardian to make decisions for you regarding your welfare and medical treatment when you're mentally or physically incapacitated and unable to make your own decisions. Your guardian can decide where you should live and what sort of medical treatment you should have, or not have.

The person you appoint as guardian must be over the age of 18. Your chosen guardian is usually a relative or close friend. Make sure you appoint someone you can trust and who's capable of making medical decisions on your behalf.

You may appoint a guardian plus an alternative guardian if the first is unable to carry out his or her duties. Or you may appoint joint guardians. However, be aware that joint guardians may argue over their decisions at a time when you're very vulnerable, so choose your guardians carefully.

To appoint your guardian you need to use an enduring guardianship form. This form must be signed by your solicitor or barrister or a register of the local court. In Tasmania the form must also be registered with the Guardianship Administration Board to be valid.

You can read more about enduring guardianship and download the appropriate forms from the following Web sites:

- ✔ **Australian Capital Territory:** Public Advocate of the ACT at www. publicadvocate.act.gov.au
- ✔ **New South Wales:** Office of the Public Guardian at www.lawlink.nsw. gov.au/opg
- ✔ **Northern Territory:** Office of the Public Trustee at www.nt.gov.au/ justice/pubtrust
- ✔ **Queensland:** Department of Justice and Attorney-General at www. justice.qld.gov.au
- ✔ **South Australia:** Legal Services Commission of South Australia at www.lsc.sa.gov.au
- ✔ **Tasmania:** Office of the Public Guardian at www.publicguardian.tas. gov.au
- ✔ **Victoria:** Victoria Legal Aid at www.legalaid.vic.gov.au
- ✔ **Western Australia:** Department of the Attorney General at www. justice.wa.gov.au

Each state and territory has its own legislation covering enduring guardianship. If you're moving interstate, you need to appoint a new guardian in that state.

Making your wishes known

When you appoint an enduring guardian or power of attorney (medical) it's a good idea to write down your wishes regarding your lifestyle and medical treatment. That way, you can specify your wishes concerning a number of issues, such as:

- ✔ The type of accommodation you would like should you become disabled and where you would like that accommodation to be; for example, close to a specific family member

- ✓ Whether you want a priest or other religious person to be present
- ✓ Whether you want to be allowed to die with dignity, with no heroic medical interference
- ✓ Whether you want to be kept on life support, and if so, for how long
- ✓ Whether you want to be resuscitated
- ✓ Whether you want your organs to be donated
- ✓ Whether you want to receive blood transfusions

Part III
Living Well in Retirement

Glenn Lumsden

'The new residents have requested that
you ditch the classical music and play more
Pink Floyd and the Stones.'

In this part ...

To make the most of your retirement and the rewards it can bring, you need to stay fit and healthy. In this part, I explain how to do just that, with pointers about health checks and exercise regimens. I also outline the Medicare system and health insurance, so you can work out what extra cover, if any, you need. I provide guidance on looking after your elderly parents or partner with a health problem, and help you to decide whether retirement village living may be for you. Finally, I take you through the pros and cons of moving house and the various options open to you, including downsizing, sea changing and tree changing.

Chapter 7

Staying Fit and Healthy

. . . .

In This Chapter

▶ Exercising for health

▶ Undergoing annual health checks

▶ Working out your workout routine

▶ Raising a sweat

▶ Getting fit and healthy without getting sweaty

▶ Staying the course

. . . .

*G*ood health is essential if you want to get the most out of your retirement. If you're not already doing so, now's the time to get involved in an exercise activity whether that means an organised activity, a group-oriented activity or simply exercising on your own.

Before you begin any exercise program, make sure you consult your doctor to undertake some basic medical check-ups: See the section 'Lining up for Health Tests' later in the chapter.

In this chapter, I discuss the physical and mental health benefits of exercise. I also outline the health tests you need to take, suggest some healthy activities and demystify the gym.

Preparing for a Healthy (Happy) Retirement

Having a regular exercise program is even more important as you age and risk becoming more sedentary. Most days you can't open the newspaper without being confronted with statistics on the rising incidence of obesity. Obesity is often linked with a sedentary lifestyle — and associated with obesity comes the threat of a number of health issues, including Type 2 diabetes and cardiovascular disease.

Exercising your way to good health

Just 30 minutes of daily exercise that raises your heart rate can dramatically improve your health and wellbeing. Thirty minutes? Doesn't sound much, does it? But if you're like many Australians, how often do you get through the day without walking 300 metres, let alone the three kilometres you need to walk to keep fit and healthy?

If you need some encouragement to get motivated and find time to add more exercise to your day, consider these facts:

✔ By exercising regularly, you may reduce your weight and your waist size, but more importantly, you lower your risk of cardiovascular disease and developing Type 2 diabetes. And if you already have Type 2 diabetes, you can use exercise and diet to help control the disease and keep you healthier longer.

✔ Regular exercise improves your mood and helps fight depression. In addition, regular exercise:

- Boosts your good cholesterol (high-density lipoprotein, HDL) and lowers your bad cholesterol (low-density lipoprotein, LDL), so your heart will thank you

- Helps lower your blood pressure

- Improves the circulation to your heart and lungs, so consequently you feel better and are able to do more

- May help prevent cancer of the bowel, breast and endometrium

- Will help you to sleep better, and even enjoy better sex

Convinced? Well, before you pull on your running shoes and set out for a jog, you need to know just how much exercise you should be aiming for, and at what intensity level.

Knowing how much exercise is enough

Although reports vary, the general consensus is that 30 minutes of moderate exercise at least five times a week is beneficial, and some studies suggest you also need to build in some vigorous activity.

Moderate exercise means you're moving fast enough to increase your heart and breathing rates but you can still hold a conversation. *Vigorous activity* means you're huffing and puffing, but you need to build up to this — never start straight away at a vigorous level.

To calculate your exertion level you can use the *perceived exertion rate*, whereby you rate your exertion level on a scale of one to 10. One means you're sitting on the couch doing nothing and 10 means you're lying on the floor exhausted after a tough workout. You should be exercising in the mid-range with a score of about five. This means you should be able to hold a conversation, even though you may be puffing, but you shouldn't be gasping for breath. Don't start exercising at 10 or you'll be lying prone on the floor — possibly for several days.

The perceived exertion rate is probably the easiest and most efficient way of rating your exercise level. It grows with you. As your fitness increases your exertion level decreases and you'll know it's time to up your level of exercise.

Calculating your target heart rate training zone

Your *maximum heart rate* (MHR) is the maximum number of times your heart can beat in a minute. This rate differs for everyone. The best way to find your MHR is to take a stress test administered by a health professional, whereby you go to a lab and run on a treadmill while connected to an electrocardiogram that measures your pulse. Exercising to your MHR is not recommended.

Your *target heart rate* is how many times a minute your heart should beat to gain the maximum benefit from a workout. Your *target heart rate training zone* is between 60 and 85 per cent of your MHR. If you exercise at a gym, you may have seen these figures listed on the cardio equipment.

You can rate your exercise level by calculating your MHR and then working out your target heart rate training zone. A simple way of calculating this is as follows:

✔ Work out your MHR by subtracting your age from 220.

✔ Work out your target heart rate training zone by multiplying the result of 220 minus your age by 0.6 and 0.85.

For example, if you're 60 years old, you calculate your target heart rate training zone as follows:

✔ $220 - 60 = 160 \times 0.6 = 96$

✔ $220 - 60 = 160 \times 0.85 = 136$

Thus, your target heart rate training zone is between 96 and 136 beats per minute. To begin with, you'd expect your heart rate to be in the 90–100 range. Moderate exercise would take it to the 110–120 range, while more vigorous exercise will have your heart beating at 130-plus beats per minute.

You can find heart rate calculators on the Web. You'll get some variation in the results depending on what you want to achieve from your training. For example, if you want aerobic conditioning you'll have a different target heart rate training zone than if you want weight reduction.

Estimating your perceived exertion level and calculating your target heart rate training zone are guides only. They don't take into account any health issues you may have. Make sure that you consult your doctor *before* you begin any exercise program.

Checking your heart rate

To check your heart rate during exercise, stop exercising and take your pulse by placing your fingers over your carotid artery — the thing beating (and possibly thumping) in your neck. Take your pulse for 10 seconds and multiply it by six to calculate the beats per minute.

You can buy a heart rate monitor that continuously takes your pulse as you exercise. The more sophisticated monitors calculate your speed, pace, distance and calories or kilojoules burnt.

Ramping it up

As you improve, you can progress to two or three sessions of more vigorous exercise (where you're puffing but still able to talk) and two or three sessions of strength training per week. Weight-bearing exercise is important for strengthening your bones and muscles. Strong muscles support your joints so you're less prone to back and knee pain.

Measuring up

When you undertake an exercise program, one of your goals may well be to lose weight. Health professionals emphasise the benefits of losing centimetres around your waist rather than obsessing about your weight on the scales. Scales were invented to weigh inanimate objects like silver and gold, not people.

The ideal waist measurement is 94 centimetres for men and 80 centimetres for women — regardless of height. If your waist measures more than this, you may be at increased risk of developing Type 2 diabetes and some cancers, including cancer of the colon, prostate cancer, cancer of the kidneys, breast cancer after menopause, cancer of the oesophagus and myeloid leukaemia.

If you're like me and have run off to get the tape measure, you need to know how to measure your waist correctly. The tape measure should sit at the hollow between the bottom of your ribs and the top of your hip. This is roughly where your belly button is.

Breathe in, exhale and then measure. Be brave — don't hold your breath in as you measure! Scary, isn't it?

Is your waist measurement more than the ideal? The good news is you can do something about it *right away*. Get a pedometer and start walking. Aim for 10,000 steps per day. For more advice, see the section 'Use It or Lose It: Activities to Keep You Healthy' later in the chapter.

If you're one of the lucky people whose waist measurement sits on the ideal, that's no reason to abandon starting your exercise program! You won't get all the health benefits of regular exercise if you don't stay active.

Lining up for Health Tests

Before you start your exercise regime, you need to consult your doctor or healthcare professional and get some health checks done.

When you reach retirement age, begin a routine of annual medical check-ups, as outlined in this section.

Essential check-ups before you start exercising

This section outlines some essential check-ups you should undergo to make sure all is well before you start your exercise regime.

Blood pressure

Get your blood pressure checked regularly — untreated high blood pressure can lead to heart attack, kidney disease and stroke.

To measure your blood pressure the doctor puts a band around your arm and pumps up the tube. This measures the pressure of the blood in your arteries as your heart pumps it around your body. Two measures are recorded: systolic and diastolic. The *systolic* measurement (the higher number) records the blood pressure in your arteries and the *diastolic* measurement (the lower number) records the pressure as your heart relaxes before its next beat.

For example, in the reading 120/80 (which is considered normal), the 120 is the systolic measurement. A reading of 140/90 is considered high and 180/110 is very high.

Cholesterol

Cholesterol is naturally found in your bloodstream and is necessary for the body to function. However, if you have too much of this fatty substance in your blood it can clog your arteries. Cholesterol has two parts: good cholesterol (HDL) and bad cholesterol (LDL). LDL clogs your blood vessels; HDL helps to unclog them. A simple blood test is all that's required to check your cholesterol level.

Diabetes

Type 1 diabetes (insulin-dependent diabetes mellitus or juvenile onset diabetes) occurs when the pancreas ceases to produce insulin. The immune system attacks the cells of the pancreas. This type of diabetes usually occurs under the age of 30, but can begin at any age and requires a lifetime regime of insulin injections.

Type 2 diabetes (non-insulin-dependent diabetes mellitus or mature-age onset diabetes) is commonly referred to as a lifestyle disease. This type of diabetes responds well to diet and exercise, although medication and eventually insulin may be needed to manage the disease.

If you have a family history of Type 2 diabetes or are inactive and overweight, you should have a blood test to check for this condition. Complications such as eye, heart, kidney and peripheral nerve damage can result from untreated diabetes.

For more information on diabetes, see your doctor or go to Diabetes Australia's Web site at www.diabetesaustralia.com.au. See also *Diabetes For Dummies*, Second Australian Edition, adapted by Lesley Campbell (Wiley Publishing Australia Pty Ltd).

Heart

Every *minute*, an Australian dies from heart disease. Heart disease kills four times more women than breast cancer. Make sure you have a regular heart check-up with your doctor. Your doctor will decide whether you need a stress test or ECG before you begin an exercise program.

Check out the Heart Foundation's Web site at www.heartfoundation.org.au for healthy living guidelines, including tips on eating and drinking, physical activity, weight management and mental health.

And while you're at the doctor's surgery ...

While the doctor is performing the essential health checks, you should also consider the following tests.

Pap smear

The National Cervical Screening Program provides a screening program for women to help prevent cervical cancer. A two-yearly pap smear can prevent the most common cancer of the cervix in 90 per cent of cases. Your doctor or health practitioner can carry out your pap smear test and send the cells to a laboratory to check. You'll be notified of the result within two to four weeks.

Find more details on the Cancer Screening Web site at www.cancerscreening. gov.au.

Prostate check

Men over the age of 40 are urged to have a yearly rectal examination of the prostate. After skin cancer, prostate cancer is the most common cancer in men. One in six men are diagnosed with prostate cancer in Australia and nearly 2,500 die from the disease annually.

Prostate cancer can be symptom-free in its early stages, but if it's not diagnosed early it can spread to other parts of the body. Don't wait for symptoms to begin — get checked regularly.

Skin cancer

Australians have a culture of sunbathing. While many people use sunscreen nowadays, when I was young like many others I loved to oil up and bake in the sun. Consequently, it's a good idea to ask your doctor to check out any suspicious-looking spots or moles. If you're very freckly, a dermatologist can make a skin map and you can check your freckles against this map every six months.

Other important regular check-ups

Here are several other checks that need to be performed on a regular basis.

Breast check

BreastScreen Australia is a national program for the early diagnosis of breast cancer. This free service is offered to women between the ages of 50 and 69 at two-yearly intervals. You don't need a doctor's referral for a screening mammogram through this service.

To make an appointment, simply telephone 13 20 50 for the cost of a local call. You'll be notified when your next appointment is due two years after your scan. Go to www.breastscreen.info.au for more information.

Hearing

Are you constantly telling your family to stop mumbling? Do you avoid noisy situations because you can't hear what's being said? You're probably suffering from hearing loss. If you can't hear you risk becoming socially isolated — as well as driving everyone around you mad. A simple hearing test can establish whether hearing aids will be an advantage to you.

Sight

Regular eye examinations are essential for your sight and can help identify the early signs of a range of diseases. Cataracts, glaucoma and macular degeneration are all serious health problems. If you have diabetes, your doctor will send you for regular eye tests.

Use It or Lose It: Activities to Keep You Healthy

This may be the first time you've thought about regular exercise since your teens or early 20s. However, it's never too late to get active. Start your exercise program gradually, and preferably with something you enjoy. If you take up an exercise that you don't really like or that you find boring, you won't stick with it. Better still, get together with a group of friends and go for a walk, a swim or a bike ride — or join a club of like-minded exercise enthusiasts.

You won't really start to feel the benefits of any regular exercise program for at least six weeks.

Responsible exercise

Before you undertake any exercise activity, make sure you've had a medical check-up. Then begin exercising slowly — don't start your running regime with a 10-kilometre race. You can expect some muscle soreness and stiffness when you start exercising or change your exercise regime, but this should go as you get fitter. If the pain is severe or doesn't go away, see your doctor or healthcare professional. The idea of no pain, no gain isn't sensible. Pain is your body's way of telling you to go easy on yourself. Tune into your body and listen to it. Take adequate rest days. Your muscles need time to repair.

For more information, see *Fitness For Dummies*, Australian & New Zealand Edition, by Kelly Baker (Wiley Publishing Australia Pty Ltd).

Walking your way to health

Walking is the easiest and most accessible exercise and has *so many* benefits going for it:

- ✔ It's low impact and easy on the knee and ankle joints.

- ✔ It's a low to moderate intensity exercise that's a good fat burner.

- ✔ It increases blood flow to the limbs.

- ✔ The only money you need to spend is on a good pair of walking shoes.

Make walking a habit. Most people can walk and it doesn't matter how slowly you begin, as long as you're moving. You'll get quicker as you get fitter. Get a pedometer and aim for 10,000 steps per day.

If you don't want to walk alone, join a walking group — you'll find all sorts of walking groups throughout Australia. You can walk and talk in Victoria, walk with attitude in Tasmania, join the Y Striders in Western Australia, walk with a four-legged friend or walk children to school. Contact your local council for information on walking groups in your area. Or type 'walking groups' into your search engine and browse the Web.

Bushwalking clubs

Bushwalking Australia's Web site at www. bushwalkingaustralia.org provides information on bushwalking clubs throughout Australia. Being a member of a bushwalking club is great fun. You have wonderful walking companions, your walks are thoroughly researched and there's always help if you run into trouble.

Many clubs offer other sports too, such as cross-country skiing and events like talks and social outings. Some organise group travel in Australia and overseas. You may find yourself taking a ferry up the coast of Alaska or walking through Italy staying in all sorts of interesting accommodation.

When you find a club in your area check to see whether you need to be sponsored by an existing member. Most clubs ask you to join them on a couple of walks before inviting you to take up membership.

Cycling around

Cycling is another low-impact exercise that won't jar your knees and ankles, but this doesn't mean you won't suffer some aches and pains. Reality check: If you ride a bike you'll get a sore bottom. Your knees and back may also suffer.

Follow these tips for a smoother, more enjoyable ride:

✔ Consult your local bike shop about the best bike for you and get your bike properly fitted.

✔ Pay particular attention to the handlebars if you're prone to back pain. A more upright position may suit you better.

✔ Select your saddle carefully: Make sure it's comfortable for you. Gel seats and overlays may help ease the aches.

✔ Set the bike at the right height for you, otherwise your knees will suffer. Your bike shop should give you advice on this when you purchase your bike.

✔ Start with short, easy rides.

You can join a club for road riders, racers, mountain bikers, tourers or recreational riders. The main advantage of belonging to a club is the contact with other riders: You can exchange information about bikes and accessories, participate in events and socialise.

The Web site of Bicycles Network Australia at www.bicycles.net.au is a good place to start if you're looking for a cycling club or other related information. The site is a free online resource for cycling-related information including clubs, shops, brands and cycling-related organisations.

Running (whew!)

You may not want to run a marathon, but some do and others just want to go for their morning jog. Whatever level you want to take your running to, you can join a running club, or take advantage of the time to be alone with your thoughts.

Running takes more preparation than other activities. You need to build up gradually. Start by walking before you advance to a run/walk schedule. Find a program on the Web or in a running book or magazine. Most programs suggest you begin with 20–30 minutes of walking three times a week. From there you can advance to a two-minute walk/one-minute run cycle for 20 minutes. Then you increase the minutes of running and decrease the walking time over a period of weeks until you finally build up to 30 minutes of running. Importantly, you should always be able to maintain a conversation as you exercise.

Depending on your fitness it may take anywhere between eight and 12 weeks before you can run for 30 minutes without stopping. It's important not to rush this so as to minimise your risk of injury.

Swimming with (or without) the fishes

Swimming is one of the best exercises for all-over fitness. Because water supports you while you exercise, you don't have to worry about jarring your joints. And swimming is a great cardio-respiratory exercise. Swimming is an excellent exercise if you have a physical disability and/or joint pain, because the water supports your limbs while you work to strengthen them.

You don't need much for swimming, just bathers, goggles and a towel. You can add in training aids like a kickboard, flippers and swimming paddles when you get serious. Most Australians are lucky to have easy access to pools and the beach, so grab your togs and towel and go for a swim.

Don't forget to stay between the flags if you swim at the beach. It's not easy to see the rips in the water, and you need to swim where it's safe.

And if you find swimming up and down a pool rather boring, here are some ideas to keep you interested:

✔ Break up your routine with a warm-up and then some 50- or 100-metre sprints.

✔ Set yourself a distance and see whether you can beat it. After you feel confident with your distance, add another 25 or 50 metres. Swimming is different from other forms of exercise — you can't just stop swimming if you run out of puff, but you can side stroke or float.

✔ Use swimming aids like flippers or a kickboard to vary your routine.

✔ Vary your stroke. Swim halfway up the pool freestyle and change to backstroke for the rest of the lap.

Taking lessons

Sign up for lessons at your local pool if you can't swim. Lessons aren't just for beginners, however. You'll also benefit from lessons if you'd like to improve your technique or learn a new stroke.

Swimming in the big pond

Each summer open-water (ocean) swimming races are held all around Australia. Open-water swimming is different from pool swimming: Without lanes, you have nowhere to focus on and take your bearings from. You need to look up to see where you're going. And you can't swim over to the side for a rest. You need to train hard in the pool over winter to be fit for this sport.

If you're interested in swimming in open water, besides the most important tip, knowing your own swimming ability, take these other simple precautions:

- ✔ **Assess the water conditions carefully before you set off.** Make sure you know what a rip looks like. If you're swimming at an unfamiliar beach, consult a life saver if you're in doubt.

- ✔ **Be safe.** Swim with a group or in an enclosed area such as a sea baths. Some ocean swim sites have regular training groups you can join. Type 'open-water swimming' in your search engine and browse the Web to find groups near you.

- ✔ **Don't lose your cool.** Open-water swimming can get your mind working in strange ways — those shapes are just seaweed (really they are).

- ✔ **Stay in your depth if you're beginning training in open water.** This means swimming along the shore line rather than out to sea.

- ✔ **Wear a wetsuit in cold water.** This keeps you warm and safe from any stray stinging creatures. Don't forget that your head, hands and feet get cold too. You may want to wear a cap and booties in southern waters.

Joan jumps in

My friend Joan competed in her first open-water swimming race in her 40s. She was used to swimming in salt water and prepared for the race by swimming in the local pool. Although the race was 1.2 kilometres, Joan aimed to swim 2 kilometres in training. She figured the tide could make a difference.

On the day of the race Joan proudly sported her competitor number on her arm. She chose to wear a wetsuit as she knew the water would be cold. But one thing Joan wasn't prepared for was the battering she got from the arms and legs of other competitors. The water was like a whirlpool, so she decided to drop back a little. As the race spread out the water calmed down.

Joan was right about the tide — it did make a difference, and while she swam out fast, after rounding the buoys for home the shore got closer only very slowly.

Joan and her family were very relieved when she finished the race. Joan was very proud of herself, especially as it was her first attempt. She hadn't aimed to win, but she was pleased she didn't come last.

Swimming with the masters

Masters Swimming Australia offers a program of stroke correction and coaching by qualified coaches at most big swimming centres throughout Australia. Competitions are run and you can compete at your own level. This program is a great idea if your swimming has started to become boring and you're losing your incentive to continue. See the Masters Swimming Australia Web site at www.aussimasters.com.au for more information.

Joining aqua aerobics

Standing at the side of the pool watching the participants' heads gently bobbing in the water, aqua aerobics looks easy. But aqua aerobics is a good all-round workout. It improves your range of movement — and consequently your golf swing.

Because water supports you while you work out, you can do exercises in the water you'd never dream of doing on dry land. Aqua aerobics is particularly great if you have an injury, arthritis or any muscle soreness or are recovering from surgery (but be sure to check with your doctor first).

A typical class is held in a pool where the water is at chest height. The instructor stands at the side of the pool. You begin with a warm-up of jogging on the spot and arm exercises. Next you travel up and down the pool with your feet both on and off the bottom (don't worry, it won't be deep). After your warm-up you push reverse dumbbells or noodles made of polystyrene through the water — this helps strengthen the muscles in your arms and chest. Sometimes you may even play games, but one thing you can count on is having fun while you get fit.

Running in the deep end

Strap on your buoyancy belt, jump in the diving pool and start running — you'll get a workout like you've never had before! Running in water gives you an aerobic workout without stressing your joints and is a great rehabilitation activity.

Hitting the Gym: Don't Be Afraid to Flex Your Muscles

To get the most out of your gym workout, use the professional advice on offer at the gym. The gym consultant may ask you what you want to achieve from your workout: set some easily achievable goals. Think about fitness and flexibility as well as weight loss. For example, you may want to be able to get down on the floor more easily — and back up again — so that you can play games with your grandchildren.

Aim to go to the gym two or three times per week and have your program reviewed every six weeks. Boredom with a program and goals that are too ambitious are among the major reasons people stop going to the gym. Don't expect to be a sylph after a few visits. It takes several weeks before exercise becomes an enjoyable habit.

Check with your doctor before you do any exercise designed to raise your heart rate.

Exploring the gym beforehand

You need to feel comfortable in the gym. Some gyms seem to be full of Lycra-clad lads and lassies who're there as much to be seen as to work out. Other gyms are dedicated to weightlifters and body builders. Check out the gym beforehand — you can usually have a free workout before committing to join — to see whether the vibe is right for you.

If you don't like the idea of joining a big gym, numerous local shopping strips have smaller gyms that offer 20–40-minute workouts including circuit work, vibrating platforms and personal training. The advantages of these centres are that usually you don't have to pay yearly up-front fees and you get more individual attention.

Gyms make a lot of money from people who pay their fees but then don't attend. Here are some things to think about *before* you join a gym:

✔ Are you self-motivated and prepared to go to the gym at least three times per week? You need to attend this regularly to get your money's worth and to see results.

✔ Can you see staff on the gym floor? Are they interacting with clients?

✔ Do you want a gender-specific gym? Are you comfortable with the atmosphere in the gym? Are the staff friendly and attentive?

✔ Does the gym offer off-peak membership? Apart from being cheaper, this also has the advantage of keeping you away from the gym at rush times.

✔ Does the gym offer group training or yoga so that you can vary your workouts?

✔ Is the gym right for you? Does it offer the programs you want? Does it have adequate equipment?

✔ What is the joining fee? Is this open to negotiation? Does the gym have specials when the joining fee is waived? Can you wait for these specials?

Exercise rehabilitation

Exercise rehabilitation is a new and growing industry of qualified university graduates. If you have an injury or illness these graduates will manage your exercise routine to help you overcome your problem. Going to the gym when you have a bad knee or back can make the problem worse. An exercise rehabilitation worker will take you through a program specifically tailored to address your problem area.

Specialised training programs

Personal trainers aren't just for movie stars. A personal trainer can get you focused on your exercise regime. If you have an injury or health issue you can discuss this with your trainer, who'll set up a program specifically for you. Your trainer will monitor your progress and motivate you. It's easy to say, 'I'll skip the gym today and go tomorrow', but not so easy if you've got someone waiting for you at the gym and you've committed to paying them.

Training with a group

Working out at the gym can become routine and boring. You need to be highly motivated to stick at a program for a number of years. One way of overcoming this boredom is to participate in some group training sessions. When you work out on your own you can slacken off in your intensity. A group session set to music makes you keep up and pushes you along.

Begin at the beginning. Don't jump straight into an advanced class unless you've done the groundwork.

Aerobics

If you enjoy exercising with a group and are looking for an overall aerobic workout, aerobics classes may be for you. You need some coordination to keep up with the routines, but you won't take long to get in step. Check that the floor you're exercising on is properly sprung to minimise jarring to your joints. Most gyms offer classes for the over 50s if you want something with a more realistic pace.

BodyPump

BodyPump classes are for those who want to lift weights in a group atmosphere. The classes combine weights with a cardio workout and work all the main muscle groups. You'll be provided with a bar, light weights and a step. You begin with a warm-up and then pump weights to music. You should attend a technique class before you begin the main classes.

Give your muscles a rest day. Don't do seven pump classes per week.

Boot camp

Boot-camp training isn't for the faint-hearted! This tough, military-style training is a great way to get fit outdoors but requires a lot of stamina. I see boot-camp devotees running up and down the beach dragging tyres or carrying sacks of sand when I go for my morning walk.

Spin

Spin classes involve riding a stationary bicycle that's weighted so you can increase or lower the resistance. You ride up hills, on the flat and flat out, all to a thumping beat. Be wary of the over-enthusiastic instructor! Spin classes are definitely not for novice cyclists — build up your fitness before you enter this class.

Enjoying Alternative Exercise Programs

Does the thought of getting hot and sweaty in a frantic exercise class leave you cold? You don't have to raise your heart rate to improve your health. By participating in exercise classes that emphasise the gentle stretching of muscles and tendons to allow the blood and life force to circulate around your body you won't raise a sweat, but you will enhance your circulatory and respiratory systems.

Digging dance

Dancing is a wonderful way to get fit and enjoy your retirement. Dance has made a huge leap forward from the stuffy church socials of my younger days. Jazz, funk, salsa and tango are just some of the styles on offer these days. You can find your nearest dance class by typing 'dance class' into your search engine and browsing the Web. My local class is called 'Le Bop Modern Jive'. I don't know what that is, but it sounds fun.

Belly-dancing and Bollywood are now major dance movements in Australia. You can learn to move your body and dress up in exotic clothes at the same time. Tap dancing is still going strong in the suburbs, with retirees donning the ankle socks and tap shoes and shaking up local halls.

Health benefits

Dancing has numerous benefits:

✔ Dancing burns as many kilojoules (calories) as walking. It can help to reduce your waist measurement and lower your risk of contracting a number of diseases.

✔ Like other forms of regular exercise dancing helps lower your blood pressure and strengthen your heart.

✔ The social aspect of dancing helps guard against isolation and depression.

✔ The weight-bearing nature of dancing works to strengthen your bones and muscles.

What to wear

Wear loose comfortable clothing. You can wear comfortable street shoes until you wish to purchase proper dance shoes.

Practising Pilates

Pilates was begun by Joseph Pilates in England during World War I to help rehabilitate wounded soldiers. He then modified the exercises for ballet dancers and now Pilates is a worldwide exercise phenomenon.

Basically, Pilates involves developing core strength that enables you to improve your posture and alignment. There are two ways of doing Pilates:

✔ On mats on the floor

✔ With equipment that uses ropes and pulleys for resistance

The classes appear to be slow and gentle, focusing on the many small muscles in the body that support your larger ligaments and tendons. However, the day after a class you'll know you've been working out because you'll feel muscles you didn't know you had.

Health benefits

Pilates has many benefits:

- As a low-impact exercise Pilates is ideal for people with injuries or osteoarthritis. Of course, if you're in severe pain, consult your doctor or health professional before starting a class.
- Pilates is a good mental workout. You have to focus on using small muscle groups and remember to breathe at the same time. The exercises have a meditative quality.
- You get an holistic rather than an aerobic workout. As you train your core muscles, you'll notice your stomach becoming firmer and flatter.
- You should be able to stand more upright and have less trouble with day-to-day tasks.

What to wear

Wear loose comfortable clothing. You can take a towel to lay over the mat that's provided by the instructor. You'll probably exercise in socks or bare feet.

Tuning in to Tai Chi

Tai Chi is a soft form of the martial arts (Wushu). It has become popular in the West because its continuous, circular, slow movements can be practised by almost everyone, anywhere. Classes are often held outdoors in harmony with nature.

Health benefits

Tai Chi classes offer numerous benefits:

- The exercises are a great way to begin the day because they allow you the opportunity to stretch your muscles in a slow and purposeful manner. Tai Chi can be helpful in freeing tight neck, shoulder and back muscles.
- Those who practise Tai Chi report feeling calmer. The movements have a meditative quality and enable you to slow down both internally and externally. Once your mind slows, you can think more clearly and sleep better.
- Your balance may improve, as well as your outlook on life.

What to wear

Wear flat-soled shoes and loose clothing.

Yearning for yoga

Yoga originated in India and isn't just an exercise regime — it's a whole life wellness tradition. It includes meditation, gentle exercises and breathing control. Yoga is about fulfilling your potential and finding the happiness within you.

Most yoga pupils begin with Hatha yoga, or the physical dimension of yoga. In some forms of yoga the postures (asanas) are gentle and reflective. In other forms (such as Ashtanga yoga) the postures are quite vigorous and demanding. You move quickly between the poses. Whichever form of yoga you try, you'll be encouraged to become aware of your body as you hold the poses.

The instructor will probably begin the class with some breathing exercises. Breathing control is an important aspect of yoga practice. The class usually ends with relaxation. Cover yourself with a blanket or towel as you lie on the floor in complete quiet.

Choose your class carefully. Some instructors are a bit gung-ho and have you standing on your head in your first class.

Health benefits

Yoga has numerous benefits:

- ✔ The breathing exercises increase your respiratory and cardiovascular efficiency, and your blood pressure may decrease.
- ✔ The poses help you develop increased flexibility and strength. Your balance and posture will improve.
- ✔ The poses also help improve your mood and concentration. Your sleep should also improve as a result.

What to wear

Wear loose, comfortable clothing.

Most instructors provide mats, but if not you'll need to buy your own.

Don't eat directly before your yoga class — or indeed any exercise activity. Also, try to arrive early so that you can put the stresses of the day behind you and begin to relax.

Holding in There

Sometimes you feel like you've been exercising for weeks without making any improvement. It's a bit like playing golf — or tennis. After a couple of years you may be disappointed with your progress, but if you take a few minutes to reflect on your first five or six games you realise how far you've come and how far you can go.

Here are some tips to help you to stick at it:

✔ **Set yourself goals and write them down.**

- In two months time I want to be able to swim for 50 minutes without stopping.

- In three months time I want to be able to walk for 45 minutes flat out without feeling puffed.

You may like to add some health goals, such as lowering your blood pressure, lowering your blood sugar level or losing 5 centimetres from your waist measurement. Make sure your goals are achievable. If you want to climb Mt Everest or run a marathon, you have to set short-term goals as well as long-term ones to help you get there.

✔ **Track your progress.** This suggestion helps you to realise your achievements and stick with your exercise regime. You can buy an exercise book or diary and fill in what exercise you do each day. Or you can set up a spreadsheet on your computer. Record how far you walk each day and how long it takes. Note down all your improvements. Take your pulse and note how your recovery improves.

✔ **Use a pedometer.** This device helps you keep track of how far you walk each day. Basic models are cheap and easy to use and measure how many steps you've taken and possibly how many kilojoules (calories) you've burned. More sophisticated models incorporate a GPS so you can accurately measure the distance you walk and upload the data to your computer.

Chapter 8

Understanding Health Cover and Insurance

Australians are lucky in their healthcare system. Medicare provides basic, straightforward health insurance for all Australian citizens, whatever their age and wherever they are in Australia — and in some overseas countries too.

In this chapter, I outline what is and isn't covered by Medicare. I discuss some of the basics about private health cover and provide some pointers to help you to decide whether you need to take out private health cover.

For more detailed information on any Medicare issues:

✔ Call 13 20 11

✔ Go to www.medicareaustralia.gov.au

✔ Visit your local Medicare office

Understanding How Medicare's Got You Covered

Medicare is a universal Australian health insurance system. If you live in Australia and hold Australian or New Zealand citizenship or have a permanent visa, you're eligible for Medicare cover. This means you receive free treatment and accommodation as a public patient in any public hospital and may get free or subsidised treatment from your doctor or specialist. If you're a private patient, Medicare will cover only 75 per cent of the Medicare schedule fee for services and procedures provided by the treating doctor (but not the accommodation).

Bulk-billing

Your doctor or specialist can choose to bulk-bill you for their services. This means that Medicare covers the whole of your medical expenses. If your doctor doesn't bulk-bill you, you can put in a claim to Medicare and it will pay 75 per cent of the scheduled fee. However, since many doctors and specialists charge above the scheduled fee, you may still be quite out of pocket. Many doctors bulk-bill pensioners and concession card holders only, although they may bulk-bill you if your consultation is short. Your doctor can provide you with a list of fees and Medicare rebates.

The Pharmaceutical Benefits Scheme and Safety Net

The government subsidises the cost of medicines on the Pharmaceutical Benefits Scheme (PBS). To take advantage of these discounts, you need to show your Medicare card when you buy any PBS medicines.

If you use a lot of medicine in a year, you may reach the *PBS Safety Net* threshold. The PBS Safety Net program helps reduce the cost of your medicine. Keep a record of all your PBS medicine purchases on a Prescription Record Form (available from your pharmacy), or ask your pharmacist to keep a record of your scripts on her computer. After you reach the Safety Net threshold, ask your pharmacist how to apply for a PBS Safety Net card, which means your PBS medicine will be less expensive for the rest of the year.

The Medicare Safety Net

The *Medicare Safety Net* protects you or your family if you have many out-of-pocket medical expenses. After you or your family reach a certain amount of medical expenses, Medicare will pay 80 per cent of your out-of-pocket costs for doctors' visits and tests. Families and couples need to register with Medicare to receive the benefit, but individuals are automatically registered.

Other Medicare benefits

Medicare doesn't only cover medical treatment in hospital or from your doctor. It also provides benefits under the schemes in this section.

Aged care

Medicare offers a number of aged-care services. Together with the Department of Health and Ageing, Medicare offers packages to help people stay in their homes and to subsidise places in aged-care and nursing homes. You can read more about these schemes in Chapter 9 or on Medicare's Web site.

Bowel cancer screening

In partnership with the Department of Health and Ageing, Medicare is implementing the National Bowel Cancer Screening Program (NBCSP). If you're turning 50, 55 or 65 between January 2008 and 2010 you may be invited to take part in this program. If you agree to participate, you will receive a free faecal occult blood test. If you're not part of the program, you can purchase the test from your pharmacy for about $15.

Visit www.cancerscreening.gov.au to find out more about this program.

External breast prostheses reimbursement

This program provides a reimbursement for external breast prostheses after a mastectomy. It doesn't provide reimbursement for internal prostheses or clothing. You can read more about this on Medicare's Web site.

General practitioner packages

If you have a chronic health issue and require treatment by allied health professionals, your doctor can give you a special *GP management plan.*

If you have a mental health issue and need to see a psychologist or psychiatrist, you can claim visits to see a psychiatrist on Medicare but you can't claim visits to a psychologist. However, under a GP management plan you can claim a Medicare rebate on six to 12 visits to a psychologist per year. To be eligible you must see a psychologist with a registered Medicare provider number. You should get a rebate of $115.05 from Medicare when you see a clinical psychologist under this plan.

If you have a chronic physical disease such as arthritis, asthma, diabetes, cancer or cardiovascular disease — one that has lasted or will last for six months or more — under a GP management plan you can claim a Medicare rebate for a number of visits to allied health professionals such as physiotherapists.

Check out Medicare's Web site at www.medicareaustralia.gov.au or the Web site of the Department of Health and Ageing at www.health.gov.au for more information.

Hearing services

If you're hearing impaired and hold a Pensioner Concession Card or gold or white Department of Veterans' Affairs card, you can obtain a hearing services voucher from your doctor or hearing services professional. This voucher will entitle you to free hearing tests and hearing aids. If you buy more expensive hearing aids, you'll have to pay for the difference. For a small annual fee, you can enter into an agreement with your hearing services professional to maintain your hearing aids and supply you with batteries.

Optometry

Medicare provides for optometrists to bulk-bill for eye examinations. If your optometrist bulk-bills, you won't have to pay for your eye examinations. If your optometrist bills you directly, you can claim a rebate of most or all of the bill from Medicare, unless you've already had an eye examination within the last two years. If you have poor vision and need more extensive tests you may be eligible for a further rebate. See Medicare's Web site for more information.

Special assistance schemes

Medicare has a number of schemes to help cover the medical costs of those caught in disasters. At present the scheme covers Bali 2005, Balimed, Drought Bus, Dahab Egypt Bombing, London Assist and Tsunami Health.

Travelling overseas

Medicare has reciprocal arrangements with some countries. To receive medical treatment in these countries you must produce your passport and Medicare card and should see a doctor who participates in the country's health scheme. Reciprocating countries are: Finland, Italy, Malta, New Zealand, the Netherlands, Norway, Sweden, the Republic of Ireland and the UK.

However, in an emergency you'll have to go to the emergency room of a public hospital and receive whatever care is provided there. You won't be insured for a medical evacuation to Australia and you may not be insured for transportation between hospitals.

Medicare strongly advises travellers not to rely on these reciprocal agreements and to take out suitable insurance cover for the period that they'll be away.

See Medicare's Web site at www.medicareaustralia.gov.au for more information.

Knowing what Medicare doesn't cover

Public hospitals often have long waiting lists for surgery such as hip and knee replacements. And if you're being treated as a Medicare patient in a public hospital, you won't have a choice of doctor — in fact, you'll probably be treated by several different doctors. If this doesn't appeal to you and you'd prefer to go to a private hospital for surgery (or in an emergency) or to choose your own doctor or specialist, you'll probably need private health cover.

Similarly, you may have to wait a number of months before you can get an appointment at a public dental hospital, unless you have an emergency. If you'd prefer to look after your own dental needs, you'll need private health cover.

In addition, Medicare doesn't cover the following:

- **Allied health professionals:** If you want to see an acupuncturist, a chiropractor, an exercise physiologist, a physiotherapist, a podiatrist or a massage therapist, for example, you need private health cover.

- **Ambulance:** Unless you live in Queensland or Tasmania where the state pays for your ambulance cover, you'll need to take out separate cover for emergency ambulance transportation. You can purchase ambulance cover through your private health insurance or directly from the ambulance service in some states. To find your local state or territory ambulance service online, type 'ambulance' into your search engine.

- **Cosmetic surgery:** Cosmetic surgery is not a life-sustaining procedure and as such isn't covered by Medicare.

- **Hearing aids:** Unless you hold a Pensioner Concession Card or gold or white Department of Veterans' Affairs card, your hearing tests and hearing aids aren't covered by Medicare. Hearing aids cost many thousands of dollars, especially if you want one of the snazzy, new, small versions.

- ✔ **Optometry:** Although your eye test may be free, Medicare won't pay for your glasses or extra eye tests.

- ✔ **Private patient hospital costs:** Although Medicare will cover 75 per cent of the Medicare schedule fee for services and procedures provided by the treating doctor, it does not cover hospital costs such as accommodation and theatre fees.

Examining Private Health Insurance

While Medicare is a one-horse race, in the private health insurance stakes you find a lot of starters. If you're interested in taking out private health insurance, you need to do some homework to decide which insurer is right for you and which schedule is suitable for you.

Check out the following Web sites for more information on private health insurance:

- ✔ PrivateHealth.gov.au at `www.privatehealth.gov.au`, where you can find out about all private health insurance companies in Australia, search a database of policies offered, and find out what private health insurers and Medicare do and don't cover

- ✔ Private Health Insurance Administration Council at `www.phiac.gov.au`, where you can find a list of registered providers as well as general information on private health insurance

Types of cover

Private health insurers usually offer the following types of cover:

- ✔ Extras cover
- ✔ Hospital cover

In addition, some insurers offer ambulance cover.

If you have ambulance cover in your policy, check that it covers you when you're travelling interstate.

Extras cover

Extras cover provides insurance for some or all of the costs associated with any treatment you receive from allied health professionals. The services that are covered vary between policies and insurers but usually include

- ✔ Acupuncture
- ✔ Dental
- ✔ Hearing aids
- ✔ Home nursing
- ✔ Hydrotherapy
- ✔ Orthodontics
- ✔ Pharmaceuticals
- ✔ Physiotherapy
- ✔ Podiatry

Some services attract a reasonable rebate, such as 50 per cent, while for others the rebate may be only 20 per cent. In addition, some policies limit the amount that you can claim for each service per person per year. This depends on your policy and the level of extras cover you have.

Check your health insurance policy carefully to confirm what services are covered and the amount of rebate offered.

Hospital cover

Hospital cover means that any hospital stays and surgery you need are covered by the health fund. Depending on the cover available, all your fees may be paid by your insurer or you may have to pay an *excess* (see the section 'Excess payments and co-payments' later in the chapter).

The top level of hospital cover should pay all your in-hospital care including accommodation (in a private room if one is available), intensive care, coronary care, nursing care, operating theatre fees, prostheses, physiotherapy and pharmaceuticals. Psychiatric care may also be covered.

Exclusions

You can get cheaper hospital cover if you elect to leave out some items of cover. You can do without items like *IVF and obstetrics* at this stage in your life, but think carefully about jettisoning items like cataract surgery, coronary care, joint replacement surgery and renal dialysis. If you rule out knee replacement and then need surgery, you could be up for about $15,000, and a coronary heart bypass could cost you up to $140,000!

Make sure your policy covers you for treatment in any private hospital, not just the hospitals associated with your fund. You get the highest rebates if you're treated at a hospital approved by your fund.

Excess payments and co-payments

To reduce the amount you pay for your policy each year, you can elect to pay an excess if you go to hospital. Policies vary: For example, this excess payment may be $200 per hospital stay or $200 for any amount of hospital stays in one calendar year.

Another way you can reduce your policy payments is to elect to make a *co-payment* if you go to hospital. For example, you may pay something like $50 per night for every night you stay in hospital.

Gap payments

While you're in hospital, your health insurance may pay the gap between the Medicare scheduled fee covered by Medicare and the actual fee charged by your doctors and specialists. However, after you leave hospital this gap may not be covered. Some health funds pay the gap if you pay a higher premium.

Check your policy carefully regarding exactly what is covered while you're in hospital. For example, does it cover the full amount of all in-hospital pharmaceuticals and physiotherapy?

Other considerations

In this section, I cover some steps you can take to ensure that you make the most of your private health insurance. Check these out:

- ✔ **Ask your doctor or specialist to advise the costs involved for any major surgical procedures you need.** That way, you know exactly how much you pay out of pocket. Remember that private health insurers usually give higher rebates if you attend a hospital that's listed by them.

- ✔ **Hunt around for the best deal for each type of cover.** You don't have to use the same insurer for your hospital cover and extras cover.

- ✔ **Reassess the restrictions and inclusions in your policy on a regular basis.** Your needs change as time goes by. Make sure that you're covered for all the services you may need now and into the future. Drop any you definitely won't need any more, so that you can reduce your premiums.

The waiting periods enforced for pre-existing illnesses may mean that you have to wait up to 12 months before you can collect any rebates on medical and allied healthcare costs related to those illnesses. If you want to take out more hospital cover or add to your extras cover, you may face an additional waiting period.

Additional waiting periods for pre-existing conditions shouldn't be enforced if you're changing funds but maintaining the same level of cover or opting for a lower level of cover. Check this with your fund.

Health-related travel insurance

If you're planning to travel overseas, your health insurance probably won't cover you and you may need to take out separate private health-related travel insurance. This travel insurance can cover you for the following items:

- ✔ Emergency medical assistance

- ✔ Hospital cash — this is an amount of money you can claim (usually about $50 per day) if you're hospitalised overseas for more than 48 hours

- ✔ Medical evacuation

- ✔ Medical, hospital and dental expenses

- ✔ Permanent disability

To obtain travel insurance you need to declare any pre-existing medical conditions. You may be asked to pay an extra amount to cover your condition — or you may be refused coverage. Chapter 11 has more specific information on travel insurance.

Deciding Whether You Need Health Insurance

Deciding whether to take out private health insurance cover may be easy if you simply can't afford it. If you can afford it, you need to decide whether you're happy relying on government-funded healthcare or would prefer the security of being able to choose your hospital, doctor or specialist and avoid the long waiting lists in public hospitals. Alternatively, of course, you can take the gamble that you remain in good health for the rest of your life.

Here are some things to consider before you make your decision:

- ✔ If you don't already have private health insurance and are over the age of 31, when you sign up for private health cover, you have to pay an extra loading for the remainder of your insured life. This loading works out at 2 per cent for *every year* you're over the age of 30 up to a maximum of 70 per cent. So, if you wait until you're 40 before you take out hospital cover, your premiums will be 20 per cent more than those of people who took out hospital cover when they were 30. This extra loading can substantially increase your premiums.

- ✔ If you pay private health insurance premiums, you're eligible for the federal government's 30 per cent rebate on private health insurance. If you're aged 65–69 you receive a 35 per cent rebate and if you're 70 or over you receive a 40 per cent rebate. You can have this rebate included in your premiums, or you can pay the full cost of your premiums and either apply to Medicare for a rebate or claim the rebate in your tax return.

  To receive this rebate you have to be insured with a registered private insurance provider. At www.phiac.gov.au you can find a list of these providers.

- ✔ If you want to choose your doctor or specialist in a public (or private) hospital, Medicare will pay only 75 per cent of the Medicare scheduled fee — you have to pay the other 25 per cent. Private health insurance should normally cover this gap.

- ✔ Medicare doesn't cover the services of allied health professionals unless your doctor gives you a general practitioner package, and even then you receive a Medicare rebate for only a limited number of consultations per year. Depending on the policy, such services are often covered by private health insurance.

- ✔ The waiting lists for non-urgent surgery like knee and hip replacements are long in public hospitals. You may have to wait several months for surgery.

- ✔ You can rely on the government to provide basic health cover through Medicare. You're guaranteed free treatment in a public hospital and will receive some if not all of the costs of doctor and specialist consultations. You also receive a Medicare rebate for private doctor and specialist care.

Chapter 9

Understanding the Aged-Care System

At this stage in your life you probably won't need to access the aged-care system for yourself, but you may need to understand it if you suddenly find yourself responsible for looking after an elderly relative. Australians are living longer, and many recently retired people find themselves having to deal with elderly parents who perhaps need a lot of attention or full-time care.

The decision needs to be taken in consultation with your relative and family, of course. If your relative is still fairly healthy and self-sufficient, staying in his or her own home is an option, but if your relative needs regular care that you can't provide, you'll need to look at an aged-care facility.

If you find yourself in the position of being responsible for the care of an elderly relative, you have three options, which I cover in this chapter.

Allowing Your Relative to Remain at Home

Probably the most-favoured option on all sides will be for your relative to stay in his or her own home. Just because your relative has reached 80 or 90 — or even 100 — he or she doesn't have to leave home. The Australian government aims to keep people in their own homes for as long as possible, so various forms of help are available for those who wish to remain living independently.

Council support

Look to your local council for support in helping your relative in the first instance. Most councils have extensive programs in place to care for their older residents. You or your relative's doctor can ring the council and ask for a care assessment. A council worker will visit your relative's home and assess how the council can help.

The council can supply some or all of the following services to eligible persons:

✓ **Cleaning services:** The council can arrange for a cleaner to clean your relative's home once a week. The cleaner has only one or two hours to complete the job. He or she will vacuum and mop the floors, clean the bathroom and toilets, wash and iron, and do other small jobs. If heavy washing like sheets is hung on the line, the council may provide someone to bring them in later in the day.

✓ **Community transport:** The council can provide community transport if your relative wants to go to the senior citizens club or one of the other social clubs in the area.

✓ **Home maintenance:** The council can arrange for a handyman to undertake any tasks your relative needs done to make his or her home safe. These include:

- Changing light globes and smoke detector batteries

- Cleaning guttering and fixing dripping taps

- Installing grab rails in the shower and toilet

- Relighting the gas heater

✓ **Meals:** Most councils provide one home-delivered three-course meal per day (soup, main meal and dessert). Australian Meals on Wheels Association is the source of most of these meals. Visit www.mealson wheels.org.au for more information on Meals on Wheels.

✓ **Personal care:** If your relative needs help with showering, shaving, dressing or eating the council can supply a personal carer to help. Your relative will be assessed as to how many care visits he or she can receive per week.

- **Respite:** If your relative has a live-in carer or main carer, respite is available to give the carer some time off. A council worker may stay with your relative at home to relieve the carer. Or your relative may be picked up by bus and taken to a special day facility to give the carer a break. This service isn't always available outside office hours.

- **Shopping and bill paying:** If your relative is able to go out but needs someone to drive or help with the shopping, the council can arrange for a carer to undertake shopping trips.

- **Social support programs:** So your relative isn't isolated at home, the council has programs that offer bus trips, gentle exercise and discussion groups.

The fees charged are calculated according to income and are heavily subsidised. You can't access these services every day — for example, in one week your relative may get two hours of cleaning, one shopping trip and help with showering for two days.

Other help

As well as getting support from your local council, don't forget to check out the following service providers:

- **Department of Health and Ageing:** The Department's Aged Care Web site at www.agedcareaustralia.gov.au has an enormous amount of information regarding services available for the aged and their carers.

- **Department of Veterans' Affairs:** The Department's Web site at www.dva.gov.au contains information on pensions, housing, health and other assistance you need if you're caring for a veteran, or war widow or widower.

- **Royal District Nursing Service (RDNS):** This not-for-profit organisation offers regular 24-hour care to elderly patients in their own homes. Anyone can be referred to the RDNS. Your relative can phone the service, or you or your relative's doctor can make the referral. The RDNS charges most clients a fee for the care provided. However, fees vary, depending on the care provided and the person's circumstances. For more information, check out the RDNS's Web site at www.rdns.com.au.

- **Senior citizens groups:** These groups can provide meals, newspapers, computer access and activities in their centres. See www.seniors.vic.gov.au for more information or contact your local council.

In addition, a number of private agencies provide aged-care services. To find one of these agencies, check in your local phone book under 'aged care' or search online. As a starting point, you could try the following:

✔ www.dialanangel.com (DIAL-AN-ANGEL®)

✔ www.silvercircle.com.au (Calvary Silver Circle)

Aged-care assessment

Does your relative require a lot more help than the local council can give? Then he or she needs to get an ACAT assessment. *Aged-Care Assessment Teams* (ACATs) are government-funded teams of doctors, nurses, social workers and others who can assess your relative's care needs and suggest suitable care options. They can help your relative to stay in his or her own home, or they can refer your relative to aged-care residential and respite homes.

Ask your relative's doctor to make the referral for an assessment, or you or your relative can simply make an appointment.

To find out how to book an assessment, check out the Department of Health and Ageing's Web site at www.health.gov.au.

After the ACAT assessment booking is made, a member of the team visits your relative at home, taking some time to assess your relative's needs. The assessor may ask your relative to walk or perform a task to check mobility. The assessor assesses any medical needs and checks other things like whether your relative:

✔ Can look after his personal care

✔ Is alert and articulate

✔ Is involved in social and community activities

✔ Has a carer

✔ Needs domestic assistance

✔ Needs help with transport

If your relative is planning to remain at home, the assessor may check the bathroom and other facilities to ensure that they're safe.

The assessor then provides a report advising which program best suits your relative's needs. ACATs provide access to the following government-subsidised care packages:

- **Community aged-care packages (CACPs):** CACPs provide similar services to those the local council provides but they're coordinated by a CACP provider.
- **Extended aged-care at home (EACH) packages:** EACH packages are designed to help the frail aged to stay in their own homes. As well as the services provided by a CACP program, the recipient may receive nursing assistance and be able to access an EACH dementia package, which provides help with behavioural difficulties.
- **Residential aged-care packages:** These packages help with high-level (nursing home) and low-level (hostel) residential care and high- and low-level respite care.
- **Transition care packages:** These packages provide assistance after the recipient has been in hospital.

Your relative may be offered a CACP if he or she is mobile and can feed and dress himself or herself. If your relative is unable to dress and feed himself or herself, high-level care residential or respite care or an EACH package may be offered.

You'll need to plan ahead if your relative would like to receive one of these packages, because there may be a 12-month waiting list for some packages.

Hold onto the ACAT report and make copies of it. Any residential home you contact may ask for a copy, even if you're simply putting your relative's name on a waiting list. This report is valid for 12 months and must be renewed every 12 months.

If your relative is recommended for a government-subsidised care package, the package is usually delivered via a not-for-profit organisation like Benetas and replaces any council care package. Your relative may be able to continue using her usual care provider, but the care will be coordinated by a different body. One advantage of a government-subsidised care package is that it provides additional services so that the recipient can get more domestic and personal carer assistance. The recipient also has a case manager to contact to discuss her needs and concerns.

Has your relative already formed a good working relationship with a council-provided domestic or personal carer? You can request for that same person to continue your relative's care. The CACP or EACH provider will engage the council to provide your relative's direct care, but your relative will make a payment or donation to the new provider. Both sides should agree on the fee and it mustn't be more than 17.5 per cent or your relative's basic pension. If your relative has a higher income, the fee may be higher. If your relative is unable to pay, he or she won't be excluded from the service.

Moving Your Relative into an Aged-Care Home

Deciding to move your relative out of his or her own home and into an aged-care facility can be a very difficult and emotional time. Some people would rather stay at home come what may, whereas others are happy to move into a facility where they'll be cared for on a daily basis. Sometimes you have no choice but to place your relative in an aged-care home if your relative has dementia or is too unwell to care for himself or herself. If your relative resists the idea, your task won't be straightforward.

Try taking these steps to ease the way:

- ✔ **Do the groundwork.** Make sure that your relative's aged-care assessment is up-to-date and investigate some homes to make a short list of alternatives.

- ✔ **Ease your relative into the idea of care by finding him or her a place in respite care for a while.** Your relative may find that he or she likes being looked after, getting ready-cooked meals and not being alone.

- ✔ **Enlist the help of your relative's doctor.** Your relative may take more notice of the doctor's advice than yours!

- ✔ **Get the finances sorted out.** Sometimes having to sell the family home is a stumbling block. You may be able to rent the home to cover costs. Talk to the managers of the aged-care home for their advice, as they'll have dealt with this situation before, or seek other financial advice.

- ✔ **Try to find a home that caters for your relative's religious or cultural beliefs.**

- ✔ **Try to find a home that's either close to where your relative lives so that your relative's friends can pop in or close to where you live so that you can visit often.**

- ✔ **Try to stay positive and point out to your relative the advantages in not having to struggle and do everything alone.**

In addition, you may like to seek counselling and/or support for yourself. This can be an exhausting time and you need to keep your energy up.

Applying for a place in an aged-care facility

You have to go through a lot of red tape before you can enter someone into an aged-care home — even for only a week of respite care.

Follow these steps to help cut through the red tape:

1. **Ensure that your relative has an ACAT assessment.**

   The resultant report will advise which level of care your relative needs (see the section 'Aged-care assessment' earlier in the chapter).

2. **Get your relative to complete an application form for respite care or permanent entry to an aged-care home.**

   The ACAT assessor can supply the correct form. Your relative must supply personal details and particulars of any full or part pension or support payment. A copy of a current ACAT report must be attached to the form. Your relative can nominate a representative to sign the form or to be contacted on his or her behalf about the form, but this person must hold the relevant power of attorney. A copy of this power of attorney should be attached to the form. (For more information on powers of attorney see Chapter 6.)

3. **Ensure that you have a good basic understanding of how to go about entering an aged-care home.**

   Accompanying the form is a booklet, '5 Steps to Entry into Residential Aged Care', which you should read carefully. The booklet contains important information about the steps you need to take to enter your relative into an aged-care home. The booklet covers the following processes:

   - Assessing your relative's eligibility for residential aged care

   - Finding an aged-care home

   - Working out the costs involved (fees and charges)

   - Applying for a residential aged-care place

   - Moving and settling in

   The booklet also outlines how your relative's income and assets are assessed. If your relative doesn't want his or her assets to be assessed, he or she won't be eligible for an Australian government subsidy to cover accommodation costs.

   You can download a copy of this booklet from the Department of Health and Ageing's Web site at www.health.gov.au.

Make sure that you understand the assets test *before* you decide what to do with the family home.

Understanding the costs associated with aged-care facilities

To understand the various costs associated with residential aged-care homes you need to grasp the main terms used:

- **Accommodation bond:** People with a low-level care rating may be asked to pay an accommodation bond on entering a home. The maximum bond is based on their assets at the time of entry. There is no set figure for the bond: It is negotiated between the resident and the home. Some homes are more up-front about this money than others. The money is kept as an income-free loan and is returned after certain deductions have been made.

- **Accommodation charge:** Those in high-level care may be asked to pay an accommodation charge, paid as a daily fee. This charge is in addition to the basic daily care fee, but is dependent on the person's assets.

- **Basic daily care fee:** This fee is charged to meet the costs associated with basic care, such as meals, cleaning, laundry and staff.

- **Concessional or assisted place:** People with assets below a specified amount are classified as concessional. This means they don't have to pay an accommodation bond. However, their choice of care may be limited as most homes have a set number of concessional or assisted places.

- **Income-tested daily care fee:** People with private income may be liable to pay this fee in addition to the basic daily care fee.

Finding the right aged-care home

While you're taking the appropriate steps for your relative to enter a home, you'll also be looking for a home that suits your relative's needs. This can be a time-consuming task but is essential if you and your relative are going to be happy with the new accommodation.

The ACAT assessor can supply a list of suitable homes. You can also search for homes on the Web or in the *Yellow Pages*.

Take the opportunity to view several homes before you decide which one to choose. You need to make an appointment to visit a home. While you and your relative are being shown around, talk to the staff and ask questions. You can also ask to chat to a resident for a moment. Alternatively, a meeting with a resident may be pre-arranged for you. Keep your eyes and ears (and nose) open.

Here are a few questions you may like to ask staff to find out more about the facility:

- **Activities:** What sort of activities are available? Are the residents taken on shopping trips or outings? Do the staff provide gentle exercise programs?

- **Air-conditioning and heating:** Does each room have air-conditioning and heating, or do residents have to purchase an air-conditioner and have it installed?

- **Alzheimer's care:** Is there a separate Alzheimer's or dementia ward? (This is important, because dementia patients have very special needs.)

- **Auxiliary staff:** Is there a resident or visiting hairdresser, podiatrist and physiotherapist?

- **Doctors:** How are doctors' visits organised? Is there a roster for visiting doctors or do residents make their own arrangements? (You may like to check whether your relative's regular doctor visits the home.)

- **Food:** What is the food like? Is it cooked on the premises? Are morning and afternoon tea provided? Does the home cater for particular food requirements? Ask to see a sample menu.

- **Friends and relatives:** Are friends and relatives made welcome? Is there a facility to have friends over to play cards or to celebrate birthdays and other occasions?

- **Language and culture:** Are the language or culture appropriate? Some homes cater exclusively for a particular culture and some have activities like newspaper readings in particular languages.

- **Laundry:** Is there a central laundry system? Can residents do their own laundry if they wish?

- **Religion:** Is there a room set aside for religious services? How often are they held? What denominations are catered for?

- **Staff:** How many staff are there? How many are trained aged-care workers? Is there a nurse on the premises?

Ageing in place

A number of aged-care facilities now have a system that is referred to as *ageing in place*. This means that if your relative enters a facility as a low-level care resident, he or she doesn't have to move to another facility when their needs become high care. The main advantage is that your relative stays in the place he or she is used to and you won't have to go hunting for other accommodation.

Caring for Your Relative in Your Own Home

Caring for an elderly relative in your own home changes the dynamic of your house. This option isn't for everyone. If your children have recently left home and you've been looking forward to an empty nest, the decision to take in a relative is a big one.

Often, your parents are able to manage perfectly well while they're both together, but when one passes away the other's financial and emotional circumstances will change dramatically. Often, the one who's left simply can't afford to maintain the house alone.

If you decide to care for your relative in your own home, don't feel that you're all on your own. Help is available for carers. Check out these Web sites:

✔ Accessibility.com has a section devoted to carers. It has information relating to carer benefits and self-education and provides a list of carer support groups. Visit www.accessibility.com.au and click the 'Carers Support' button under 'Health Topics'.

✔ Ahm Total Health at www.totalhealth.ahm.com.au discusses the issues surrounding caring for aged parents. Browse the site by typing in 'carer' to the search facility.

✔ The Department of Health and Ageing's Aged Care Web site has advice on respite care and getting in touch with other carers. Check out www.agedcareaustralia.gov.au.

Your local council will also have information on carer support networks.

Chapter 10

Moving House

*R*etirement is a time of change, and moving house is one of those discussions that tends to crop up at some time — either while you're making your retirement plans or after you've retired. You may be feeling 'out with the old and in with the new'. Perhaps you'd like to move somewhere more appropriate for your new lifestyle? You may be contemplating a radical change from town to country or want to live nearer a golf course — or your children.

Don't act on impulse. Before you commit to selling up you need to make sure that you're *completely* happy with the decision. Buying and selling property can be expensive in terms of solicitors fees, agents fees and stamp duty — and if you make the wrong move, the added stress can impact on your health and wellbeing.

If you're not happy with the change, you may join the growing group of Australians who sell up the family home in the suburbs, move to the country, find the move doesn't satisfy them and then try to relocate back to the suburbs. Unfortunately, in the meantime the increase in suburban house prices compared to rural prices means you may have to be satisfied with a lower standard of accommodation than you want — or worse, you can't re-enter your preferred market at all.

In this chapter, I look at the pros and cons of moving house. I also take you through downsizing, sea changing, tree changing and village living.

Making the Decision to Move

Making the decision to move isn't something that can be taken lightly. You need to think carefully about your options. If you're living with a spouse or partner, you need to agree whether you actually both *want* to move, and where to. If you live your own, you don't have to agree with anyone but yourself — although sometimes even this can be problematic.

Here are a few suggestions to help you with the decision-making process:

- ✔ Give yourself some time to work out what's most important to you about where and how you live. For example, do you prefer ease of access to shops, libraries and transport, or is being near your family of paramount importance?
- ✔ Consider whether you want to get away from the city or move closer to a city or town centre.
- ✔ Find out whether the area you want to move to has adequate medical facilities and other services — unfortunately, you're not getting any younger. Also investigate the area for activities and entertainment you enjoy. Can you join the local theatre, cycling club or outriggers group?

Check out Chapter 2 for some exercises to help you with the decision-making process.

Negotiating a change of address with your partner

This is what you've been waiting for: You've finally got time to really get to work on your vintage car collection — or perhaps extend your garage into a you-beaut craft room. And then your partner announces that it's time to sell the suburban plot, move to a city apartment and enjoy the cultural whirl of museums, theatres and galleries.

Or perhaps it's the other way round: You may long to get away from the area and try something different, but your partner is strongly attached to your house and neighbourhood and doesn't want to leave it.

If you're going to move house and make any sort of big change at retirement, you *both* need to be happy with the new lifestyle — or it simply won't work.

Unless you've constantly moved house over the years because of your job or other circumstances, your current house will hold all sorts of meanings for you. But you and your partner may have totally different relationships with your house and your community. Perhaps you see where you live as a safe haven from the working week and want to retire there in peace, while your partner is happy to leave it all behind and can't wait for the excitement and adventure of trying something new.

If you and your partner don't immediately see eye to eye over whether to move house or not, try these positive steps to make sure that you're working in harmony:

1. **Individually work out what's important to each of you.**

   See Chapter 2 for ideas on how to approach this task.

2. **Sit down together and discuss your findings.**

3. **Try to come up with four basic wants and needs you have in common.**

   Talk about how these will affect your lifestyle in the future.

Your common ground will give you a base to negotiate from. For example, if:

✔ Conservation is important to both of you, a tree change may be the answer

✔ You both want to travel, you may want to downsize to an apartment or a retirement community

✔ You're both worried about health issues, you may decide to locate near good medical facilities

✔ Your family is important to both of you, you can consider moving to be near family members

Finding somewhere new to live

After you've decided on the four most important aspects of your life, you can begin the process of finding a new place to live. If you've always had a dream location, this may not be a problem. But if you have only a vague idea of where you want to relocate, you need to put in a lot of research.

Make a list of your wants and needs concerning your new location. At the top write the most important aspects, but don't forget the mundane essentials like access to transport, medical facilities and shops.

Your list may look like this:

- ✔ No more than an hour's drive from family
- ✔ Existing home in need of renovation
- ✔ Close to a surf beach
- ✔ Good computer and telephone links
- ✔ Access to a golf course
- ✔ Close to public transport
- ✔ Big enough to accommodate family and friends
- ✔ Access to good medical facilities

Or this:

- ✔ Close to a major city with museums and galleries
- ✔ Within 20 minutes' drive of family and friends
- ✔ Walking distance to shops, library and public transport
- ✔ House ready for immediate occupancy — no renovations *at all*
- ✔ Close to cafes and restaurants

Or even this:

- ✔ Away from *everyone*
- ✔ Room to keep animals and grow vegetables
- ✔ Ability to create own energy sources
- ✔ Availability of recycled building materials

Your list gives you a starting point to search for your new home. If you can't find what you want, you'll need to compromise on some of your list items.

You also need to put a dollar amount on how much you can afford to spend. Make sure that you understand your superannuation and other investments and have some idea how much money you need to live on — see Chapters 3 and 4 for more information, and talk to your financial adviser. Have your house valued.

Investigate the area where you intend to live and compare house prices with the value of your own home to see whether there's a shortfall or you'll come out ahead.

More things to think about before you move

Before you sell up make doubly sure that you and your partner really want to move. Draw up a list of all the people and services you'll miss and try to work out ways to compensate for them. You need to work through these basics to ensure that your move will be successful.

Here are some issues to consider when you're contemplating your new location:

- **Activities:** Are there enough activities to keep you occupied? Is there a bushwalking club, golf course or sailing club nearby? Can you find a fishing club, book club or knitting circle?

- **Entertainment:** If you like going to the theatre or pictures, investigate what's available in the new neighbourhood. Do the picture theatres show only blockbusters or can you find some art house movies? Consider joining a local film society.

- **Family:** Is your family within easy reach? If you have elderly parents or grandchildren, are you close enough to keep in contact?

- **Friends:** Be prepared to make new friends, especially if you move a long way from your old neighbourhood. Join clubs, take up an activity and make sure that you become involved in community life so you can avoid social isolation.

- **Medical facilities:** While you're healthy this isn't an issue, but be aware that smaller towns don't have the same medical facilities as larger cities. Do some research and find a good doctor you can trust. If you have a medical condition, make sure that you can find specialist care without going too far afield.

- **Part-time or full-time work:** After the initial excitement of retirement and moving house has settled down, you may want to return to some form of work. If you think this may be an option, check out the local papers to see what work's available.

- **Transport:** Besides making longer trips back to friends and family, how will you get around your immediate community? If you're away from the town centre, can you easily get to the shops if for some reason you can't drive?

Future planning

Are you planning to move house for the long term or the short term? If your move will be long term think carefully about how your situation may change as you age. Some of the important issues for future planning revolve around transport and easy access to your local shops and medical facilities, as well as to community centres, your local church or hobby club. It's vital to stay connected to others as you age. Also consider the layout and situation of your house. In later years you probably won't want to be walking up and down stairs — unless you see it as a way to keep fit. And if you're at the top of a hill and the shops are at the bottom, walking up the hill with shopping may become difficult as you get older.

If you think your move may be short term and you'll soon relocate nearer to family and friends or into a retirement village, your new house needs to be easy to sell. Keep this in mind when you're looking at properties.

Moving Closer to Family

The rising cost and scarcity of childcare is having an impact on retirees. As more women return to the workforce after maternity leave, often grandparents are left minding the children.

Although this is a wonderful opportunity for bonding between grandparents and grandchildren, it also impacts on where retirees choose to live. Some retirees relocate to be nearer their children and grandchildren, others delay their sea change or, if they do move, commit to travelling as required to babysit.

Be aware of the pitfalls of selling up and moving closer to family members. At a minimum, do the following before you sell your house:

  ✔ Ask whether family members are actually planning to stay where they are for the foreseeable future, especially if you need to sell your house to be near them.

  ✔ Check out the social scene in the new area — are there enough suitable activities to keep you occupied? You need to make new friends in your new location.

  ✔ Investigate the medical facilities available. Some smaller towns don't provide extensive (or any) hospital and specialist care.

> ✔ Work out any family issues before you move, because these issues are unlikely to go away with time. Sometimes people move to be near family but find that all their old childhood grievances come back to haunt them.

A good option is to rent a place in the area first, to see how things work out. And rent out your house too, so that you've got somewhere to return to if things don't go to plan.

Downsizing

After your family grow up and leave home, you may think about *downsizing*. After all, how many rooms do you need? Well, if you're like me — a bit of a hoarder — lots. But if you're prepared to face a more minimalist lifestyle, downsizing may be for you.

Of course, as a result an inevitability about downsizing is having to dispose of *a lot* of stuff. Give yourself plenty of time for sorting. Excess stuff can be sold at a garage sale and/or given to a charity shop. Your heavy furniture, that old piano, the contents of the garden shed … all have to go.

Ask your children to take all the old clothing, comics, school assignments and sporting equipment they're storing at your place too.

Going home

Although my friend Michael was born in Adelaide and spent his young life in that city, in his mid-20s he moved to Melbourne for work. When retirement became imminent, Michael thought carefully about his future. He had made many friends in Melbourne and had become involved in the local football club, but he decided that as he aged it was important to be close to his family.

So Michael bought a house in Adelaide, but he waited for a year before selling his Melbourne house. At first Michael travelled between Melbourne and Adelaide regularly, then he began to settle into the Adelaide lifestyle. He had fun playing golf with his brother and enjoyed the company of his sister-in-law and nephews. He joined Rotary and volunteered to help out at his old school.

Within a year Michael had settled into his new lifestyle and knew it was time to sell his Melbourne house. He still visits his Melbourne friends, and they're always welcome in his home in Adelaide, but he's now happily returned to his roots.

You still need somewhere to store possessions you don't use every day — like golf clubs, bicycles and potting mix — so make sure you have access to storage in your new place.

One of the biggest difficulties many people face with downsizing is putting up with the cramped quarters when their grown-up children return to the nest. You may have left home at 18 with the understanding that you weren't going back, but one of the biggest generational changes these days is the number of 20- and 30-year-olds returning home so that they can save to buy a house of their own. If you don't love all the to-ing and fro-ing of a big household, buying a really small apartment will ensure that your children won't be able to come home permanently.

Also, when you leave your home, you may be leaving your neighbourhood, your friends and your support. This can take some adjusting to. You may find yourself driving back to your old neighbourhood for a while to visit your doctor or dentist or to see your favourite shops. Give yourself time to explore your new surroundings: You'll soon find alternatives. However, I have to admit that I still drive back to my old suburb to visit my dentist after leaving seven years ago. There's something about the trust between me and my dentist that takes time to establish.

Some Australians see downsizing as a way to boost their retirement savings. If you own a substantial home in a pricey suburb, swapping it for an apartment can put more money in the kitty. But beware — many city apartments and townhouses are more expensive than big homes. As the population ages, more retirees are moving from suburban houses with big gardens to homes with less upkeep. Naturally, this pushes prices up.

Rising high

Some people opt for the high life, whereas others keep their feet firmly on the ground. Here are some issues to consider if you're contemplating high-rise living:

- **Lifts:** As a high-rise dweller, you're dependent on the lift's smooth operation — unless you want to keep *very* fit.

- **Neighbours:** Instead of just two or three neighbours, you have a lot. Make sure you understand how your building works — and I don't just mean from a structural point of view. Find out how things get done and how you can have a say in what happens in the building.

- **Noise:** Many high rises are in the city or on the city's edge. You hear more traffic noise and screaming sirens. You may also hear more noise from the neighbours.

✔ **Pets:** High-rise living presents special issues for pet owners. Pets can't run in and out of the doggie door to relieve themselves: You have to be on hand to take them outside. Alternatively, get a more contained pet like a snake or lizard. Some apartment buildings don't allow pets at all, so if you have pets you may have to make a difficult decision.

✔ **Security:** A high-rise apartment with a security door can be very comforting. If you're on the 20th floor you probably won't have to lock your windows.

✔ **Wind:** Sitting outside on your balcony and having a barbecue or admiring the view may not always be on the agenda when you're 20 floors off the ground: You'll find things can get very windy up there.

Living in the city

For many Australians downsizing means leaving the leafy suburbs and moving to the inner city. If you're not used to city living, you may be in for a bit of a culture shock. For a start, you aren't buffeted from your immediate neighbourhood by your garden: When you step outside you're on the street — with its traffic, people and noise. And although getting around the city may be easy enough, getting out of the city may be a tedious long run of traffic jams.

However, if you can get over the culture shock and don't mind the hustle and bustle, the plusses are aplenty:

✔ Transport is likely to be a short walk away.

✔ You have easy access to galleries, museums, public lectures and other forms of entertainment.

✔ You have the opportunity to eat out more at cafes and restaurants.

✔ You may get to know your neighbours better than you did in the suburbs. They're less likely to emerge from behind big gates in their 4WDs and more likely to be walking to the shops with you.

Accommodating a relative or growing hobby

Although many retirees downsize their property, if you have a hobby that requires a lot of space or want to accommodate an elderly relative, you may find you need to move to a *bigger* home, not a smaller one. Alternatively, you may prefer to renovate your existing home, or add a new wing or a granny flat. You're not releasing the equity in your house, but you're investing in the capital value. Perhaps you can use your new big property to begin a bed and breakfast or become self-sufficient.

Making a Change

Tired of urban or suburban living? Fed up with the traffic? With retirement you have an opportunity to resign from the rat race and move to the country or seaside. You can sell the family home and get away from it all. Or you can finally build your dream home.

You may even like to buy a mobile home and join the Grey Nomads. Chapter 12 has the low-down on taking to the road.

Sea change

If you've had beach holidays at a particular place for several years, you may consider living there permanently when you retire. If you're lucky, you may already have a beach house that you can renovate and move into. Otherwise, you'll find that prices have risen dramatically over the last few years, especially in resorts that are an easy one- or two-hour drive from a major city.

As with any move to a new location living the sea change dream requires some preparation. You're leaving behind your old neighbourhood and all its familiarities and taking on a whole new set of circumstances. You have to seek out new medical and allied health professionals. Your friends will love to visit at first, but you need to make new friends too as time goes on.

Holidaying in a seaside town and permanently living there are two different things. While you're on holiday you have a sense of escape from your everyday life. After you relocate to the seaside, your daily life comes with you.

 Being in an area with a lot of rentals won't bother you while you're holidaying, but you may find that having neighbouring houses rented out to groups of party makers all year round is a real nuisance. Also, if you're in a heavily treed area, the threat of bushfires may be made worse if surrounding holiday homes aren't maintained and made fire safe.

These annoyances can all be forgotten when you get up in the morning, head for the beach and fill your lungs with sea air — or crest that first wave.

Tree change

Many Australians choose to leave the noise and bustle of the city and its traffic behind and make a new life in a more laid-back and restful style. On your own little piece of dirt you can grow your own food and become self-sufficient if you wish.

Once again, you need to make some preparations for such a move. You'll be leaving your current community with all its associations and conveniences, and unless you want to become a complete hermit, you need to find a way of fitting into the new community.

On top of all the usual considerations when you move, country living entails extra issues. For many people country living means a larger property, so looking after your property is a much bigger task. On a half-acre block in town the job won't be too onerous, but on a couple of acres or more you need to maintain fences and control vegetation — slashing, clearing, stick-picking, weeding, burning off ... the list goes on. Depending on the size of your new property, you could find that maintenance takes a considerable chunk of your time. While some will revel in this new role, you really need to consider whether you can make the commitment. Unless you want to spend your life maintaining your property, consider buying a much smaller acreage or a property in a country town.

The whole idea of buying a country property is often to have a few chooks and cows, and maybe a sheep or two and some ducks or geese. Do a short course at TAFE so you know how to look after them properly. You have to factor in vets' fees as part of your new lifestyle. Remember, if you keep a few sheep they'll need to be shorn — unless you run a special breed of sheep that loses its wool naturally.

 Bushfires are a major threat to most of rural Australia. Take the advice of your local Country Fire Authority on how to fire-proof your property. Decide early on whether you'll leave your property if a fire comes or stay and fight the fire.

If you decide to move to an out-of-town property, here are some further issues you need to consider:

- ✔ Broadband and mobile phone services aren't available in some rural areas. Check with your telecommunications supplier to make sure that you can stay connected.
- ✔ Natural gas isn't available in many country areas. Remember that electricity and bottled gas are more expensive than natural gas.

✔ Rather than the post being delivered to your home, it may be delivered to a cluster of letterboxes on the nearest main road.

✔ You'll probably have to be self-sufficient in terms of water supply, because town water isn't often available out of town.

✔ Your newspapers may not be delivered — and you'll have to travel further for your morning cappuccino.

Keeping one foot in town — or not

One way of settling any debate about where to live is to sell your house and with the proceeds buy a flat in the city and a house in the country. This way, you have the security of keeping a foot in the city door. If you find country living isn't for you or if you need to return to the city to be close to family or medical facilities, you've kept your options open so the move can be swift and fairly painless.

Talk to your financial adviser before you end up with two properties so you understand all the ins and outs: You don't want to over-commit yourself. Owning and running two properties has a downside, of course: They eat into your income. You have to pay two sets of utility bills and rates, and maintain two properties and perhaps two gardens. If you and your partner each spend time at separate properties, you'll be burning gas and electricity to heat and cool two houses at the same time. You'll also use more petrol travelling between the properties.

Making the decision to sell one of your properties can be quite difficult, especially if you've always dreamt of living in the bush and keeping a place in town to be near family and entertainment venues. You have to take many things into account when deciding which property to sell, such as the state of your finances and the practicality of each house.

You may decide to sell one property and invest the remaining money. If you decide to live in your country property and sell your town house, you can use rented accommodation or stay in hotels when you're in town. On the other hand, giving up your beach house or bush shack may mean you're free to travel more often. You won't feel tied down to one place or obliged to be there all the time.

Having a place in the country and a pad in town is a lifestyle choice. You need to work out what's important to you.

Building your dream home

Have you always had an interest in architectural design? Would you like to live in a totally environmentally friendly house? Do you have the perfect block of land? Perhaps you want to take the opportunity in your retirement to build your dream home?

Building a new house is exciting, but it can also be a fraught time. You need to do a lot of planning and be well-prepared. Work out exactly what you want. Although your finances will dictate the style and quality of fixtures and fittings, you can do a lot to make sure your house works for you. Here are some points to consider:

- ✔ Are there enough storage cupboards? Do you have a linen press, and sufficient kitchen and bedroom cupboards?

- ✔ Can you work comfortably in the kitchen? Is there enough bench space? Can you easily take food from the stove or fridge to the bench top?

- ✔ Do you want a house on one level or two — or more? Are you happy going up and down stairs every time you want to go to the bedroom or the kitchen?

- ✔ How wide do you want the doorways and hallways? Will you need to carry big items through the house, or push a wheelchair or pram through?

- ✔ Is it a house for just you, or will you have guests staying over?

- ✔ Should the house integrate with the garden? Are decks necessary to join the two? Is there convenient access from indoors to outdoors?

Do your homework thoroughly. The Web site of the Department of Families, Housing, Community Services and Indigenous Affairs at www.fahcsia. gov.au has plenty of advice on building a new house. The topics covered include buying land, choosing a builder, protecting yourself against building defects, planning for energy efficiency, building contracts and certificates of occupancy.

Retiring to Village Life

Perhaps your idea of retirement living is a village with facilities and new friends close at hand? Many lifestyle resorts are specifically aimed at the active over-55s and are designed to offer everything from bowling greens, tennis courts, swimming pools and gymnasiums to high-class restaurants. However, they still give you peace of mind, with 24-hour medical assistance available should you need it.

Retirement villages come in all shapes and sizes, from the basic units clustered around a community centre to individual villas built around a swimming pool and restaurants. Some villages are run by church or community not-for-profit organisations, while others are commercial ventures funded by the residents.

Levels of living

Self-care villas provide occupants with the privacy of their own home. You can do all your own cooking or take advantage of the central dining room (usually at an extra cost). You can even have guests to stay. These villas offer security and peace of mind if you wish to travel. In addition, they usually have a call-button facility that you can use in an emergency.

As you age, you may prefer a higher level of care. *Serviced apartments* are aimed at residents who may need more help with their personal care and who prefer to have their meals cooked for them. *Nursing home facilities* are designed for those who are no longer able to look after themselves. These facilities offer a high level of personal and medical care.

Choosing a village

Choosing where you want to live is a very personal decision. Your financial and social needs will help inform your choice. Before you move to a retirement village you need to carefully assess all the financial, legal and lifestyle implications of such a move. Here are just some of the essentials to check when choosing a retirement village:

- ✔ **Day-to-day living:** A whole raft of things affect whether your daily living is pleasurable or not so pleasurable. Enquire about the following *before* you enter a village:

- Are you near to public facilities such as churches, hospitals, parks, restaurants, shopping centres and public transport?

- Can you keep pets? If other residents have pets, can you be assured that you won't be annoyed by yapping dogs or wandering cats, for example?

- Do you agree with the rules imposed by management?

- Does the village provide you with the security and medical attention you require?

- Is there ample car parking and storage space?

- Will your villa be serviced by housekeeping if you wish?

✔ **Departure fee:** If you sell your villa, the owner or operator of the village may charge you a departure fee. You need to understand the nature of this fee *before* you enter the village. The different fee structures can have very different financial outcomes. The departure fee may be calculated on percentages or the operator may be entitled to up to 100 per cent of the capital gain on your villa. Visit some of the Web sites listed at the end of this section to find out more about departure fees and how they may affect you.

✔ **Financial considerations:** When you purchase a villa or an apartment, you don't necessarily purchase the freehold title. You may buy a lease (the term used in the industry is 'tenure'). If so, you need to check whether the landlord can cancel your lease at any time or whether you can cancel it if you want to move out of the village. Each state and territory has specific legislation covering this arrangement.

✔ **Management rules:** After you enter a village you are bound under the rules of the village management. You need to know how much of a say you have as a resident in decisions taken by management.

With the number and diversity of retirement villages available, you may have difficulty knowing which one will suit your lifestyle. Make sure that you check out the village thoroughly before you buy, especially regarding the financial side.

Check out the following Web sites if you want to find out more about retirement village living:

✔ It's Your Life at `www.itsyourlife.com.au` has a complete rundown of what retirement village life is all about and an Australia-wide directory of retirement villages.

- ✔ Law Institute of Victoria at www.liv.asn.au explains what retirement villages are and how they operate on a financial level. The information supplied is relevant for other states and territories.

- ✔ Retirement Village Association at www.rva.com.au has developed a set of standards for retirement villages. To be accredited, villages must be assessed as having met these standards.

- ✔ Seniors.gov at www.seniors.gov.au covers types of retirement villages, legislation covering villages, costs and departure fees.

Part IV
Using Your Time Wisely

Glenn Lumsden

*'I'd love to help, but I'm far too busy.
You should've rung before I retired.'*

In this part . . .

You have many exciting opportunities open to you in your retirement. How would you like to spend your time? Like many retirees you probably have the travel bug, and I offer tips to help you to decide what sort of travel you want (and can afford) to do, including short breaks, long trips and packing up your caravan to become a Grey Nomad. To keep your mind stimulated, I provide ideas on courses to study and ideas for returning to work. I also give you ideas for staying involved with the community through volunteering. Finally, I provide information on expanding your hobby into a small business.

Chapter 11

Indulging Your Travel Dreams: Short Takes and World Tours

In This Chapter

▶ Organising family and finances for your trip

▶ Exploring your own region

▶ Venturing much further afield

*Y*ou may have put your leisure plans on hold while you raised your family and built your career, but now you have the time to indulge your travel dreams.

In this chapter, I look at the travel options available to you now. I also include information on taking short breaks in Australia and making longer trips overseas.

Considering Your Options Before You Travel

So travel is one of the items on your retirement to-do list. The question is, what sort of travel? You can tour the world in an endless variety of ways. Would you like to hike, bike, sail by barge or glide by balloon? Take a berth on a luxury liner? Or buy your own yacht and sail away? Do you remember Adam Troy from the television show *Adventures in Paradise*? I'm sure that show inspired a generation to dream of sailing around the South Pacific!

Of course, your budget may have an impact on where you can travel, and for how long. You may also have family constraints to consider.

Deciding what sort of travel you want to undertake

Your travel plans may depend on a number of factors — financial, emotional and health issues all take part in this decision. Travel options in retirement roughly fall into three groups:

- **Extended trips:** You keep your house but make it secure so you can be away for one to six months per year.
- **Long-term travel:** You sell your house and buy a caravan, motorbike and tent or cabin on a cruise ship and make the road (or water) your home.
- **Short breaks:** You keep your house, and the cat and dog, and see the sights nearer home.

The type of travel you choose also depends on how attached you are to your creature comforts. You're probably one of the following:

- **Intrepid adventurer:** You have a good pair of hiking boots, a backpack and a tent that'll take you anywhere.
- **Luxury traveller:** You like a hot shower, a comfortable bed and a decent meal while seeing the world.
- **Middle of the roader:** You want to travel in luxury, but for budgetary, moral or environmental reasons you prefer to take the middle road, wanting nothing too flashy, but nothing too cheap either.

Of course, you move between these groups when finances permit or aching bones force you indoors.

Understanding financial considerations

Sometimes outside forces affect your travel choices — financial constraints usually being one of the highest on the list.

To work out how much money you need to set aside to pay for your trip, you need to prepare a travel budget.

Setting your travel budget

Begin making your budget by setting some goals so that you know how much money you're aiming for. For example, is your goal to see as much as you can of Europe, or to spend time touring Australia in comfort?

A very conservative budget for two months in Europe is $10,000 per person. Approximately $2,000 of that amount goes on air fares, leaving $8,000 for living — which is only $133 per day. Unless you're backpacking, this is a pretty tight budget.

Some luxury travel in Australia costs $10,000 or more for a short trip. For example, a Heron Airlines 21-day air tour circumnavigating Australia costs $13,000 plus per person.

You may decide to take the Grey Nomad path and buy a 4WD and caravan so that you can take various-length trips around Australia. A big 4WD and caravan can cost more than $200,000. For more information on this option, see Chapter 12.

After you have a figure to aim for, start keeping track of your everyday expenses and commitments to work out how to save this amount. Break down your bills into weekly or fortnightly costs so that you know how much you need to live on and what you can afford to save.

Don't forget to set aside an amount of money for contingencies like medical bills or a new washing machine. You can work out how much you may need from past experience.

Maximising your savings

As a general rule, retirees are good savers. Look at where you can make savings in your everyday living expenses. The most obvious areas are food, fuel and entertainment. Here are some ideas:

- ✔ **Consider walking or taking public transport instead of driving.** This benefits your health, the environment and your hip pocket.

- ✔ **Cut down on treats.** Many retirees get into the habit of having one or two glasses of wine with their meals. By forgoing a $10 bottle of wine each night you can save $70 per week — or more than $3,500 per year.

- ✔ **Go back to basics.** A friend of mine had at least one meal of baked beans a week and put the money she would've spent on a more elaborate meal into her travel piggy bank.

- ✔ **Make the most of a Seniors Card.** If you're over 60 you can apply for a Seniors Card, which gives you discount fares and shopping at some supermarkets. You can also use your card for free Sunday train travel and country bus travel in some states. Visit www.seniorscard.com.au or check out Chapter 3 for more information.

How much you're prepared to cut costs depends on how keen you are to travel. You've got to weigh up the short-term pain against the long-term gain.

Here are two further ways you can boost your travel coffers:

- **Investigate which financial institutions offer special interest rates.** Some financial institutions have special savings accounts with bonus interest awards. If you leave your money in the account without making a withdrawal for a certain period of time, you earn extra interest (although this amount will be subject to tax).

- **Use your credit card to amass frequent flyer points.** You can then use these points to reduce the cost of your air fare or to upgrade to business class on long-haul trips. If you're good at paying off your card each month, consider making all your purchases by card, thereby earning more points.

Are you struggling with the concept of saving? The federal government has a Web site dedicated to helping you to budget and save. Go to www. understandingmoney.gov.au where you can download a handbook of useful information and advice.

In addition, take a look at *Sorting Out Your Finances For Dummies*, Australian Edition, by Barbara Drury (Wiley Publishing Australia Pty Ltd). This book has some great in-depth information about budgeting for your daily financial requirements and looking at what you can realistically afford to save each week.

Refining your travel budget

After you've calculated how much you can set aside for travel, you can work out what level of comfort you can afford for your chosen destination. Will it be Europe on a shoestring or the outback in luxury?

To work out your options you need to refine your travel budget. This requires some research, using either the Internet or a travel agency, or both. Some people are happy to plan their trip from beginning to end using the Internet; others like to do the preliminary research online and then have the security of a travel agent making the final arrangements.

One way to begin your research is to attend an information evening on the trip you want to take. Such evenings are usually held by travel agents who have undertaken the trip themselves. As well as seeing photos of your destination, you get information about weather conditions, clothing requirements and sightseeing options.

You can save on travel costs by booking early. This may mean booking a year or more in advance, but you can save a substantial amount of money and may even qualify for some upgrades. Look in the travel section of your newspaper for deals.

Package tours help you set your budget fairly exactly, as most expenses are included. If you take a cruise or tour you need only budget for extra sightseeing options and shopping.

As a rough guide, the more expensive the tour, the less additional spending money you need. The more inclusions in the tour — especially meals, tipping and excursions — the easier you find it to budget more precisely.

However, if you're travelling under your own steam, you need to budget for some essentials:

- **Accommodation:** Look for accommodation that suits both your pocket *and* your preferred level of comfort. If you're happy in hostels and tents, your accommodation options will be cheap. Otherwise, consider serviced apartments or villas rather than hotels to save money.

- **Air fares:** Shop around for the best deal, but don't discount comfort on a long-haul flight. Some people board a flight and fall asleep instantly, but if you aren't one of these lucky people, give some thought to seat dimensions, in-flight entertainment and seating position. Log onto the Seat Guru at www.seatguru.com for information about seat pitch and width plus everything else you want to know about commercial aircraft. You can also find lots of blogs on the Internet debating the value of one seat over another.

  If you're an especially bad traveller, upgrading to business class is an option, albeit a more expensive one. However, not all business class is created equal. You can get cheaper options if you're prepared to go on less well supported routes or airlines.

- **Entertainment:** It's hard to go to New York without seeing a Broadway show, so put a major show into your budget. On the other hand some of the best entertainment is free. Street festivals, buskers and even laundromats provide free or very cheap entertainment.

- **Food:** Meals can be expensive in some overseas countries, especially if you're on a special diet. Search the Web for help and advice. For instance, Work Gateways at www.workgateways.com/working-cost-of-living.html gives a rundown of food (and other) costs in Britain.

- **Shopping:** You want some souvenirs of your travels. Budget some money to spend on a beautiful leather coat from Florence or a cosy Aran sweater from Scotland.

- **Sightseeing:** A one-day bus tour of your destinations can be well worth the money. It gives you an orientation of the city. When you know where you are, you can make your way around on your own.

✔ **Transport:** You can hire a car, rent a bike or take the train to your destination. Once at your destination, you still need to get around to see it. If you're staying in capital cities, you can walk or take cheap local transport.

You get what you pay for. Check out the airline, bus company or ship's track record before you book your trip. Talk to people who've travelled with that particular company. People love to share their horror stories, but you can also ask them what was good about their trip. The best way to do this is to attend any information nights available.

Always *overestimate* how much you need to spend. Don't forget to add in something extra for emergency travel contingencies — and for that great end-of-season bargain that you know you won't be able to resist.

Whether you opt for a package deal or decide to make your own travel arrangements, you need to bear the following in mind when you're refining your budget:

✔ Before you go, you may have additional expenses such as obtaining a passport, undergoing a medical check-up and having vaccinations.

✔ Equipment rental, excursions and entertainment are usually extras. And if you're going to Las Vegas or Monte Carlo, for example, you may need a gambling budget!

✔ Tipping is important, especially in the US, where you're expected to tip for every service provided. At the hairdresser, for example, be prepared to tip the hairwash person, the cutter, the colourist and the person who sweeps the floor. You also need to tip the toilet attendant at public conveniences — even if you find it a bit unnerving having your towel handed to you.

✔ Travelling on your own can be cheaper as far as transport is concerned, but single accommodation is often more expensive.

Some tour operators and guidebooks provide a rough 'spend per day' estimate of how much spending money you can expect to go through while travelling through a particular country.

Marie goes under

My friend Marie suffers from claustrophobia, and so was terrified at the thought of having to spend 14 hours on a plane to visit Vancouver in Canada. The more Marie thought about her upcoming trip, the worse she felt. To overcome her fear, she decided to see the hypnotist who had successfully helped her niece to give up smoking. Part of the hypnotist's solution was that Marie look at and take notice of everything around her — all the people and shops at the airport, everyone on the plane — and look forward to arriving at her destination and exploring all there is to see.

Marie had a good flight to Vancouver, but on arrival there the hypnotist's advice morphed into a shopping obsession. This was unusual for Marie; she is renowned for going shopping and returning empty-handed. Three leather coats, several necklaces and numerous souvenirs later, Marie left Canada. Now she knows that if she travels, she shops — so she budgets this into her plans. She figures this is a small price to pay for being able to travel and see the world.

Taking family into consideration

You've raised your children, worked hard and are now ready to see the world. You may expect to be free from family obligations at this stage of your life. The truth is, times have changed. People are living longer and are being encouraged to stay in their own homes until they need nursing care. Many retirees find they have the care of an elderly parent and/or grandchildren to take into consideration when making their travel plans.

Elderly parents

If you're responsible for the care of an elderly parent, talk about your travel plans with your family and see whether you can come to some possible solutions together for the time you're away. You may be able to suggest someone who can take over the care of your parent during this time, or perhaps someone may volunteer for the role.

If no-one is available, you have several options:

- ✔ **Your parent can move temporarily into respite care.** You need to arrange this well before you plan your travel dates, as places in care facilities are usually limited. Respite care is easier to access if you're able to pay for your parent's place. Some government-assisted places are available, but they're more difficult to get.

Every person requiring aged care, even for only two or three weeks, needs to undergo an aged-care assessment to determine what level of care is required. Chapter 9 and the Department of Health and Ageing's Web site at www.health.gov.au have more information about this.

✔ **Your parent can stay at home with the help of outside assistance.** Local councils generally provide assistance to the elderly with the aim of allowing them to stay in their own homes. This includes cleaning, maintenance, shopping and showering services. A number of agencies also provide private aged-care services. See Chapter 9 for more information.

If your elderly parent has to go into an aged-care facility while you're away, the next obstacle may be to persuade your parent to do so. Chapter 17 has some tips on how to tackle this subject and other detailed information about sharing the care of your aged parent.

Grandchildren

If you care for your grandchild or grandchildren, you don't need to give up the idea of travel altogether. Talk to your family and relatives about your travel plans. Perhaps another relative can provide short-term care while you're away. Or one or both of the child's parents may be able to arrange time off work to care for the child while you're away.

If you're the only person who can provide the care required — or maybe you just can't bear to be away from your grandchild for too long — consider these options:

✔ **Take short breaks instead.** Check out the 'Discovering the Gems in Your Own Backyard' section later in this chapter.

✔ **Take your grandchild with you.** These days, grandparents travelling with their grandchildren are not an uncommon sight.

Health insurance constraints

Australians are well looked after when it comes to healthcare cover at home. You can choose to be covered solely by Medicare or take out private health insurance. Unfortunately private health insurance doesn't cover you when you travel outside Australia, so you need to take out travel insurance for overseas trips.

Neither Medicare nor the Royal Flying Doctor Service has waiting periods for treatment of pre-existing conditions. However, when you join a private health fund you have to wait for periods of up to 12 months to receive rebates on medical treatment for any pre-existing conditions. To find out more, see Chapter 8.

Medicare

Australian and New Zealand citizens are eligible for Medicare cover. The Medicare system provides you with free treatment in any public hospital and free or low-cost care at any doctor's surgery or optometrist anywhere in Australia. This care is transportable, meaning that you can take advantage of the system wherever you travel in Australia.

In addition, the Medicare system covers Australians for the cost of emergency in-patient care in public hospitals in some overseas countries, among them New Zealand, the UK and Italy.

For more detailed information, visit the Medicare Web site at www.medicareaustralia.gov.au or enquire at your local Medicare office.

For more information on medical cover while travelling overseas, see the section 'Travel insurance' later in the chapter.

Carry your Medicare card with you when you travel, otherwise you won't be able to access the services offered. Don't leave your card at home.

Royal Flying Doctor Service

The Royal Flying Doctor Service (RFDS) is a free health service available to the residents and travellers in outback Australia. If you're unfortunate enough to have an accident, become ill or get bitten by a snake or spider while travelling in the outback, you can call the RFDS.

The organisation's Web site at www.flyingdoctor.net has more information about the service, as well as general tips about travelling in outback Australia.

Ambulance cover

Even if you're in an ambulance fund in your home state, you may not be covered when you travel interstate. Or you may find that you're covered for emergency treatment like being taken to hospital, but not for an ambulance ride back home or between hospitals. If you have private health insurance, check your policy to see whether you're covered.

Check out the reciprocal rights between your state and the state(s) you're visiting. The Lets-get away Web site at www.lets-getaway.com has a rundown of which states cover what services. The Parliament of New South Wales Web site at www.parliament.nsw.gov.au/ also has more information.

Special needs

Travel can be difficult if you're on a restricted diet for conditions such as coeliac disease or diabetes. You need to know where you can get a suitable meal and find medical assistance.

Check out the following Web sites for more information on travelling with these conditions:

- Coeliac Society of Australia at www.coeliac.org.au
- Diabetes Australia at www.diabetesaustralia.com.au

Likewise, if you have a disability you may need advice on how to travel safely. The following Web sites contain information and guidance for travellers with disabilities:

- Department of Civil Aviation and Safety at www.casa.gov.au. As well as tips on how to prepare for travel (such as finding out whether the plane seats have fold-down arm rests) the site covers topics such as medical requirements and mobility aids.
- Disability Lifestyles at www.disabilitylifestyles.org.au. This site offers information about travel agents, cruise ships, destinations and accommodation for the mature disabled traveller.
- Disability Travel and Recreation Resources at www.makoa.org/travel.htm. This site has numerous links to other Web sites useful to travellers with disabilities.

Discovering the Gems in Your Own Backyard

Tourists often see and do more in your home town than you do. Think about exploring your own neighbourhood. When you reach 60 you can apply for a Seniors Card, which entitles you to discounted and sometimes free travel and entry to museums, theatres and other entertainment. See Chapter 3 for more information.

Short getaways (just a few days)

After you've been retired for a while and have done the big trip around Australia or overseas, you may find that your calendar is suddenly filled with all sorts of commitments, such as golf, study, writing, lunches and dinners, not to mention medical and dental check-ups — it's amazing how many small things start to go wrong when you reach retirement age.

You may not want to take on a big trip each year, so this is the time for short breaks. Here are some ideas for shorter trips closer to home:

- **Arrange a house swap with an interstate friend or relative, or rent a house for a short break in the off-season in a nearby regional town.**

- **Pick an area of interest and read up on the local history, then visit the key places of interest in that area.** You may be amazed how well the history of many areas, like Beechworth in Victoria, is presented.

- **Plan a short trip around an event.** Each state and territory has a tourist Web site with a long list of events in that state. Some events are international in scale, like the Grand Prix, others are national, like football finals, while others still are smaller regional affairs like the Wandiligong Nut Festival in the Victorian high country.

- **Think about a themed holiday.** Golfers have the perfect reason to travel: Playing at other courses is always fun. Even better, make up a group and challenge members of the course you're visiting. Foodies may like to go in search of the best fish dish in their state; and health aficionados may want to try out all the local spas to find out which gives the best value.

- **Travel around your state.** If you want to be organised, sit down with a map and divide your state into a grid. Check out the tourist information Web sites for each area and pinpoint all the attractions you want to see over a few days.

- **Visit your local area.** Your immediate region is probably filled with interesting places to see. I usually notice new places or things to see when I'm driving visitors around. Take note of these local places of interest and plan a trip to visit them.

Day trips

You may be surprised just how many enjoyable day trips are available in your local area. Best of all, day trips are often easy on the hip pocket. Check out the following ideas.

Wanderer for a day

Get a map of your local city or another city or town within easy reach and go walking for the day. Explore the laneways, small boutiques and art galleries that you normally pass by on your usual errands. Or you can base your walk around several themes.

Local history

Find a book on a local character at your library and investigate his or her haunts. On your wanderings you may find small plaques on seemingly ordinary houses denoting who once lived there. These heritage site identification markers should be listed on your council's Web site. Check this Web site before you begin your walk, as it may provide a map detailing the sites of historic significance.

Farmers' markets

Farmers' markets are becoming very popular. You can base your wandering around buying fresh produce and supporting the local community. If you type 'farmer's markets' into your Internet search engine, you can find sites that list Australian and local markets. Your local community newspaper should also provide information on market days.

By shopping at farmers' markets you are buying produce that hasn't travelled very far. To help reduce the effects of climate change, some people suggest only buying food that has travelled less than 100 kilometres. Some local markets advertise the number of kilometres the produce has travelled to get from the producer to you.

Walking close to home

Walking tours are a great way to see the countryside and enjoy a short break. Many options are available in Australia's national parks, ranging from walks of just a few hours in duration to longer treks over several days. The Australian National Parks Web site at www.australiannationalparks.com has further information.

Cradle Mountain in Tasmania, for example, offers several walking trips, ranging from very short walks of 30 minutes to all-day treks. Two of the walks have wheelchair access. Cradle Mountain is also the beginning of the Overland track, a 65-kilometre trek that ends at Lake St Clair and takes six days or more to complete, depending on the weather. You can take either a guided or a non-guided walk. You need to be prepared for all eventualities: it snows even in summer. See the Tasmanian Parks Web site at www.parks.tas.gov.au for more details.

Inner-city walking tours

Nearly all capital cities and many regional towns offer guided or self-guided walks around the city centre. Guided walks are usually structured around a theme, and you pay for the service. For example, you can go on a chocolate walk, hearing about the history of chocolate and stopping for tastes along the way. Or you may prefer a spooky ghost walk, where you listen to eerie tales as you trek the city's historic sites after dark.

When you visit a town, visit the tourist information centre or log onto the local Web site for details of self-guided walks in the area.

Bushwalking

Check out the bushwalking available in your local area and plan a day trip — see Chapter 16 for more information on bushwalking, including joining your local bushwalking club.

Always notify someone before you set off for a bushwalk. An easy two-hour bushwalk can turn into an overnighter if something unexpected happens. Take plenty of drinking water and wear sunscreen, a hat and sturdy shoes.

Exploring bike paths and rail trails

Cycling is a favourite Sunday pastime in most capital cities. You can't miss the colourful lycra-clad cyclists as they zoom around the streets and congregate in roadside cafes — on the other hand, if you're driving a car, I hope you do miss them.

Cycling is fun, cheap exercise, but riding on the road can be dangerous. Fortunately, Australia has an extensive system of bike paths and trails you can take advantage of.

Bike paths

Many cities and towns now have dedicated bike paths. These paths are a lot safer for cyclists than roads. Watch out, though, for the poles that councils plonk in the middle of the paths to keep out other vehicles — I didn't, and fractured my thumb.

If you're cycling through a tourist area, be prepared for people stepping out in front of you. Always be on the lookout for small children and dogs running across the path.

And don't overdo it on your early rides: Remember, you have to get back home.

Rail trails

Rail trails are shared-use paths. They often run along abandoned railway lines and can be used by cyclists, walkers and horse riders. You find rail trails in all parts of Australia, although some states have more trails than others. Note that some trails are incomplete and others are yet to be developed, so visit the rail trail Web site at www.railtrails.com.au or check out a rail trail book before you go.

Don't forget to check the condition and gradient of the track beforehand too. Some country trails are suitable only for walkers or mountain bikers and very fit riders.

Several cities and regional towns have sealed, level trails that take you past markets and cafes. These are a great way of seeing a city. Some trails, such as the Hervey Bay Links Mobility Corridor, are suitable for cyclists, walkers, wheelchairs and prams.

Think safety. Always wear a helmet and take enough water to stay hydrated throughout the ride. Wear bright, colourful clothes so that you're easily seen, and make sure that your bike is well lit at night. Keep to the left side of the path unless otherwise indicated.

You'll find a huge variety of bikes to choose from, including road, hybrid, mountain and touring bikes. Getting the right bike for you is important, so get advice from your local bike store and shop around until you're happy with the bike and the price.

Travelling Overseas

An overseas trip is the ultimate travel dream for many Australians. You may spend some time researching your travel options, but when you've finally made up your mind where you want to go you can book your trip.

Before you go, don't forget to also take the following measures, which can take some of the hassle out of your trip:

- ✔ Ensure you have all the necessary inoculations (see the section 'Keeping healthy' later in the chapter).
- ✔ Obtain adequate travel insurance for the whole period that you will be away (see the section 'Travel insurance' later in the chapter).
- ✔ Register your travel destination(s) with the Department of Foreign Affairs and Trade (see www.dfat.gov.au).

Booking your trip

Do you feel comfortable booking your whole trip yourself online, including all your flights and accommodation? Or would you rather go to a travel agent and use the agent's expertise to help you design and book your trip?

Booking online

To book your trip yourself online, you must be organised. Work out your itinerary in detail so that you know where you want to be and at what times. Don't forget to factor in changes in time zones — you don't want your next flight to leave before your connecting flight arrives at the airport.

When booking your air fares online, you have two options:

- Book directly through your chosen airline's Web site, such as www.qantas.com.

- Use one of the numerous online discount travel Web sites (try searching online under 'discount air fares'). If you use a discount operator, contact the airline you're flying with to check your flight details. Make sure that you have booked to go to the correct city in the correct country, and double-check your dates.

Likewise, you can book your accommodation directly using the hotel or company's Web site. But if you want to save money and are prepared to book at the last minute, you can save a substantial amount — sometimes up to 75 per cent — by using a discount travel site. Try www.wotif.com or www.lastminute.com for last-minute deals.

You can also save money on a cruise if you're prepared to book a long way ahead or at the last minute. Check out www.vacationstogo.com for cheap cruises.

If you're booking a holiday package online, make sure you do some extra research to find out what you're really getting. For example, check out the accommodation yourself by calling the hotel directly. Here are some questions you may like to ask:

- Does the hotel have a restaurant, or are there food outlets nearby?

- Is the accommodation within walking distance of the beach, city centre etc?

- Is it near places of interest or on public transport routes?

Make sure that you're clear about your liability for all taxes, transfers and other costs.

Booking online can leave you with no protection if you buy a product that doesn't exist or isn't what you think it is. What you see in a photo isn't necessarily what you get. Before you book, see whether you can find any reviews of the accommodation or holiday package online — and remember to read the small print.

Alternatively, if you don't want to book all the components of your trip individually, you can use an online travel agency. Make sure that the agency is licensed and contributes to the Travel Compensation Fund (TCF). The TCF is used to reimburse travellers if they have problems with their travel arrangements. See www.tcf.org.au for more details and travel tips.

Using a travel agent

A licensed travel agent offers peace of mind as well as the benefit of the agent's experience. By using a licensed agency that contributes to the TCF you can claim compensation if the agency collapses and you lose your holiday.

Travel agents can put together the whole travel package for you. They know which airport is best and easiest to access, how long it takes to get from A to B, and changes in time zones. They provide full details of taxes, transfers and other costs, which may not be made clear when booking online.

Ask your travel agent whether he or she has stayed in the accommodation you're looking at or has had any word-of-mouth referrals. A package holiday that looks good in the brochure may not live up to the advertising.

Check whether your travel agent offers an information night about your travel destination where you can speak to people who've been on a similar trip and find out about suitable clothing to take with you and sightseeing trips.

Renting an apartment overseas

Hotel accommodation in capital cities is often horrendously expensive. For $200 per night or more you get a tiny room and a muffin for breakfast. Don't expect the room to be equipped with a mini bar or tea- and coffee-making facilities.

On the other hand, you can rent a holiday apartment for about the same price as a hotel room on a daily basis — maybe a bit less if you're staying for a month or more. Depending on the price, the apartment will have a bedroom, sitting room, kitchenette and bathroom. Some apartments even have access to a pool and gym. An apartment is ideal if you intend to stay for a week or more, but you can rent them for shorter stays.

If you're travelling with family or in a group, a two- or three-bedroom apartment is an economical option. After the fun of eating out has passed and you realise how much money you're spending on food, you'll be happy to explore local markets and supermarkets and have the occasional home-cooked meal.

An apartment in a capital city makes a good base for exploring other parts of the country or continent. An extended stay means the rate will be cheaper, and you can take short trips and keep your main luggage in the one place.

If you're looking at renting an apartment in the US or Europe, try these Web sites:

- ✔ vacation.new-york-apartment.com/en/liste for apartments in Manhattan, the Bronx, Queens and Brooklyn in New York

- ✔ www.nyhabitat.com for apartments in New York, Paris, the South of France and London

- ✔ www.iloveparisapartments.com for apartments in central Paris, the Dordogne, the Loire Valley and London

Staying in a Tuscan villa

Who hasn't dreamt of renting a villa in Tuscany, exploring the region, sampling the food and drinking the wine? Staying in a villa gives you the opportunity to become familiar with a district. You can have a break from packing and unpacking your suitcase and simply relax and soak up the local atmosphere. Or you can take a cooking class or a short language course to brush up on your Italian. Some villas have swimming pools and offer maid and cooking services. You can rent a villa to sleep one or 21.

Tempted? Check out these Web sites:

- ✔ www.tuscany-villas.com has photos of the villas it rents out and someone to talk to about your booking.

- ✔ www.tuscanynow.com claims to have seen every single property that it rents out.

- ✔ www.tuscanyretreats.com offers luxury villas and a phone number to call to speak personally to the agent.

Book well in advance if you want to rent during the high season (the European summer). If you want more personal service, see a travel agent. Ask whether the agent has inspected the villas he recommends or has had positive feedback from previous clients. Do your research and talk to anyone you can find who's rented a villa.

Taking a bus tour

Touring is an easy and convenient way to travel. If you want some free time on the trip you can combine a tour with longer stays at either end of the planned tour. Budgeting is easier when you book a package tour as nearly everything is paid for in advance, including tips. In addition on a tour your suitcase is unloaded from the bus and taken to your room for you, rather than you having to lug your case around with you.

A number of bus companies cover the same routes but have different cost structures. Looking at their itineraries, you may wonder why some charge more. They go to the same places, have the same number of meals and offer the same sightseeing excursions. Look closely at the bus dimensions and carrying capacity. The top-range tours may carry fewer passengers, which means more leg room and general room within the bus. When you're on the bus for long stretches at a time, the 'get what you pay for' mantra becomes real.

Extremes of climate at the various stops along the way on your tour mean you have to take a range of appropriate clothing. If you have the time, you can buy this at your destination, but if you're arriving the day the tour departs you need to buy your clothing beforehand.

Dress in layers so you're always at a comfortable temperature. In cold climates, you need all your layers on outside, but inside it'll be warm — sometimes much warmer than Australians are used to.

The tour guide on the bus is extremely important to the enjoyment of your trip. Unfortunately, you have no say in appointing the guide. Check before you book whether the driver and guide receive incentives for taking tours to specific cafes or shopping centres (thereby reducing the time you have to see the sights). On one trip to the US my bus tour guide stopped for hour-long breaks at big, soulless shopping centres and only half an hour in picturesque villages.

Inevitably, someone on the bus will irritate you. No, you can't vote them off — no matter how much you want to. Try following these tips for an enjoyable trip:

✔ Dress in comfortable clothing. Bus trips involve sitting around a lot, as well as constantly getting on and off the bus and walking around.

✔ Enjoy your meals, but remember that you're part of a group booking and have to stick to the choices offered.

✔ Have your suitcase packed and ready for pick-up at the appointed time. If that means 7.00 am before breakfast, take your toothbrush in your carry-on luggage.

✔ Relax — and go with the flow.

✔ See as much as you can during the appointed stops. Go for a walk and talk to people.

✔ Understand that tours run on a tight schedule, so shopping time's limited. Don't be late for a scheduled departure time or you'll face rows of stony-faced people — or, if they're Australians, a bus full of rowdy travellers giving you the slow handclap.

Even if you're not planning an extended tour, taking a bus tour of each new city you visit is invaluable. In an hour you get stories of the inhabitants and useful tips about the city.

Walking, trekking and cycling holidays

From walking the Kokoda Trail to cycling in Mongolia, you can take a walking, trekking or cycling tour just about anywhere in the world. These trips are graded from introductory to challenging, so you know how fit you need to be for each level.

Walking tours

Walking holidays range from fully guided luxury experiences to do-it-yourself adventuring. Options for overseas walking tours include the following:

✔ **Do-it-yourself walks:** Everything is left up to you. You carry your own pack and sleep in shelters or tents along the way. You set up the camp site and do your own catering.

✔ **Guided walks:** An expert guide leads the walk, pointing out things of interest along the way. Your luggage is transported between camp sites and you carry a small day pack. Your meals are provided and the overnight accommodation is usually a permanent tent or lodgings with ensuite facilities.

✔ **Self-guided walks:** You have the option of exploring the region on your own but with the knowledge that you have a meal and comfortable lodgings awaiting you at the end of your day.

Walking in the footsteps of pilgrims

For a really long walk, you can journey to Spain and make the pilgrimage known as el Camino de Santiago, or The Way of St James. To qualify for the compostela, or certificate of accomplishment, walkers must cover at least 100 kilometres and cyclists must ride for 200 kilometres to the Cathedral of Santiago de Compostela in Galicia in northwest Spain. Some choose to ride horses or donkeys, as was done in medieval times. You can start the walk from any one of a number of towns in the Pyrenees or inside the French border. Visit www.santiago-compostela.net for more information and stories about this walk.

Before you embark on an active walking holiday, make the following preparations:

- ✔ Buy your walking shoes well in advance rather than at the last minute. Get properly fitted shoes and walk them in. Walking is a major part of the travel experience.

- ✔ If you're going to carry a backpack on your trip, train with a weighted backpack before you go. Tins of fruit added to a pack make it suitably heavy for training.

- ✔ Take note of the training regimen suggested by the travel company. Walk regularly every day before you go.

- ✔ Test all your equipment ahead of the trip. You need to find out about malfunctions before you go.

- ✔ Wear in your clothing before you go to make sure nothing rubs. Some clothes can be itchy or irritating to the skin and some aren't as sweat-proof as the manufacturers make out.

Cycling tours

You find cycling tours in some of the most scenic areas of the world. Bicycles Network Australia at www.bicycles.net.au/links/tours.html has a detailed list of Australian and international cycling tours and travel logs. You can also use the Web site to find a partner to ride with.

The start of your cycling tour is *not* the time to realise you haven't ridden a bike for 40 years. For an enjoyable holiday, follow these tips before you go:

✔ **Get on your bike and put in some miles.** Practise on hills as well as the flat. Some people (including me) find it more difficult and scary to go down hill than up, so train as much as you can. Seek out some dirt roads and practise stopping on gravel. Know your limitations. If you're going to be covering 20 kilometres per day on your trip, make sure that you can accomplish that level before you leave. The bike you get on your trip will probably be heavier than the one you're used to, but at least you'll know you can keep your balance.

✔ **Practise riding with a load.** A steep hill in the Pyrenees isn't the place to test out your balance with a packed bike.

You also need to get the correct gear. You don't have to be lit up like a Christmas tree or have the latest matching apparel, but comfortable bike pants and a visible top are essential. You need layers of clothing. It can be cold riding into the wind and hot going up a hill.

Enjoying a leisurely cruise

Now that people don't need to take a six-week boat trip to get from Australia to Europe, many people are opting to do just that. These days ocean liners are like floating luxury hotels. On board you find a wide range of entertainment, all of which is included in the fare — from theatres and cinemas to casinos, nightclubs, games and even libraries if you want a quiet time.

Cruises are a relaxing way to travel. You move from one city to another while unpacking your suitcase only once. You don't have to be up at 5.30 am with your bag outside the door ready for another day on the bus.

Cruises are also a great way to meet people. Some friendships begun on board last for years, with the friends getting together every few years to travel somewhere different.

If you have a chronic illness or disability, cruises are an easier travel option. The ships have a medical facility on board and lifts to take you between levels. If you opt for a cruise that takes you close to shore, you can see the sites from the balcony of your cabin. For example, on the inside passage from Vancouver to Alaska you can see bears, otters and whales from the comfort of the ship.

You can cruise on a luxury liner around the world or hire a barge to take you down the canals and rivers of Europe. Combining air travel and a cruise is a good way to get the most out of your cruising experience without having to be away for too long.

If you're thinking of taking a cruise, here are some things to consider before you book:

- ✔ **By booking very early, or very late, you can get a cheaper fare.** Book early if you want a particular cabin, such as a balcony cabin; book later if you want a heavily discounted fare and aren't so fussy about your cabin.

- ✔ **Consider the type of cruise you want.** If you're going with your family, a 'fun' cruise that focuses on nightclub life may not be for you. Likewise, if you're single and looking to meet people and have lots of fun, you may not enjoy a cruise that is dedicated to observing the wildlife outside the ship.

- ✔ **Look at the staff-to-customer ratio.** The higher the ratio, the better the service.

- ✔ **Pay attention to clothing guidelines.** You may need to dress for dinner or other functions. Cruisers like to dress up and most wear evening attire. Some people resent wearing evening clothes on their holiday and carting the clothes around is a drag, but — depending on the cruise company — there's usually at least one dress night per cruise.

On a cold-climate cruise don't forget to take layers of clothes so that you can peel off the outer garments after you've promenaded around the deck. A hat and gloves are essential near glaciers.

You can save up to 70 per cent on the cost of the cruise if you're prepared to embark at short notice.

Putting 'caring' into your travel

Have you waited your whole working life to explore the world? Perhaps you held down a job and brought up a family, putting your dreams to one side. But now that you're ready to head off, you're in a dilemma. Air travel is responsible for a huge amount of carbon emissions. In addition, the more you see and hear about other countries, the more you realise how well off you are. If you want to give something back to the world, think about undertaking volunteer work as you travel.

Literally hundreds of organisations around the world have projects requiring volunteer help. The list of positions is endless. For some of this work you need a formal qualification such as a medical certificate, but you can find numerous opportunities to help out whether you have such a qualification or not.

As a volunteer you have to pay for your trip. However, most likely the accommodation will be with a host family, so you have the chance to learn about the local culture and language.

Chapter 15 has more information about volunteering at home and abroad.

Keeping safe and healthy

You need to take several precautions before you travel to ensure that your trip is as safe and enjoyable as possible.

Travel insurance

Travel insurance covers such things as cancellation fees, lost deposits, medical emergencies, accidental death or injury, and theft or loss of money, luggage or travel documents. A number of items are excluded from travel insurance policies, with medical exclusions being the most common.

If you have a pre-existing medical condition you need to notify your insurer, who will make a decision whether or not you need a doctor's assessment of your travel fitness. For some conditions such as asthma that haven't required hospitalisation in the past 12 months you may have to pay a small fee to obtain coverage.

If you have a serious disease or condition you need a doctor's or specialist's assessment of your fitness to travel. Each insurer has a different idea of exactly what constitutes 'serious'. Leave plenty of time before you travel to make the necessary doctor's or specialist's appointments.

If you develop a medical condition between the time you buy your insurance and your departure date, contact your insurance agency. You may find the insurer will prefer to refund your costs rather than insure you.

Insurers are not created equal. Your travel agent can give you some advice about which companies are more likely to insure against existing medical conditions. You can also check out travel insurance policies on the Web.

Make sure you read the fine print of any policy and look out for the following:

✔ **Medical conditions for which you may be refused travel insurance.** This includes conditions that need ongoing treatment, such as cardiovascular disease and stroke. If you have such a condition, you need to decide whether you want to take the chance of not needing medical care overseas or paying for a medical evacuation.

✔ **Policy exclusions.** These may include acts of terrorism, certain extreme sports and lost luggage:

- If a terrorist act occurs in an area that was considered safe, the insurer may pay for death, medical and emergency evacuation costs. However, if there are warnings against travel to a region on the Department of Foreign Affairs and Trade's Smart Traveller Web site at www.smartraveller.gov.au, you probably won't be covered in the event of a terrorist attack or outbreak of war in that region.

- Some extreme sports such as rock climbing, bungee jumping and snowboarding are not covered, so if you're planning on enjoying anything like this while you're away, you probably need extra insurance. Ask your insurer about this.

- If you're going on a tour that offers extreme sports, take a careful look at the tour company's travel insurance policy. The policy may cover only climbing at certain sites or walking on certain tracks. If you decide to take off on your own and put your life in danger, you may not be covered by the policy.

- If your bag or its contents are stolen when not under your care, you may not be covered by insurance, so be careful about leaving your baggage unattended. (And don't forget, if you do leave your bag unattended, it may be shot by a robot or confiscated.)

Australia's Medicare system has a reciprocal agreement with some countries whereby you can receive emergency medical care while travelling in these countries, but you still need private health insurance for non-emergency healthcare. For the full list of reciprocating countries, see Chapter 8 or go to Medicare's Web site at www.medicareaustralia.gov.au.

Staying safe

Check the Department of Foreign Affairs and Trade's Smart Traveller Web site at www.smartraveller.gov.au before you travel. The Web site lists those countries you're advised not to travel to and those where the Department recommends you rethink your travel arrangements. The Department also suggests you register your travel details on its Web site, so that you can be contacted easily in an emergency.

Use commonsense when travelling overseas and make sure that your important documents are safe. Deposit your documents and valuables in the safety deposit box at your hotel — don't leave them lying around in your hotel room.

Make two copies of all your documents including credit cards, your insurance policy and itinerary. Carry one set with you, separate from the originals, and leave one set at home, preferably with someone you can contact easily if you lose the documents. If your passport is lost or stolen, you can report it online or at the nearest Australian Embassy, High Commission or Consulate.

Keeping healthy

See your doctor before you travel concerning any vaccinations you need and any medications you have to take with you. Give yourself plenty of time to have these vaccinations, because some are administered in more than one dose over a period of four to six weeks.

Australian prescriptions can't be filled overseas, so you need to carry enough medication for the whole trip. Always carry any medication in its original container and clearly label the container with your name. Ask your doctor to give you a signed list of your prescription medications. If you have an EpiPen, syringes or an insulin-injecting device, you need a letter of authorisation from your doctor. You may have to show this letter at airport security.

Don't take any chances if you're unsure about the water quality in a country you're visiting. Boil your drinking water for five minutes or drink bottled water. Avoid raw foods or foods that may have been washed in water, such as salad items, and don't include ice in your drinks.

Chapter 12

Becoming a Grey Nomad: For a Year or Forever

*R*etirees who travel extensively within Australia, usually with their campervan or caravan hitched to their car or in a motor home, are known as *Grey Nomads*. A life on the road as a Grey Nomad sounds alluring for many retirees. Perhaps you didn't backpack around Europe when you were young, instead settling down and having a family. Now that your family has grown up, however, the open road beckons.

In this chapter I cover the many things you need to think about before you hit the road. And it's a very long road: Plan to be away for at least nine months, but preferably 12 or more if you want to do the round Australia trip.

Before you embark on your trip, get Internet savvy. The Internet is the cheapest form of communication and is a great way to keep in contact with family and friends back home.

Selecting the Right Vehicle

Whether you decide to leave your old life for good or just go on an extended holiday, you need to choose your accommodation and a motor vehicle to pull it. You have several options:

✔ Drive your standard sedan and tow a caravan.

✔ Lash out on an American-style motor home.

✔ Plump for the traditional 4WD and caravan or camper trailer option.

If you plan to tow a caravan or camper trailer, you need to consider whether you're going to stay on the bitumen or go off-road. Unless you go off the tar, you may not actually need a 4WD — a conventional car will take you right around Australia. In fact, you can tow a caravan or camper trailer behind many modern sedans. If you already have a sedan, check out the maximum weight or aggregate trailer mass (ATM) your vehicle is permitted to tow. A caravan can weigh up to 2,500 tonnes — don't forget that it weighs more when fully loaded.

Instead of changing from your sedan to a 4WD, you can take the option of driving your car on the bitumen and hiring a 4WD for off-road trips. Or you can join various 4WD tours along the way.

Buying a car and caravan or a motor home is a big decision. One way of finding out whether your chosen combination suits you is to hire it for a short holiday. This may seem like an expensive option, but you quickly discover what you're getting into. And such an option is far better than setting off on your big trip only to return a few days later because you don't have the right equipment or you can't handle towing a caravan.

4WDs

Despite the variety of 4WDs on the market, not all are suitable for tackling the extreme conditions found in the outback. Most 4WDs are fine if you intend to stay on some sort of made road and offer additional clearance and traction on dirt roads. However, to go off the beaten track, you need a heavy-duty 4WD such as a Toyota LandCruiser or Nissan Patrol.

Buying a 4WD

Expect to pay from $32,000 to $44,000 for a smaller 4WD like a Toyota RAV 4 or a Honda CRX. A more powerful Nissan Patrol can cost from $55,000.

A LandCruiser comes in at $70,000+ (and by 'plus' I mean add another $10,000). If you want to travel in style, consider a Land Rover Range Rover at more than $170,000. Note that these are approximate prices only. Go online or see your local dealer for more information.

The ExplorOz Web site at www.exploroz.com has a comprehensive guide to choosing a 4WD. The site includes descriptions of the various vehicles available, the pros and cons of petrol versus diesel models, and the availability of spare parts. You can also use the site to plan your trip, find out about permits and accommodation, and read the blogs of others on the road.

Learning to drive the beast

If you intend to travel off-road to remote places and aren't familiar with driving a 4WD, you need to enrol in a course where you can master the basics of driving safety and maintenance. Such a course should cover

- ✔ Being safe around your vehicle
- ✔ Caring for the environment you are driving in
- ✔ Knowing how to read the local terrain, and understanding where you can safely drive your vehicle and where not to go
- ✔ Maintaining your vehicle
- ✔ Safely tackling ascents and descents and starting the car after a stall on a slope
- ✔ Understanding 4WD transmission and how to use it

When you buy your 4WD, ask your dealer whether a free driver training course comes with your purchase. Or ask for a course to be included in the package.

Here are just some of the many companies offering 4WD education and training courses that you can book online:

- ✔ Australian 4WD Driver Training & Tours at www.australian4wd.com.au/btrain.php
- ✔ Great Divide Tours at www.greatdividetours.com.au
- ✔ Murcotts 4WD/AWD at www.murcotts.com.au
- ✔ Ultimate 4WD Training at www.ultimate4WDtraining.com.au

In addition, Autosource at www.autosource.com.au lists various 4WD training Web sites throughout Australia.

To improve your driving skills and confidence level after you've completed your driving course and before you head off solo on your big trip, you can join a short tag-a-long tour using your own vehicle. Such tours offer all the adventure of four-wheel driving with the added security of skilled instructors and guides being on-hand. The tours give you the chance to drive to places like the Simpson Desert and The Canning Stock Route — some of the most isolated off-road tracks in the world — with the knowledge that you're not alone and help is readily available.

Camper trailers and caravans

If you want to tow your accommodation behind your vehicle as you travel, you can opt for either a camper trailer or a caravan. If you're unsure which option is best for you, this section highlights the pros and cons of each one. Whichever you choose, you can buy your vehicle off-the-shelf or have it made to your specifications — try browsing the Web for layout specifications and designs used by other travellers.

Camper trailers

A camper trailer is compact and provides a sleeping platform and roll-out kitchen. It should be easy to erect and pack away. You won't get a shower and toilet in a camper, but some of the larger ones have a pottie room. Most provide large annexes to extend the living space.

A camper trailer is easier to tow than a caravan due to its lower profile, lighter weight and streamlined configuration. You don't need a highly specialised vehicle to tow a camper, and if you're nervous about towing a caravan, a camper trailer may be a suitable option for you.

An added advantage of a camper trailer is that you can often take it to areas where it's impossible to take a caravan. For example, you can tow an off-road camper trailer off the bitumen and enjoy camping in out-of-the-way places.

On the downside, you have to pack and unpack your camper trailer at every stop. Furthermore, unlike a caravan or motor home, you can't pull over to the side of the road and pop inside for a cup of tea.

A very basic new camper trailer costs $3,000 to $5,000. If you want a model with more features and more robust construction expect to pay $11,000 to $14,000.

For more information about buying a camper trailer, go to the campertrailers.org Web site at www.campertrailers.org. This not-for-profit organisation provides a forum for discussing camper trailer experiences and has a useful checklist to use when buying a camper trailer. The site also provides technical tips, trip reports and get-togethers. The site advertises that it's not affiliated with any manufacturer or supplier.

Caravans

A caravan can be your home away from home. The larger more luxurious ones have a bedroom big enough for a queen-size bed (as well as extra sleeping accommodation); a stove top, oven, microwave and dishwasher in the kitchen; and a toilet and shower.

The bigger the caravan, the bigger the vehicle you need to tow it.

The price range for caravans varies enormously. Before you decide to buy a new model, look at the huge range of second-hand vehicles available. Second-hand caravans range from $30,000 to $99,000. New caravans cost anywhere between $50,000 and $200,000 for a custom-made version with all the extras.

Alternatively, if you aren't confident towing a larger van, or have less money to spend, consider a pop-top. One of the most popular caravans for travellers is the 15- or 16-foot pop-top. When buying a pop-top, make sure that the van has a solid roof, a waterproof and mildew-proof canvas, and it pops up easily. With a pop-top you have to do some work setting up when you stop for the night, but usually this is minimal. Lower-end-of-the-range pop-tops don't have a toilet or shower, but some have a roll-out kitchen — otherwise, you have to cook on an outdoor stove.

A second-hand basic pop-top costs from about $7,000, and an off-road version costs around $25,000. For a new model expect to pay anywhere between $30,000 and $70,000+.

These prices are averages. Make sure you do your homework before you purchase such a big-ticket item.

As well as cost considerations, you need to answer the following questions to help you decide which type of caravan to buy:

  ✔ **How long are you going to be away?** Do you want the van for short, impulse trips or one long trip? For a long trip you may opt for a full caravan with fitted beds, kitchen and bathroom facilities. If you intend to do short trips, a pop-top or camper trailer may suit you, because they're less expensive and easier to store.

✔ **How many people do you need to sleep in your van?** If you're considering taking friends or grandchildren with you, you need a larger van, or the ability to add a sleeping annex.

✔ **How much roughing it can you take?** This question is important. If you don't like sharing bathroom facilities or digging a hole in the ground, you need a van with a bathroom. This means you need a caravan or a high-end pop-top.

✔ **What sort of vehicle do you have to tow the van?** If you aren't planning to change your vehicle, you need to check how much weight your car can tow.

✔ **Where are you going?** Will you be staying on sealed roads or going off-road? If you're going off-road, you need a caravan made for this purpose. It has to be energy self-sufficient, have a sturdier chassis, and have waterproof and dust-proof doors.

✔ **Where will you keep the van?** Is there a height restriction for garaging your van? If so, consider a pop-top, which has a lower profile for storage.

Check out the Web site of the Caravan & Camping Industries Association of South Australia at www.caravanandcampingsa.com.au for information on the types of vehicles needed for towing a caravan. You can also view a series of videos on towing caravans.

The Caravan, RV & Accommodation Industry of Australia (CRVA) provides lists of caravan parks and retailers throughout Australia on its Web site at www.welovethiscountry.net.au, as well as descriptions of different types of vans. The site also has the following useful information and tips:

✔ Issues to consider when buying a caravan

✔ Issues of caravan safety

✔ Things to pack

✔ Towing a caravan

✔ Travel insurance considerations

✔ Travelling with your pet

Towing your van

You must know how to tow your van safely. Book into a course that gives you the key points of caravanning, including

- ✔ Choosing the correct vehicle to tow your van
- ✔ Cornering, braking and parking
- ✔ Correctly weighting your tow-ball
- ✔ Hitching and unhitching
- ✔ Manoeuvring in heavy traffic
- ✔ Packing your van for safe towing
- ✔ Setting up your mirrors

Tow-Ed's Web site at `www.tow-ed.com.au` lists towing courses in most states and territories.

Motor homes

Travelling in a motor home takes the stress out of towing a camper trailer or caravan. However, you're like a snail carrying your house on your back. And like a snail, you can't unhitch your house and leave it in the caravan park while you go off exploring. If this is a concern to you, choose a motor home with a chassis that enables you to tow a small 4WD, or take a couple of bikes with you.

You can drive most motor homes on a standard driver's licence. However, you need a light truck licence for a motor home that exceeds 4.5 tonnes.

When you buy a motor home, you're buying a vehicle and a van in one. The advantage of the smaller models is that you need only a standard driver's licence. However, you also have to consider the engine power of the vehicle and the driver's comfort.

Motor homes range in price from about $90,000 to more than $600,000. A four-berth bottom-of-the-range model usually includes a small kitchen and bathroom, although the bathroom may have a small shower module with a pull-out shower.

A top-of-the-range motor home such as the Winnebago Classic, which looks like an up-market bus, costs at least $600,000. It has a Cummins 300 HP six-cylinder turbo diesel engine and has a large shower, washing machine and dryer, air-conditioning, wall-to-wall carpets, a water control system and satellite TV among other features.

The Motorhomes Australia Web site at www.motorhomesaustralia.net is a great resource and includes

✔ A chat room

✔ Design layouts of various motor homes

✔ Technical motor home information

✔ Travellers' tales

Dealing with the House

Having made the decision to take off on the great Australian adventure, you need to think about what to do with your house in your absence. You have several options:

✔ Sell up, so you have nothing to worry about

✔ Downsize to an apartment, so you can lock and leave your premises with peace of mind

✔ Rent out your house for the time you're away

✔ Get a house-sitter

Coming home

Jan and Murray sold their house in suburban Sydney and bought a caravan and 4WD. They had enough money left over to buy a small mobile home in a trailer park in Northern Queensland. They intended to spend the rest of their days travelling around Australia, using their mobile home as a base. This plan worked well for the first eight years, but then Jan fell ill and Murray was unable to give her the care she required. They realised that they needed to be around their family and medical facilities and decided to return to Sydney. Unfortunately, during the years they'd been away house prices had skyrocketed and they found themselves unable to buy back into the market.

Selling up

Selling the family home and taking to the open road sounds ideal and works well for some people who are still happily travelling in their 80s. But the pitfalls are many:

- Perhaps the most important of these is the time you're out of the property market if you find you then have to move back to the city. You may discover that you can no longer afford to live where you want to be. You need a contingency plan in case you have to return from travelling for some reason. The biggest problem most travellers encounter is when a partner falls seriously ill or dies.

- If you receive a pension and sell your house without buying another property, your assets will be recalculated. Your house isn't an asset when you live in it, but when you sell your house and invest that money, the money from the sale becomes an asset. This can affect your pension entitlements.

- If you sell your house and have no fixed address, you may find it difficult to get insurance for your caravan or motor home.

Talk to your financial adviser *before* you take the big step of selling your house. Your financial adviser can also recommend how best to invest the proceeds from the sale of your house while you're away.

Renting out your home

Unless you intend to stay away indefinitely, the option of renting out your house will give you some security and an income stream. However, you need to bear these important points in mind:

- **Consider using the services of a rental agency.** You won't be there to check up on your property — many people have entered into a private rental agreement with those they thought to be trustworthy only to find their property was not looked after. Using an agency also takes the hassle out of chasing rent if the lessee falls behind in payments.

- **Handle the renting out of your property as a financial transaction.** Whether you use a rental agency or go it alone, you must know your rights as a landlord. At the Consumer Affairs Web site for your state you can download guidelines for tenants and landlords containing information such as privacy laws, bond money, condition reports, meter reading and entry to premises. Go to the Web site of the Ministerial Council on Consumer Affairs at www.consumer.gov.au and click on your state for the address you need.

✔ **Make sure you're aware of the basics, whether you use an agency or not:**

- Document the condition of your home. Take photos.

- Give seven days' notice of any inspections. You can carry out only four inspections in a 12-month period.

- Keep in contact with your agent.

- Organise urgent repairs as quickly as possible and carry out other repairs in a reasonable time.

- Review how much rent you receive every 12 months.

- Screen your rental applicants. Make sure they give you or your agent references from employers and previous landlords.

- Take out landlord insurance.

Be mindful of capital gains tax when renting out your house. Even if the house is your main dwelling, you're limited on how many consecutive years you can rent it out. The Australian Taxation Office Web site at www.ato. gov.au has more information.

Finding a house-sitter

Instead of renting out your property, you can engage the services of a house-sitter. Sitters come from all walks of life. Some are retirees who'd rather see the country by house-sitting in different places than by towing a caravan.

The usual arrangement is that the sitter does any small jobs around the house and pays his or her own utility costs, but doesn't pay rent. If your home requires more work than normal — for example, if you have a large number of pets or run a small property — then you pay all the costs the sitter accrues. However, if your house is easy to manage, you can charge a suitable rent.

You can advertise for a house-sitter through one of the many dedicated Internet sites such as Aussie House Sitters at www.aussiehousesitters. com.au. Usually, advertising for a sitter is free.

As with renting out your property, you need to bear several important points in mind:

✔ Give your house-sitter all your contact details plus the contact details of someone you trust. You may have to authorise that person to spend money on repairs to the hot-water service, television etc. Also leave contact numbers for your local vet if you have pets.

✔ Keep in contact with your house-sitter and your neighbours. Explain the situation to your neighbours and ask them to keep an eye on the place. They can then contact you in case of an emergency.

✔ Make sure you're adequately insured for any mishaps that may occur while you're away. Check your insurance policy carefully.

✔ Take photos of your house and grounds so you have something to refer to if there's any damage.

Setting a Budget

It doesn't matter where you are, it still costs you money to live. When you take to the road you have to factor in costs such as fuel, food and camping fees. Even if you're self-sufficient and used to roughing it, at some stage you have to pay fees for camping sites and national park access. So it makes sense to budget how much money you'll need for the basics *before* you go.

Fuel

One of the biggest costs for travellers is fuel. You may think that fuel is expensive in the city, but outback it's a lot dearer.

To estimate how much fuel you may use per trip, and therefore calculate how much money you need to set aside for fuel, you need to know how much fuel your vehicle uses per kilometre.

Your fuel consumption depends on the type of car you drive, the size of the caravan you're towing and the speed at which you travel. Various fuel-saving devices are on the market. Research these carefully before you buy.

To help with your calculations, log onto www.exploroz.com.au where you can find a table submitted by readers detailing the roads they've travelled, the date, engine and fuel type, fuel used, fuel carried, distance travelled and kilometres per litre. The site has posts for trips such as The Canning Stock Route, the Simpson Desert, Fraser Island and the Darling River Run.

Food

Your diet probably won't change much when you're on the road. If you like to prepare your own food, you should incur roughly the same costs as you do at home, so you can budget on a similar amount while you're away. Obviously, you spend more if you decide to eat out and socialise regularly.

Stock up on canned goods and other non-perishables at supermarkets in big towns, because smaller centres often have less choice and may be more expensive. Many regional towns hold farmers' markets where you can buy seasonal produce to supplement your diet.

Camping

Camping under the stars in the wilderness of the outback costs nothing. However, camping outside designated camping areas isn't always possible — or legal. At some point you have to camp in a national park or a commercial camping ground. To help you budget how much you need to set aside for accommodation, this section outlines some of the fees charged by national parks and commercial camp sites.

Camping at national parks

National park camping areas with a pit/composting toilet can cost as little as $3 per person per night. For an unpowered camp site with flushing toilets and an amenities block expect to pay $14 per person per night.

Some parks charge daily entrance fees. If you intend to visit a particular park or a group of parks more than once per year, you can buy an annual pass, which saves you money. For instance, a park that charges $9 for a day pass may charge only $17 for an annual pass to that park or group of parks.

If you expect to visit a number of parks in one state or territory you can buy an all-parks pass. The cost varies from state to state, from approximately $75 to nearly $200. Seniors receive a 20 per cent discount on the cost.

Some pensioner and concession card holders get free entry to national parks. Remember, however, that with this pass you still have to pay nightly camping fees.

Check out the following Web sites for information in each state and territory:

- **Australian Capital Territory:** The National Parks Association of the ACT has a description of its national parks at www.npaact.org.au. For camping ground bookings visit the bookings and reservations Web site at www.bookings.act.gov.au.

- **New South Wales:** The Department of Environment and Climate Change Web site at www.environment.nsw.gov.au has detailed information on NSW national parks. The site provides a list of camping grounds in NSW parks, details of the facilities and access available, and activities and cultural sites.

- **Northern Territory:** The Natural Resources, Environment, The Arts and Sport Web site at www.nt.gov.au/nreta/parks has details of national parks in the Territory. The Parks and Wildlife Service has a four-tiered system of camping fees. Category A and B sites, which have water and flushing toilets, range from $3.30 per person per night to $6.60. Category C sites are youth and education training camps, and Category D sites are commercially run camps, whose prices and services vary.

  You need a permit to enter some parks, like Garig Gunak Barlu National Park. The entry fee is currently $232.10 if you enter by road, which covers the camping fee of $220 plus a transit fee of $12.10.

- **Queensland:** The Environmental Protection Agency's Web site at www.epa.qld.gov.au has detailed information about camping facilities in Queensland national parks. Generally, before you camp you must obtain a camping permit and pay your camping fee, although some camping grounds allow you to pay on-site. To obtain a permit and pay in advance go to the Web site or call 13 13 04.

- **South Australia:** The Department for Environment and Heritage Web site at www.environment.sa.gov.au/parks is somewhat complicated to use and you need to go through each park's page for information. The Caravan Parks Association of South Australia Caravan & Camping Guide Web site at www.sa-parks.com.au has more accessible information.

- **Tasmania:** The Forestry Tasmania Web site at www.forestrytas. com.au gives a comprehensive guide to camping in and enjoying the Tasmanian wilderness. Camping and caravanning are allowed in most areas but some camp sites need to be booked in advance. See the Web site for more information.

✔ **Victoria:** The Parks Victoria Web site at www.parkweb.vic.gov.au has details of national park camping sites within Victoria, including camps that allow dogs. No overall price structure is in place, but you can find out the facilities and costs of each camp site on the Web site.

✔ **Western Australia:** The Tourism Western Australia Web site at www.westernaustralia.com has a comprehensive guide to camping and caravanning in this state. The Department of Environment and Conservation Web site at www.calm.wa.gov.au also has information on camping in national parks, as well as a downloadable map of the region.

Commercial camping and caravan parks

A powered caravan site in a commercial park costs from about $26 per night. An en-suite powered site costs from $30 per night, and a luxury cabin can cost more than $200 per night. Caravan parks are becoming harder to find because many are being sold to developers. You need to book ahead in the popular holiday seasons.

With an on-board toilet, shower and cooking facilities, you need to dump your sewage and sullage at regular intervals. Many caravan parks provide these dump points at a cost of a few dollars.

Knowing where you can and can't camp

Each state and territory has its own laws and regulations concerning camping outside designated camping grounds. Local councils usually post signs advising whether camping in public areas such as beach car parks is legal or not.

If you pull over in a rest spot beside a highway to camp overnight, be aware that many truck drivers also use these rest spots and may run their noisy refrigeration units all night.

In Western Australia you may now camp for 24 hours outside of designated camping sites or rest areas. See the WA 4WD Association's Web site at www.wa4wda.com.au/WARCO/warco.htm for more information.

Preparing To Go

Now the fun really begins. With such an enormous country to cover, you have a lot of planning to do.

Packing the essentials

Like most people, I always over-pack when I travel. When you're packing for a long trip in a confined space you have to rationalise what to take and what to leave behind.

Here are some of the essentials you can't leave home without:

- **Clothing for all weathers:** The days may be hot but the nights can be freezing, so take clothing suitable for both conditions. Also take a pair of solid walking shoes as well as thongs or sandals, a hat, sunscreen and insect repellent.

- **Communication devices and spare batteries:** See the section 'Choosing your communications technology' later in the chapter for help with choosing what equipment to take.

- **Fire extinguisher:** Place the extinguisher where you can reach it easily.

- **First aid kit:** Take a first aid course, too, before you leave.

- **Fuel and water:** You need to make sure that you're carrying enough fuel and water when you're in remote areas. Carry at least five litres of water per person per day, plus extra for emergencies.

- **Maps:** Good maps can be obtained from your local automobile club, such as the RACV, RACQ, NRMA or RAA.

- **Medications and repeat prescriptions:** Take everything you need. Don't rely on having your prescriptions filled in remote communities. As a back-up, take a detailed medical history from your doctor.

- **Tools to change tyres and do other vehicle maintenance:** Pack a jack, winder, wheel brace, spanners, screwdrivers, spare fan belt, hoses and fuses. Also pack two spare wheels, a tow rope and shovel.

Log onto the NRMA's Web site at www.openroad.com.au/packing_the_tuckebox.asp for some very useful tips on packing food, such as getting your meat vacuum-packed at the butchers rather than taking frozen meat.

Taking a first aid course

Before you leave, enrol in a first aid course. If you don't have time for a complete course, at least learn the essentials of cardio pulmonary resuscitation (CPR). Check your local community newspaper or consult the Internet or your phone book to find one of the numerous providers of first aid training.

The Australian Red Cross offers a range of courses that can be booked online (see www.redcross.org.au). The Basic First Aid course covers CPR, shock, bleeding and wound care, and breathing emergencies. The Senior First Aid course also includes treating musculoskeletal injuries, burns and scalds, and extremes of heat and cold.

Choosing your communications technology

Like most Australians, Grey Nomads embrace new technology. You can often see a caravan with a satellite dish trundling along the road. Obviously, you want at least one form of communication device to stay in touch with loved ones while you're away and in case of an emergency. You have several options.

Mobile and satellite phones

At the very least, most Grey Nomads carry a mobile phone to communicate with family back home. However, mobile coverage in Australia is patchy. The best coverage is in towns and cities and on their outskirts, and along major highways. A more reliable option is a satellite phone, but do your homework to compare the costs of operating a satellite phone.

Emergency locator beacons

For off the beaten track, take some form of emergency locator beacon. You have a choice among three different types of beacons:

- ✔ Emergency Locator Transmitters (ELTs) are designed for use in aircraft.

- ✔ Emergency Position Indicator Radio Beacons (EPIRBs) are designed for marine use.

- ✔ Personal Locator Beacons (PLBs) are designed to be carried in a pocket. They need to be operated manually.

The Australian Maritime Safety Authority (AMSA) Web site at www.beacons. amsa.gov.au describes the different beacons and their uses. The AMSA advises buyers to purchase a 406 MHz beacon, because from February 2009 the 121.5 MHz beacon won't be received by the Cosaps-Sarsat satellite system.

If your 406 MHz beacon incorporates a global positioning signal, the signal should be picked up by a geostationary satellite within seconds. The signal will pinpoint your position within a range of 120 metres.

Satellite broadband

Stay connected with the world with a satellite dish on your caravan. Many Grey Nomads set up their own Web sites before they embark on their travels so that they can keep in contact with family and friends. Communication via satellite broadband is reliable and inexpensive. What's more, you can keep updated with other travellers through Web sites such as www.exploroz. com.au.

High-frequency radio

High-frequency (HF) radio bounces signals off the atmosphere rather than using satellites or relay towers. With an HF radio you can make telephone calls, be in immediate contact with the Royal Flying Doctor Service (RFDS) and contact other users.

The RFDS recommends you purchase an RFDS-compatible HF radio from a two-way communication centre or hire one from its base. HF radios vary in price: You can pay up to $4,000 for a new top-of-the-line model or you can purchase a second-hand model for a lot less.

You need to figure out how to use your HF radio and which frequencies are available to you. You must also be part of a network and obtain a licence from the Australian Communications and Media Authority (see the Web site at www.acma.gov.au). You can join the not-for-profit Australian National 4WD Radio Network at www.vks737.on.net.

Avoiding dangers on the road

The key to safe driving, particularly in the outback, is preparation of yourself and your vehicle. Have your vehicle thoroughly serviced before you leave and find out how to change a tyre and fan belt, plus any other car maintenance you're capable of. If you're towing a van, make sure that you know how to handle the towing before you leave.

Follow these important tips for staying safe on the road:

- **Avoid driving at twilight and dawn, when wildlife are particularly active.** If you meet animals on the road, slow down and stop. Don't try to swing out — you may lose control of your car on the loose gravel.

- **Be extremely careful when passing road trains.** A road train can be the length of 10 cars (approximately 50 metres). Make sure that you have at least one kilometre of clear road ahead to pass a road train. You need to pull out wide to avoid the turbulence created by the train.

- ✔ **Carry sufficient water to avoid dehydration.** You need at least five litres per person per day, plus extra for emergencies.

- ✔ **Check out the local weather conditions where you'll be travelling.** Avoid travelling in extreme heat or rain. Many roads can flood without warning. Don't attempt to cross a flooded road if you're unsure of the depth.

- ✔ **Don't drive through dust or smoke.** In such conditions your visibility will be reduced, which is obviously very dangerous.

- ✔ **Equip yourself with good maps and find out in advance where you can buy fuel.** Fuel maps are available from the ExplorOz Web site at www.exploroz.com.au. Work out your travel distances and carry the appropriate amount of fuel. Don't go wandering down side roads unless you've accounted for the distance in your fuel calculations.

- ✔ **Give your itinerary to the local authorities if you're going off the beaten track.** Arrange to call in with your position at certain times. Take the correct communication equipment such as a satellite phone or an HF radio.

- ✔ **Stay with your car if you break down.** Your car provides you with shelter and water and is easier to spot. Activate your personal locator beacon if you have one. Carry matches so that you can light a signal fire.

Check the RFDS Web site at www.flyingdoctor.net for more information on travelling in outback Australia.

Working as You Travel

Whether you plan to look for work while you travel depends on your budget and the length of time you want to stay away. You may be able to get casual work while you travel.

Paid casual and seasonal work

Look under the 'Help wanted' heading on the Grey Nomad's Web site at www.thegreynomads.com.au and you can find details of employers looking for people who can stop by for a few days or weeks to help out with chores around their properties.

These chores range from weeding and general garden maintenance, to painting and renovating, to mechanical assistance. Travellers are offered a free caravan site with power and water or a cottage in exchange for their labour. Some employers include food as part of the deal.

Grey Nomads are also in demand as seasonal fruit, vegetable, nut and flower pickers. Such work requires a longer stay of two to three months depending on the length of the season.

Try the following Web sites for help in finding work while you're travelling:

- ✔ The Australian government's job search Web site at www.jobsearch. gov.au under 'Harvest jobs'
- ✔ The Grey Nomads Web site at www.thegreynomads.com.au
- ✔ CareerOne's Web site at www.careerone.com.au

To check out how casual work will affect your pension entitlement, go to the Centrelink Web site at www.centrelink.gov.au. You may be able to average a few weeks' work over a 12-month period without losing any entitlements.

Campground host

Campground hosts are used in national parks to provide visitor information and orientation and to act as contacts for park rangers. Hosts are offered a free camp site in exchange for their services. The length of time hosts are employed varies from seven days to six months. To be a host you need some training in first aid and the culture of the local people. You also require a police and Working With Children check.

Check out the following sites for more information on the Campground Host Program:

- ✔ Department for Environment and Heritage South Australia at www.parks.sa.gov.au
- ✔ Parks & Wildlife Service Tasmania at www.parks.tas.gov.au
- ✔ Parks Victoria at www.parkweb.vic.gov.au
- ✔ Western Australia Department of Environment and Conservation at www.dec.wa.gov.au/index.php

Volunteer work

If you volunteer your services, you'll get an excellent reception wherever you go. Note that some volunteer situations require you to undergo a police check.

If you're a member of a service club such as Rotary or Lions, you can contact the local chapter in your area of travel to find out what volunteer positions are available. Otherwise, hospitals, churches, community centres, local communities and not-for-profit organisations all need volunteers. Here are just two examples:

✔ The shire of Barcaldine near Longreach in Central Queensland hopes to harness Grey Nomad power to help with a list of volunteer work. This work includes Grey Nomads speaking at local schools about their previous careers, helping with nature projects and working in the shire's heritage centre. If you're considering spending some time in Barcaldine, visit www.barcaldine.qld.gov.au for more detailed information.

✔ Earthwatch Institute Australia at www.earthwatch.org/australia provides opportunities for people to help save the environment as they travel. You don't need any scientific knowledge, just a desire to help.

You can find out more about volunteering in Chapter 15.

Socialising on the Road

One of the best things most Grey Nomads report about their travel experiences is the number of new friends they make. These friendships can be long-lasting and may be very helpful if you break down or need medical assistance.

Two big ways to socialise include

✔ **Happy hour:** Many caravan parks have a happy hour when campers are encouraged to get together. Entertainment, such as talks about the local district and poetry readings, is organised and guests can bring out their guitars or sing a song and join in the meal cooked on the barbecue or camp oven.

✔ **Clubs:** Consider joining a club for travellers and going to meetings and rallies. Clubs such as the Campervan & Motorhome Club of Australia (at www.cmca.net.au) and the HF Radio Club (at www.hfradioclub.com.au) provide opportunities to meet like-minded people and gain useful information.

Chapter 13

Returning to Study

Many people use retirement as a time to study. Heaps of reasons exist to hit the books again. Perhaps your studies were interrupted by work and family or never got started at all. You may want to learn more about your hobby. Or retirement for you may be an opportunity for a career change.

The benefits of returning to study are greater than the specific knowledge you gain. You learn about yourself and others. Your horizons are widened by the people you meet. You have to concentrate, get organised and plan your time. You also have to get up, get dressed and participate in discussions — unless you study online, then you can stay in your pyjamas.

Exercising your mind as well as your body is important, so don't sit back and watch others participate in further study because you don't have the necessary qualifications. You can easily get your skills up to speed with a bridging course and dip your toe in the water by studying a single subject.

In this chapter, I explore the many options available for studying in retirement, whether you prefer to commit to a full-time degree or simply want to sample a subject for pleasure. I also offer advice for getting back into study mode.

You're never too old to learn. In fact, constantly learning something new keeps your brain ticking over.

Undertaking Informal Study at Your Local Neighbourhood House

Neighbourhood houses are run by the local community for the local community. More than 1,000 houses throughout Australia play an important role by providing support to individuals and families. The houses offer a number of programs and activities, covering subjects such as the following:

- Belly dancing
- Boat operator's licence
- Cooking
- Gardening
- Introduction to computers
- Languages
- Local history

In addition, many houses offer coffee mornings, games nights, book clubs, men's sheds and free legal aid.

Many activities are free or require just a small donation. Specific classes such as yoga and languages charge a fee, usually no more than $80–$100 for a six- or eight-week course. Some classes require you to enrol for the course, but others charge on a casual basis.

To find your nearest house, go to your local council Web site or visit the National Link of Neighbourhood Houses and Community Learning Centres Web site at www.nationallink.asn.au. Most neighbourhood houses do leaflet drops in their local area or advertise classes in the local newspaper.

Testing the Waters with a Short Course

If you don't want to undertake a year-long course but want to get an insight into a new area of study, the TAFE (Technical and Further Education) system and adult learning centres offer heaps of suitable short courses. You can study a wide variety of subjects, such as massage therapy, fashion and sewing, photography and first aid. Or you may want to brush up on your computer or language literacy.

Short courses are more expensive per subject than certificate or diploma courses and they usually aren't accredited, so you won't necessarily get a formal qualification at the end. However, you learn a lot. A few short courses do offer qualifications — for example, you can study an accredited TAFE module, which may help you gain entry into a certificate or diploma course.

Courses usually run by semester and are offered as two- or three-hour classes one or two nights each week, although some courses are held over the weekends. You can also take a short course online. Courses cost up to $500 or more if materials are required. Be prepared for classes with any necessary materials and be ready to contribute.

You can access short courses through a variety of institutions. Check your local TAFE college, university, adult learning centre or private education provider for more details. To find a private education provider in your area, look under 'TAFE colleges' or other education providers in your local phone book.

Centre for Adult Education

The Centre for Adult Education (CAE) is a Victorian education institute that receives funding from the Victorian government to run accredited education programs. The CAE offers a variety of courses, including access programs in literacy and numeracy, English as a second language, Years 11 and 12 VCE, art and craft courses and language courses, as well as nationally accredited training qualifications.

The CAE runs the Melbourne City Library located in Flinders Lane, where you can use the computers, go online and access books, CDs and DVDs.

The CAE also has a book club program. If you like reading and want to discuss books in an informal atmosphere, click on 'Book Clubs' at the CAE's Web site. You can join an existing book club or start your own. The CAE has a catalogue of more than 1,000 books that it can distribute anywhere in mainland Australia. The cost of being in a book club varies depending on your location. For instance, for a Victorian-based group to receive 11 books per year the cost is $125 per member ($75 concession) and $67 for the secretary. You do not keep the books. They are boxed and sent to you each month along with discussion notes and a newsletter.

The CAE can be contacted online at www.cae.edu.au or at 253 Flinders Lane and 21 Degraves Street, Melbourne.

Studying by Correspondence with Open Universities Australia

If you're happy to stay at home to study or live in a remote region with no local university, the *Open Universities scheme* may be for you. You can study at home in your own time using the Internet and graduate from one of 15 universities and colleges.

Meeting the entry requirements

Open Universities Australia has no entry requirements. You can begin your study in March, June, September or December, and you can study one or two units or go straight into a degree course.

If you're unsure how to cope with studying again, you can begin by taking *Quick Skills Modules*. These modules take only a couple of hours to complete and teach you how to project manage your study time so that you have the best chance of completing a full course.

Checking out the courses offered

Unilearn Bridging Units are designed to help you bridge the gap between your early education and university. You have 12 months to complete each unit. You don't have to sit an exam at the end of the course, but if you do you get a grade and receive a certificate. Some units include individual support by tutors. You may need to purchase various textbooks and software and have access to a DVD player.

The following Bridging Units are offered:

- ✔ **Academic Literacy Skills:** Understand the concept of academic writing and reading. Master the skills of essay writing, summarising, referencing and editing.
- ✔ **Biology:** Study modern biology and gain an understanding of microbiology covering viruses, bacteria and fungi, zoology (animals) and botany (plants).

- **Chemistry:** Gain an understanding of chemistry beginning with knowledge of the periodic tables and the gas laws.

- **Introductory mathematics:** Discover the basis of mathematics from percentages and trigonometry to introductory algebraic manipulations and elementary statistics.

- **Physics:** If you want to study applied sciences, engineering and technology then brush up your knowledge of physics with this course.

- **Senior mathematics:** Take your maths to a higher level beginning with coordinate geometry and logarithmic and periodic functions through to calculus, mathematic modelling and data analysis.

- **Successful study skills:** Plan your study, write assignments, work in groups, manage your time and prepare for exams.

To ease yourself into study, you may like to begin with *First Units*. These units are offered in the humanities, business and information technology, and the sciences. Subjects covered include psychology, introduction to Asia, introduction to Australian politics, introduction to financial planning, information methods, biology and mathematics.

After you feel confident you can go on to study in the arts, business, education, health, information technology, law or science programs. If you want to study in the business area, you can obtain a certificate or diploma, a degree or a postgraduate qualification such as an MBA.

Go to the Open Universities Australia Web site at www.open.edu.au for more details.

Working out the costs involved

Open Universities Australia units aren't as expensive as university courses but are more expensive than TAFE courses. You pay several hundred dollars for one subject. However, you may be able to apply to FEE-HELP for a student loan. Other costs involved may include buying textbooks, Internet access and software packages. Also, if you sit any exams you may need to find someone to watch over you and this service may cost up to $100.

Combining study and travel

If you want to combine travel and study, why not join a travel group centred around acquiring knowledge? What better way to develop your interest in art than to take your art classes in Tuscany. Perhaps you're sick of your garret and would like to write your novel in Bali — or learn French in France? All this is possible in the world of cultural travel.

Imagine painting in Florence surrounded by wonderful churches and museums. You can also paint in southern France, the Lake District — pretty much anywhere you choose. By joining an art tour you can study art, you can practise art, or you can combine the two. Some tours offer studio space as part of the package. Most art tours include lectures on art history, visits to galleries and other tours.

Finding the time to sit down and write is often hard. Writing is a hidden art. You usually labour away for years before your work sees the light of day. But by joining a writing tour for a week or more you're surrounded by like-minded people and you have the time to write. To get the most out of your writing tour, you need to know what sort of writing you want to do. Fiction or non-fiction? Do you want to be a travel writer, a photo journalist, a screen writer, a novelist, a poet, a documentary maker? You can write travelogues that make people laugh or make them think. Or perhaps you prefer to write crime novels or dramas?

If you're looking to develop your green thumb, you're spoilt for choice with gardening tours. The Internet lists thousands of different tours. It all comes down to deciding how and when you want to travel: for instance, small group or large group? Gardening and dining, gardening and history, or gardening and culture? Public or private gardens?

Learning a language in its native country gives you the added bonus of being able to practise your skill when you walk out the school door. Most language classes are held in the mornings, so you have the rest of the day free to explore your surroundings and practise your new-found skills.

You can take a language course for a week or much longer, depending on the level of expertise you want to acquire. Are you a beginner with no knowledge of the language, or do you know some simple phrases already? Some people like to take a short language course before they leave Australia, so that when they arrive at the school overseas they can order food and drink and find out where the toilet is.

Many language schools arrange accommodation with host families. While hostels may be a cheaper option, if you live with a host family you get some meals and hopefully a chance to practise your conversation. Alternatively, you can stay in youth hostels or treat yourself to rental or hotel accommodation.

The Internet should be your first port of call to find out more about the various courses available for studying abroad. For example, Transitions Abroad at www.transitions abroad.com caters for senior travel programs and has links to a number of other travel sites.

Alternatively, if you prefer to know the people you're travelling with, check out your local learning centre or private classes. Many centres include overseas travel packages in their programs or as add-ons. Your local paper is also a good source of information.

In addition, numerous universities and colleges offer study abroad programs. These courses last for a semester or a full year. You need to satisfy the usual prerequisites of the unit to enrol in such courses.

Entering the TAFE System

The TAFE system is a nationwide education system catering for students who want to gain a practical education. Most of the courses are delivered via industry-based national competency modules. Students complete practical placements and so gain valuable workplace skills.

Use TAFE as a stepping stone to university studies, to update your qualifications or to retrain in a new area. Mature-aged students are welcome. If you have a hobby such as raising goats, making cheese or wine, writing travelogues or painting, for example, you can take advantage of a TAFE certificate or diploma course to enhance your knowledge and skills.

The courses on offer cover a vast number of subjects, from art and architecture to yachting safety and youth work.

Find your local TAFE provider by visiting the Web site for your state or territory:

- ✔ **Australian Capital Territory:** www.cit.act.edu.au
- ✔ **New South Wales:** www.tafensw.edu.au
- ✔ **Northern Territory:** www.cdu.edu.au
- ✔ **Queensland:** www.tafe.qld.gov.au
- ✔ **South Australia:** www.tafe.sa.edu.au
- ✔ **Tasmania:** www.tafe.tas.edu.au
- ✔ **Victoria:** www.education.vic.gov.au/tafecourses
- ✔ **Western Australia:** www.tafe.wa.edu.au

In addition, the Web site of the Department of Education and Early Childhood Development at www.education.vic.gov.au/tafecourses offers a directory of accredited courses offered by TAFEs nationally.

Meeting the entry requirements

Check the entry requirements for each TAFE and course of study. Some courses require you to apply directly to the institution, or you may need to apply through the university admissions centre in your state. You must abide by the dates set out for completing the application forms. You may have to supply a folio of work and attend an interview.

To contact the university admissions centre in your state or territory, go to

- ✔ **Australian Capital Territory:** www.uac.edu.au
- ✔ **New South Wales:** www.uac.edu.au
- ✔ **Northern Territory:** www.cdu.edu.au
- ✔ **Queensland:** www.qtac.edu.au
- ✔ **South Australia:** www.satac.edu.au
- ✔ **Tasmania:** www.prospective.utas.edu.au
- ✔ **Victoria:** www.vtac.edu.au
- ✔ **Western Australia:** www.tisc.edu.au

Applying for alternative entry

If you don't have a Tertiary Education Rank (TER), you can apply as a mature-aged student. You may be required to complete the following:

- ✔ Bridging course, which raises your skills to entry-level standards
- ✔ Personal Competency Statement, which outlines how your work and life experiences suit you for study
- ✔ Special Tertiary Admissions Test

You'll be expected to demonstrate your ability and readiness to participate in tertiary study.

Looking into bridging courses

Bridging courses are designed to help students who've been away from study for some time. For example, if you wish to enter a course with an emphasis on maths, you can take a bridging course to bring your maths skills up to standard. Bridging courses also offer instruction on assignment writing, study habits, research skills, literacy and numeracy.

Offering Recognition of Prior Learning

The TAFE system offers Recognition of Prior Learning (RPL), so that you can get credits for skills already learned. Rather than being about subjects previously studied, RPL is concerned with the learning covered in training modules. This learning can take place in a formal setting or it can be a part of work or general life experience.

Contact the institution where you plan to study for the correct documentation. You must supply supporting evidence. This evidence can include a portfolio of work such as completed assessments, workplace visits, interviews and other assessment tasks such as trade tests or oral exams. Any workplace evidence must be authenticated by your supervisor or employer.

Checking out the fees involved

TAFE doesn't cost as much as university. Diplomas and advanced diplomas are the most expensive courses. For example, the annual fee for a diploma is about $1,000, or $3,000 over three years.

Aboriginal Australians and Torres Strait Islanders may be exempt from fees. If you receive a Commonwealth benefit or allowance, your fees will be greatly reduced. To find out whether you're eligible for a concession, contact your campus before enrolling. You need to take evidence of your benefit or allowance on enrolment day if you wish to pay a reduced fee.

Apprentices are eligible for an Apprenticeship Training (Fee) voucher valued at $500 if they're in a skills shortage area as defined by the National Skills Needs list. This list includes bakers, cooks, fitters and joiners among others.

Some courses charge fees for protective clothing or uniforms. You can't enter the learning area if you don't have the required protective clothing. You also have to pay materials fees for any materials supplied to you as well as buying textbooks and study manuals. The general service fee covers the costs of services, facilities and activities and is compulsory. You must pay this fee up-front on the day of enrolment.

TAFE students can't get loans under university loans schemes. Your TAFE may offer you a student loan facility, otherwise you need to get a personal loan.

Entering University as a Mature-Aged Student

You don't have to feel alone if you want to go to university when you retire. A growing number of mature-aged students in the 45-plus age bracket are now studying at post-secondary school level. You can graduate in your 80s if you like.

Universities are becoming easier to access for mature-aged students. You find a range of pathways to university other than by completing secondary school education. Your life experience is valued. You can study for your degree part-time or full-time, and either on or off campus.

Meeting the entry requirements

The conventional way of entering university is by completing your secondary education. If you haven't already done so, you can complete Year 12 by going back to secondary school or by attending courses at TAFE or an adult learning centre. In addition, some neighbourhood houses offer various Year 12 subjects.

However, you don't have to complete Year 12 to enter university. You can demonstrate your capacity to study at a tertiary level in numerous other ways.

Gaining alternative entry

If you've completed any studies at a post-secondary level, such as TAFE studies or a bridging course, or have gained professional or para-professional qualifications, these can be taken into consideration in your application.

Special Tertiary Admission Test

You can use the Special Tertiary Admission Test (STAT) as an alternative method of university admission. This aptitude test is administered in each state by the appropriate university admissions centre.

The test comprises a two-hour multiple-choice test and a one-hour written English test. Of the 70 multiple-choice questions, half are verbal and half are quantitative. You're tested on reading, analysing a passage of writing and interpreting graphical displays of information. You're required to use mathematical relationships and apply reasoning to tables of data. The one-hour written test requires written responses to two themes.

When you register to sit for the STAT test, you receive some sample questions. Or you can download the sample questions from the Australian Council for Educational Research Web site at www.acer.edu.au.

Check the admissions policy of your chosen university to make sure that it accepts the STAT as an entry pathway for your particular course. The STAT may satisfy some prerequisites in English and mathematics.

To find out more about the STAT, contact the university admissions centre in your state or territory (see the section 'Meeting the entry requirements' earlier in the chapter).

Your work and study history

Some universities take into account your personal work and study history when considering your application. This information may be used in conjunction with your STAT (see preceding section).

Document any professional or para-professional qualifications you've acquired. You need a copy of any original documents certified by a Justice of the Peace.

Also document your employment history. Include your job title, period served and major tasks undertaken. Include any skills, whether from paid or voluntary employment, that show you're capable of undertaking tertiary study.

TAFE diplomas and advanced certificates

If you successfully complete the first year of a TAFE diploma or advanced certificate IV course, you may be eligible for entry to some university courses. If you complete the whole diploma, you may receive credits in some university courses. To receive credits, you have to meet any requirements the university places on you regarding level of achievement in your TAFE studies.

Gaining entry to university by completing a TAFE diploma can dramatically lower the cost of your degree. However, before you enrol in a TAFE course you must find out whether the diploma will be credited by your chosen university.

University preparatory classes

Many universities offer foundation or bridging studies to help students prepare for university entrance. These courses are designed for those who've been educationally disadvantaged or have been away from study for some time. Graduates from these courses are eligible to apply for many different university courses.

Each university has its own particular preparatory program. Some universities require you to choose from a set of year-long units. Most bridging course units include language skills and successful study skills. You can opt to take maths and basic science as part of your core studies.

If you intend to use a bridging course as a stepping stone to a degree course, you must contact the administrator of the course you wish to enter to make sure you're eligible to apply for enrolment on completion of your bridging course.

If you don't mind studying online, Open Universities Australia offers a variety of bridging programs as well as degree programs that don't require any academic prerequisites.

The completion of a bridging course doesn't guarantee your entry to university. You must still apply for entry as determined by the institution. However, the bridging course gives you the confidence to move onto further study and in most cases it's taken into account along with your work and life experiences.

Starting with a single subject

Returning to university, or studying at university for the first time, can be a daunting prospect. You may feel out of date or unable to keep up with the younger students. To help boost your confidence, consider starting with a single subject rather than jumping straight into a major course. A single subject allows you to study the content in depth without worrying about the deadlines for your other subjects. This step is a great way of easing yourself into study mode.

Many universities offer single subjects that you can undertake either on or off campus to show your potential for tertiary study. Most single subjects require you to have some demonstrated ability to cope with the study, but this need not be formal academic qualifications. Single subjects are usually offered at a lower fee than for a formal university course but you have to pay up-front.

By enrolling in a single subject you should gain access to the library and other facilities within the university. In addition, you can elect to study the subject for your own enjoyment, rather than being assessed and credited for another course.

Single subjects are subjects from university undergraduate or postgraduate degree programs. You attend normal classes with other university students.

If you choose to be assessed, you have the same workload as other students and an academic mark will be recorded for you.

Good results in a single subject may earn you entry into a degree or postgraduate degree course: You'll have demonstrated your ability to study at tertiary level. You have to apply to have this subject credited to your degree.

If you decide not to be formally assessed, you attend the same lectures and seminars as other students and do the same reading, but you don't have to hand in any work or sit exams. And, of course, you won't receive an academic mark.

To find out how to apply for a single subject, go to your chosen university's Web site. Alternatively, university handbooks are kept on reserve at most local libraries.

Paying for university study

University study is expensive. However, most students at government-funded universities have a Commonwealth-supported place, which means that the government pays part of their fees. No age limit or asset tests are attached to these places but they are subject to citizenship tests. You can apply for a Commonwealth-supported place through your local university admissions centre.

If you have a Commonwealth-supported place, you can also apply for a HECS-HELP loan. Once again, no age limit or asset tests apply. You're provided with the necessary forms for the loan when you accept your university place.

You begin to repay your HECS-HELP loan when, and if, your income reaches $39,824 per year. Until then, you make no repayments. The loan doesn't attract interest and is indexed against the CPI each year. If you die before you finish repaying the loan, no demands will be made on your estate: The debt isn't passed on to your heirs.

Universities also offer some fee-paying places, whereby you pay the full cost of the course with no government subsidies. However, you can apply for a FEE-HELP loan to fund your place. You must request this form from your university. Visit the student services counter at your university or check out the university's Web site for more information.

Check all the relevant details of any student loan you apply for. See www.goingtouni.gov.au or www.ato.gov.au for more detailed information.

Australian Postgraduate Awards

Australian Postgraduate Awards of about $20,000 per annum are available for students in Masters by Research and Doctorate by Research degree programs. Each award covers two years of a Masters degree and three years of a Doctorate, with a possible extension of six months. To apply, contact your chosen university.

Other scholarships

You may want to use your retirement as a time to further your research in a specific area or to begin a new career. Perhaps you've always dreamt of being a teacher or lawyer, or you may want to research the perfect grape. To fund your studies you can access various scholarships, bursaries and grants. Industries, charitable institutions and universities all offer funding.

Here are just a few examples:

- ✔ **General scholarships:** The Australian Federation of University Women — South Australia Inc. Trust Fund awards bursaries to assist people undertaking studies at Australian universities. The funds are mainly awarded to those studying at Masters or PhD level. Visit www.afuwsa-bursaries.com.au for details.

- ✔ **Maths/science scholarships:** For those intending to become secondary school teachers, maths/science scholarships are available at the University of Tasmania. Visit www.education.tas.gov.au for more information.

- ✔ **Scholarships for Indigenous women:** The Padnendadlu bursaries are awarded specifically for Indigenous Australian women studying at South Australian universities. Go to www.afuwsa-bursaries.com.au for further details.

- ✔ **Scholarships for land workers and fishers:** The Commonwealth and state governments offer bursaries, grants and scholarships for land workers and fishers to gain management and other skills. Check out your state or territory government Web site.

- ✔ **Wine industry scholarships:** The wine industry offers students financial assistance and opportunities to make contacts in the wine industry. These scholarships recognise academic achievement.

The University of the Third Age

If you want to extend your knowledge on a subject in a non-threatening atmosphere, try the University of the Third Age (U3A). This international movement focuses on helping those who are ready to launch into a new phase of their lives. U3A is a true coming together and sharing of knowledge within the community.

You don't need any qualifications to join in the activities of U3A. Most of the work at U3A is done by volunteers, so the fees are kept low.

Courses are wide-ranging and are limited only by the number of people willing to volunteer their expertise. U3A also offers social outings and get-togethers.

U3A has an extensive online network. You can join classes online and you can use the ideas exchange facility, which is open to all U3A members. You can find more information about your local U3A branch through your local council or from your local newspaper.

Returning to Study as a Mature-Aged Student

This section gives you some useful pointers for coping in the classroom once again and getting back into a study routine. It also offers tips on handling the various types of course assessment. The most important thing to remember is that you have so much life experience to offer. Study these days doesn't simply involve memorising a stream of facts.

Getting prepared before you start your course

You need to understand how your education facility works and be able to use the resources — both human and technical — available to you.

You must have some knowledge of the Internet. Some classes are taught through the Internet medium of Second Life, whereby you log onto the Internet to access your lectures. At a minimum, readings and assignments are posted to the Net.

Your student diary contains a lot of information about the institution, particularly semester start and finish dates and cut-off dates for lodging various forms.

If you wish to defer your course or take a leave of absence, check your institution's Web site or ask at the administration centre. Be careful to note the cut-off dates for forms to be lodged.

Checking out the library

Find out where the library is and book in for a library session. Libraries are very different these days. You need to understand the computer system so you can order books and articles online. You can access articles from anywhere in Australia or the world, but you need to be signed up. If you're a postgraduate, the articles will be delivered to you.

Getting oriented

Orientation isn't necessarily about getting drunk — it's about finding out as much as you can. You're given a tour of the facilities and have the workings of your course explained to you. You also meet your tutors and lecturers. Some institutions require you to have a security pass, and this along with other forms is issued during the orientation sessions.

Reading the info

Read all the information that's sent to you. This material includes the campus layout, which can be tricky at a big university or TAFE college. Pay particular attention to the Hubs and other administration centres. You must know where to enrol and how to get your student card, which gives you access to the library and computer system. If you enrol online, which many people do, don't put off getting your student card. Many universities are fairly paperless and you need to use the computer system to keep track of your enrolment, results and class work.

Making the most of your study experience

You'll mix with all sorts of people — some who undoubtedly will try your patience, but others who'll be an amazing source of information.

Here are some ways to make the most of your classroom experience:

- **Ask questions.** If you don't understand something, you can bet no-one else does either. Most tutors would rather have the discussion in the classroom than answer a whole lot of individual queries later.

✔ **Be open to learning from your fellow students as well as your tutor.** Go for coffee after class. You'll glean useful information and make valuable contacts.

✔ **Make an effort to contribute in every class.** Even if you feel like the know-it-all mature-aged student, your tutor will appreciate your contributions: Talking for two hours to a blank audience is no fun. The other students will listen to you more carefully if they think you have an understanding of the topic. You'll be surprised how the age gap can be bridged with mutual respect.

Also, get involved! Don't hang back waiting to be invited to participate in group events. Some students like to organise events and everyone else just tags along.

At a minimum, do the following:

✔ Form alliances with other students and get their email addresses so that you can take notes for each other in emergencies.

✔ Go on any tours that are offered.

✔ Obtain staff email addresses. Most communication between staff and students is carried out by email.

Your student ID card may also get you discounts at cinemas and other venues. So get out there and enjoy life.

Coping with study once again

Most importantly, ensure that you attend the first lecture for every subject you're studying. This way, you should get the course outlines and assessment information.

Look into the postgraduate facilities in your faculty. You may have a quiet room and a computer terminal available to you.

Being organised

Tertiary institutions seem to generate a lot of paper. Even if you take notes on your laptop, you soon acquire a stack of hand-outs, lecture notes, excerpts from articles, and other bits and pieces. Some lecturers and tutors may present their lecture notes on disc or through Second Life, but others still prefer paper.

Follow these tips for staying organised:

- ✔ **Back up your back-ups.** If you're working on a big project, keep a copy of your work off-site.
- ✔ **Break large tasks into smaller ones.** By tackling tasks and projects in smaller chunks you aren't overwhelmed by them and can keep on top of things.
- ✔ **Keep a diary.** You should get one free when you enrol. Enter all assignment deadlines and reminders about the deadlines two weeks beforehand.
- ✔ **Keep up with technology.** Many students take notes on their electronic notebooks in class.
- ✔ **Keep your notes together.** This may sound simple, but as the weeks go by you'll generate and receive a lot of notes.
- ✔ **Reserve your books at the library as soon as you get your reading lists and assignments.** If you don't reserve them immediately, you may not get hold of them for weeks.

Skimming the stacks

Go to the library or online and get a selection of books and articles. Read the contents pages, indexes and abstracts to decide whether material is of interest to you.

Don't read everything, because you don't have time. Discover how to skim read for important passages. Skim reading can be easy — remember this: Each paragraph has one main idea contained in a key sentence. Read this for the main information. Then breeze though the rest of the paragraph.

Making a note of everything you read

Library computer systems allow you to bookmark your reading list. You need to reference everything you write so note down all the books and articles you read. You could go mad if you have to go back to the library to find a quote or statistic from a book you've already returned. You must note the title, author, date, publisher and place of publication. If you use a direct quote in your writing — that is, you quote a passage from another publication word for word — put the text in quotation marks and write down the page number and publication details where you found the quote.

Pay attention to the referencing system required for your course. Several different ways of referencing exist. Your faculty can direct you as to which system to use.

Handling course assessments

Although some courses still have written exams, many subjects are now assessed through a variety of means, including a group assignment, an individual presentation and an individual written component. If you're doing a course like woodwork you'll also have to complete a practical assignment.

Tackling group assignments

More than likely, some of your overall marks will require you to work as a member of a group. You need to lay some ground rules at the beginning of the group exercise to make sure that the process works smoothly. This is where your life experience comes in: You can manage people. Unfortunately, some students won't have your work ethic.

Try these tips for keeping your study group on track:

- **At each group session, sit close together and make sure everyone can hear.** This may sound fundamental, but even young people can have hearing difficulties if two or more people are talking over the top of each other.

- **Hold a brainstorming session at the beginning of the exercise.** Include everyone's contribution, no matter how odd.

- **Ensure that everyone understands the need for leadership.** Acknowledge a leader early in the process.

- **Make sure that everyone understands the group's objective.** Sometimes instructions are not clear: Check any anomalies with your tutor.

- **Make sure that each group member is clear what he or she has to do.** Assign tasks, take notes and get feedback.

- **Encourage everyone to contribute.** Again, your skills will be useful here. Some people are not natural contributors, but they may have good ideas.

- **Encourage everyone to listen.** Often, people think that they listen more than they do. Listening is a skill many people have to practise.

- **Be prepared to be the expert at times and to hold back at others.** Mature-aged students need to be diplomatic.

- **Don't be the workhorse.** If you take on the workhorse role because you want to control the group, you may end up resentful of others who don't contribute.

Making class presentations

When you give an oral presentation to the class, make sure you're well prepared. If the presentation is short, say, 10 to 15 minutes, you won't be able to convey much information. Rather than rushing through the whole topic, concentrate on clearly presenting the key point and one or two minor points.

If you have longer, say, 30 minutes or more, use some form of media like a short film clip or a pithy hand-out and try to get your classmates involved. Remember, you'll be lucky to keep their attention for 10 minutes at a time. Have some questions ready to ask or give them a short quiz.

Don't read from your notes with your head down. Your audience will fall asleep.

Here are some pointers for making a successful presentation:

- ✔ Know your subject. Make sure that you understand what's being asked of you.
- ✔ If you're making a PowerPoint presentation or using an overhead projector — yes, they're still in use — keep your slides clear and simple with only three points to a page.
- ✔ Book the equipment you want to use in advance — resources are usually scarce in colleges and universities.
- ✔ Find out the position and number of power outlets. You may need to bring an extension cord. (I know that life is supposed to be wireless, but *never* underestimate the power of the gremlin.)
- ✔ Check that your PC/DVD is compatible with college equipment.
- ✔ Check that all the equipment is working and practise using it.
- ✔ Practise your presentation in front of your family or a mirror — or the dog.
- ✔ When you're asked to make your presentation, face your audience.
- ✔ Introduce yourself. In a big class, not everyone will know your name.
- ✔ Begin by telling people the title of your talk. Many speakers don't do this.
- ✔ Don't pass hand-outs around while you're speaking: You'll lose your audience's attention. Leave the hand-outs to the end or allow your audience five minutes to go through the material.
- ✔ Finish by saying, 'In conclusion', and then sum up.

In an oral presentation, humour always helps.

Completing written assignments

Most assignments take the form of written work. You need to find out exactly what form your written work should take — for example, an essay, a report or a literature review. Take note of the word limit. You won't get extra marks for going over the limit and in fact you may be penalised. If your tutor is unclear about what he or she wants, ask for an example.

When writing an assignment, follow these steps to success:

1. **Don't begin writing until you've completed your research.**

    Your lecturer isn't interested in what you think unless it's backed up by research. Nor is your lecturer looking for your accumulated wisdom or a stream of consciousness. Document your research and include quotes and footnotes/endnotes. Check your sources carefully. The tabloid press and Internet sites aren't usually seen as adequate sources unless they're backed up by academic research.

    Every course has its preferred method of referencing. You'll receive a sheet directing you to the correct method for your course. Following the required referencing style is important so make sure that you follow the instructions.

    Ask questions. Make sure you know exactly what you have to do. Chances are if you don't know the required way of referencing or the form your report should take, others won't either.

2. **Finish your research, formulate your theory, make sure all your references are in order and then begin to write.**

    The actual writing phase should take only 20 per cent of the overall time allotted for your assignment.

3. **Don't cram your paper full of ideas.**

    You don't want a jumble. Be clear and concise. Plan your work carefully. You may find it helpful to actually map out what you want to say in point form so that you can see how it flows. Each paragraph should have one main idea, backed up by research. Your assignment needs only three to five main ideas. The rest of the work will be taken up with the research to support your theories.

    Never plagiarise. Plagiarism is the mortal sin of education. You may think that you've found an obscure source that you can copy outright, but believe me, spotting where a student's original work finishes and the plagiarism begins is *very easy.* Your lecture notes will outline the penalty for plagiarism. It may be instant dismissal from the university.

4. **When you've finished writing, read over your work and do some editing.**

   Your computer's spell checker is a useful tool, but it's not clever enough to know whether you mean to write 'below' or 'bellow'. Make sure that all your quotes and statistics are referenced correctly, with page numbers as well as dates and sources.

5. **Before you hand in your assignment, ensure that you've included the appropriate cover sheet.**

   Fill this in with your lecturer's name, the title of the assignment and other relevant information. If cover sheets are not handed out, ask for one.

6. **Hand in your assignment on time.**

   If you're going to be late, speak to your tutor. You can lose marks for work submitted late.

If you're experiencing difficulties with your studies, don't just drop out. Speak to your tutor. He or she will be able to help you with your work or perhaps arrange an extension of a deadline. These days, no-one wants you to just drop out. The staff are anxious for you to complete your course successfully.

Chapter 14

Working in Retirement

*W*ork is many things. You probably think of work as something you do to earn money, but work can be paid or unpaid. You're working when you clean the house. You may consider retirement to be the end of your working life, but unless you sit under a tree for the rest of your days, you may always be working in some form — just not necessarily making money. The beauty of retirement is that you can work on your own terms.

In this chapter, I provide advice if you're still employed but are looking to retire shortly, or if you're already retired but want to return to some form of paid or voluntary work.

Understanding Your Reasons for Working

Retirement may have seemed like a good idea at the time — or perhaps you had no choice in the matter. Either way, at some point in your retirement you may begin to think about taking on some type of paid work again.

Here are some reasons you may be thinking about work again:

✔ **Boredom:** Some retirees start to feel bored or can't come to terms with the lack of physical and mental stimulation. Unless you become involved in other activities, retirement can be a lonely time. Work provides you with social stimulation and feelings of self-worth you may miss when you retire. Check out Chapter 2 for more about getting involved in the activities you enjoy.

✔ **Helping your children or grandchildren:** Perhaps your children need a helping hand or maybe you just want to give them one. Rising house prices, divorce and health problems may mean your children are struggling to buy a house. Or you may want to invest in a private school education for your grandchildren.

✔ **Money:** Maybe your money isn't stretching as far as you thought it would? Because most Baby Boomers' superannuation is invested in the share market, their investments rise and fall with the market. If the market is having a very bad time, your investments may not be able to pay the pension you want.

You may want to turn your hobby into a job — Chapter 16 has advice on doing just that.

Remaining in the Workforce

If you're still in the retirement planning stage and haven't stopped work completely, you may want to take advantage of the government's transition-to-retirement pension (TRIP) strategy, which allows you to access your superannuation in pension form before you retire. You also may want to add to your super fund before you retire. You have several alternatives:

✔ Salary sacrificing

✔ Super top-ups

✔ The Pension Bonus Scheme

This section helps you to consider all your options.

Over 55 and still working

Under the government's transition-to-retirement pension strategy, you can access your super in the form of a TRIP before you retire, whether you're employed or self-employed. To qualify for the strategy, you must've reached your *preservation age*. Your preservation age depends on your date of birth. The calculation is done on a sliding scale, so if you were born before 1 July 1960 your preservation age is 55, and if you were born after 30 June 1964 your preservation age is 60.

You can't take a lump sum, but you can begin to receive a pension. By taking advantage of the strategy, you can

- Reduce the hours you work
- Supplement your part-time wages with a superannuation pension

This means that you can wind back your working hours and still retain roughly the same level of income. You don't have to stop working completely to receive your pension. And you don't have to earn less money by working part-time.

Your TRIP must be in the form of a *non-commutable pension*. You can't convert your TRIP into a lump sum, although you may be able to do so when you retire or turn 65. You can draw down no more than 10 per cent of the balance of your super fund each year. The aim of the TRIP strategy is to keep you working, not to give you unlimited access to your superannuation.

Your super fund may not offer a non-commutable income stream, so you may have to pay a fee to change to a fund that does offer a pension scheme. Make sure your workplace agreement allows you to sacrifice as much of your salary as you need to, to make this option viable. Don't forget the salary sacrifice contribution limits.

Most importantly, you need to speak to someone who can give you reliable financial or tax advice on this strategy. You must fully understand all the taxation and superannuation implications of this strategy before you proceed.

Salary sacrificing

By upping the amount of your wages you put into super (salary sacrificing) you build your super fund quicker. Because super contributions and TRIPs offer generous tax advantages, you can retain your standard of living while growing your fund. You can find out more about salary sacrificing in Chapter 4.

If you sacrifice all of your salary to super, you miss out on the tax-free threshold for the first $6,000 of your wages.

Visit the Australian Taxation Office's Superannuation Web site at www.ato. gov.au/super for full details of the salary sacrificing options.

Contribution limits

You're limited on how much you can contribute to superannuation. If you're aged 50 or over, the maximum amount you can contribute to superannuation for a pension as a concessional contribution, which includes salary sacrifice, is $100,000 per annum. This is due to change on 30 July 2012, when the limit will be reduced to $50,000.

Co-contributions

If you earn between $30,342 and $60,342 (2008–2009 figures), you may be eligible for the federal government's Super Co-contribution Scheme. Basically, under the scheme for every after-tax dollar you voluntarily contribute to your superannuation fund the government gives you up to an extra $1.50 tax-free to put into your super fund, up to a maximum of $1,500 per year. This contribution must be *separate* from your salary sacrificed amount.

See Chapter 4 for more details about the Super Co-contribution Scheme or consult your taxation adviser.

Topping up your super before you retire

You can continue to contribute to your superannuation fund until you're 75. If you're under 65, you can contribute to your super whether you're working or not. Don't forget the contribution limits — see the section 'Contribution limits' above.

Between the ages of 65 and 74, you can contribute if you've worked 40 hours in a continuous 30-day period in the financial year in which you plan to make a super contribution. After you turn 75, you cannot contribute to your super fund yourself — any contributions must be made for you by your employer.

Chapter 4 has more information about superannuation payments and schemes.

For more details, check with your super fund and talk to your financial adviser.

The Pension Bonus Scheme

Men can qualify for the age pension when they reach the age of 65. Women qualify on a sliding scale. For those born before 30 June 1944 the qualifying age is 63, and for those born after 31 December 1948 the qualifying age is 65.

If you qualify for the age pension, or a Veterans' Affairs service pension, but decide not to take the pension and continue working, you can accrue a *pension bonus* under the Pension Bonus Scheme. This bonus is a one-off lump sum payment.

A number of conditions apply to the Pension Bonus Scheme:

- ✔ You can't accrue the bonus if you already receive the age pension.

- ✔ You must accrue the bonus for a minimum of 12 months and for a maximum of five years. You must work at least 960 hours per year during that time.

- ✔ You must keep a log of your working hours during this time.

- ✔ You must satisfy asset and residency tests to qualify for the bonus.

You have to weigh up the pros and cons of this scheme for your own situation, because if you forgo the pension in favour of the scheme you may lose the benefits attached to your Pensioner Concession Card. Your spouse's income may also be taken into account and reduce your payment.

For more details on the Pension Bonus Scheme, contact your local Centrelink Customer Service Centre or visit www.centrelink.gov.au and type 'Pension bonus scheme' into the search facility.

Do your homework on this scheme. You may find it useful to read some blogs on the Internet about people's experiences with the scheme.

Getting Help When Job Hunting

If you've already retired and want to return to the workforce, you should find that help is available for the mature-aged job seeker. On the Internet you can find information on government services available for job seekers, as well as tips on how to write your resume and post it on the Web. You may like to join a government-run self-help workshop or consult a private careers counsellor. Or you could join with others in your situation and offer each other support and guidance.

For specific information on creating a resume for today's competitive working environment, writing covering letters and answering key selection criteria, see *Australian Resumes For Dummies*, by Amanda McCarthy (Wiley Publishing Australia Pty Ltd).

Government services

Centrelink provides a service for job seekers called *Employment Self Help*. In the public contact area of some Centrelink offices you can find job search kiosks, telephones and fax machines, newspapers and other job search help. Visit Centrelink's Web site at www.centrelink.gov.au for more details of this service or to find your local Centrelink customer service centre.

Many government services aimed at helping job seekers can be accessed online. To be eligible for some of these services you need to be over 50 and receiving a government allowance, but other services are available to all job seekers.

Here are some of the online government services that you may find useful:

- **Australian JobSearch** at jobsearch.gov.au supplies employment services to support job seekers and provides special assistance to mature-aged job seekers. Registration is free and you can get help creating a resume, preparing for a job interview and finding a job. The JobSearch database lists more than 80,000 jobs that are advertised in newspapers and public service gazettes as well as those that are lodged by employers and job placement organisations. By registering with the service you can be matched to these jobs.

- **JobWise** at www.jobwise.gov.au/Jobwise was set up to help address the shortfall in the labour market by helping mature-aged people to remain in the workforce or to find work. Two of the services offered are JobWise workshops and self-help workshops. The self-help workshops help job seekers to brush up on their job-seeking skills. However, the workshops are scattered throughout Australia and aren't offered in every state.

- **Mature Workers Career Options** at www.matureworkers.com.au provides information about the Mature Aged Workers Transition Program, which enables mature-aged workers to become trainers or mentors. The site also supplies lists of government agencies that can help mature-aged job seekers, and explains Recognition of Prior Learning and how you can use your workplace skills to replace learning modules in the TAFE system.

✔ **Seniors.gov.au** at `seniors.gov.au` is designed as a source of information for the over 50s, such as details of apprenticeships for the over 45s, career information centres and job placement centres. You'll receive help writing your resume. Your resume will then be posted on a national job vacancy register and automatically matched with job vacancies requiring your skills set. Note that some of the job-seeking services on offer, such as a personal adviser, are available only to those on certain government allowances.

Private online providers

Type 'job search' into your preferred search engine and you get over half a million responses. On the Internet you can find thousands of private job-seeking services. Some companies give you tips on preparing for a job, such as writing your resume and covering letter, and surviving the job interview. Other companies are recruitment agencies for particular companies, government departments and religious groups.

Some of the many Web sites targeted to helping mature-aged people to find work include

✔ Adage at `adage.com.au`

✔ OVER 40 Recruitment at `www.over40recruitment.com.au`

✔ Wiser People at `www.wiserpeople.com.au`

In addition, certain occupations may target mature-aged professionals. For example, the Master Plumbers and Mechanical Services Association of Australia is looking for mature-aged plumbers to retrain and fill a number of roles in the industry. See `www.plumbingcareer.com.au` for more information.

Register with a recruitment agency and receive job advertisements and a facility to send your covering letter and resume to advertisers. The recruiters' Web sites usually make the facility very easy to use — just follow the prompts.

When you apply for a position via the Internet, make sure you receive an electronic acknowledgement. If the system malfunctions or you misunderstand the process or the technology, the advertiser may not receive your resume. If you don't receive an acknowledgement, contact the company in person if possible.

In addition, a number of companies offer the facility for you to post your resume online and be head-hunted by employers. Check out the following:

✔ Autopeople at www.autopeople.com.au

✔ CareerOne at www.careerone.com.au

✔ JobSearch at www.jobsearch.gov.au

Online support groups

Online support groups can help you in your search for a job by offering you the support of other users. You can easily feel isolated and depressed when you're job hunting, but swapping stories and information with others in the same situation can give you a positive boost in your job-seeking efforts. You won't feel so alone and you often get useful tips from other members of the group. The Web sites listed below offer very relevant and useful information.

✔ The About Seniors Web site at www.aboutseniors.com.au provides seniors with information about federal government financial incentives to encourage seniors to keep working. The site has links to other sites with special job search information as well as to Centrelink and the Department of Veterans' Affairs. You can access the meeting place on the site, post your own blogs and catch up with others.

✔ The Australian Council on the Ageing (COTA) is Australia's leading seniors' organisation and its Web site at www.cota.org.au/index.html has links to the COTA branches in each state and territory. Via COTA, you can contribute to discussions on issues relevant to retirees, including working and volunteering.

Company Web sites

If you know which company you want to work for, log onto that company's Web site to find more information about the company, including its recent annual report. Check whether the site has details about recruitment options and read all the information you can find about working conditions at the company. The company may encourage you to register with it so that it can send you job alerts and listings that fit your profile.

By researching the company you wish to work for, you can familiarise yourself with the company and its workplace practices and be in a better position to handle interview questions. Use the Web site to find out the following:

- ✔ Career and development opportunities and prospects at the company. Are employees able to study or take advantage of training courses? Do they have access to global opportunities?
- ✔ The company's history and vision for the future
- ✔ The company's involvement in environmental and/or community programs
- ✔ The company's plans for expansion

Job hunting the old-fashioned way

Online job searching is only one way to find work. Wherever possible, use all the avenues open to you, including the ones in the following sections.

Cold calling

Cold calling involves contacting companies by phone or email and asking whether the companies have any job opportunities or positions available. You can also ask whether you can send your resume in on spec. Some companies keep a bank of resumes on file, which makes it easier to fill positions when they become available because the positions don't have to be advertised.

Information gathering

Information gathering involves calling the relevant person from the company where you'd like to work and asking that person for an interview to try to find out more information about the company. The point of the mission is to find out how the company works, whether it's amenable to hiring mature-aged workers, whether a job opportunity exists for you and whether the company suits your needs.

You need to stress that this is a knowledge-gathering exercise rather than a job-hunting exercise. Most people enjoy talking about themselves if they have the time.

Be prepared. Have a list of questions to ask and keep the interview brief. If the person hasn't got time to be interviewed, ask whether you can email some questions to them.

Networking

If you're still working and plan to return to work some time after retirement, begin networking before you leave. If you've already retired, you have several options for finding people to network with.

Networking before you leave work requires some extra effort, but you need to take positive action to build your network. Try the following ideas:

- ✔ **Look at the wider community.** Find areas where you can help others. By joining different community groups, in addition to contributing your expertise you may make valuable contacts.

- ✔ **Open yourself to new experiences.** Accept extra work that puts you in touch with people outside your immediate sphere of influence. Attend professional seminars, conferences and dinners, and seek out opportunities to speak in a professional capacity.

- ✔ **Talk to people and really listen.** Often, you work with people without really appreciating the extent of their skills and knowledge. Talk to the people around you. They may be able to give you advice on training opportunities, new developments and community programs, or they may offer support.

Begin networking after you retire by drawing up a chart of all the groups you know personally. Consider the following suggestions:

- ✔ Business associates

- ✔ Charity organisations

- ✔ Church, synagogue or mosque groups

- ✔ Family members

- ✔ Friends

- ✔ Sports club members

Think about what these different groups can offer you in the way of information and contacts. Tread carefully though: Talk to people and listen to what they're saying instead of pumping them relentlessly for information.

Reading newspaper career sections, both local and national

Check your local paper for jobs in your immediate area and national newspapers like *The Australian* for jobs on offer around Australia.

Newspaper career sections offer more than just lists of jobs: They often interview workers in different careers to find out how these people got started and what their careers offer them in terms of job satisfaction and advancement, and they may also include articles on job applications, interview techniques and other job-seeking skills.

Make sure that you take notice of any instructions in a job advertisement to contact the company for a position description. If you ignore such instructions your application may be rejected.

Creating your own job search group

One of the major problems with job searching is the despondency that comes with frequent rejections. Dealing with rejections is hard when you're job-seeking alone, but you'll find strength in numbers.

You can set up your own job-seeking self-help group by approaching your local community centre or church. Call or visit the centre and explain that you're a mature-aged job seeker who wants to set up a group to support like-minded people in their search for work. You need an outline of your aims and how you envisage the group will progress. If the community centre gives your group the go-ahead, it'll advertise the group in its brochures and the local newspaper. To raise awareness, you could also give an interview to the local paper about your group.

Some of the issues your group may like to discuss include being successful in the following areas:

✓ Being interviewed — you can role-play interviews and video them for analysis

✓ Cold calling

✓ Job searching on the Internet

✓ Making phone calls

✓ Networking

✓ Writing resumes and covering letters

Hopefully, the centre permits you to use some space rent free or for a small fee. If you're lucky, you'll have access to the centre's computers as well. The centre may offer to help you raise funds for your group or to put you in touch with government agencies that can help you raise funds.

Boosting your confidence

Often, one of the biggest hurdles retirees need to overcome when preparing to return to work is lack of confidence. If you've recently left work and stepped straight into another job this won't be a problem. However, if you've been out of circulation for a year or more, the prospect of resuming your work persona can be daunting.

Try these ideas for building your confidence and keeping up to date in your field:

- **Attend local and regional discussion groups in your profession.** By attending conferences, you'll not only hear the latest information but also meet people currently in the field. Keep up your professional memberships and look out for conferences to attend.

- **Don't be afraid to add to your skills.** Take a short course at a TAFE or adult learning centre to fill in any gaps in your skills base. If you'd like to change careers, investigate the certificates you need to obtain to branch out into this new career path. See Chapter 13 for more information.

- **Join a library and learn how to use it properly.** Through your local library, you can request to borrow material from all around Australia.

- **Make a list.** Assess what you have now in terms of qualifications, training and personal development. What do you need to update to land your ideal job?

- **Search the Internet for information relating to your area of work.** For example, you'll find blogs, research papers and pod casts related to your field.

- **Socialise with your former colleagues.** Keep in touch with workmates and go along to relevant events. Listen to what your colleagues say about their work.

- **Train online.** You can train in many different areas and study for university and college qualifications without leaving your house. Some of this training may be government-funded. For example, with Open Universities Australia you can study in your own time. Visit www.open.edu.au or see Chapter 13.

- **Volunteer for charitable services like Rotary, Lions and Probus.** You'll gain contact with the business community and you'll be socialising with others, which is a very important part of maintaining confidence and good mental health.

- **Volunteer to mentor at your local school or business college.** Mentoring helps you to keep your skills up to date as you learn from your student. See the National Mentoring Association of Australia Web site at www.dsf.org.au/mentor or the Australian Women's Mentoring Network Web site at www.womensmentoring.com.au/ for more information on mentoring in the community.

- **Volunteer your services to local community and church organisations.** Contact your local community provider or council and discuss the services you can offer. Whether you teach computer skills or help out with a men's group, you'll boost your self-confidence.

You'll be amazed at how much help you get by belonging to a group. You'll receive positive feedback, discover new techniques and generally feel good because you're sharing your expertise with others.

Confidence building involves a two-pronged attack: You need to socialise and get used to being around people again as much as you need to brush up on your work skills.

Returning to Work Part-Time

If you're retired and thinking about returning to work, a part-time position will probably be on your list. Some jobs lend themselves to part-time work, such as lecturer, consultant or tour guide. Some jobs require academic qualifications, whereas for others you need only complete a short training course before you can use your skills in new ways.

Lecturer

If you enjoy your work, you may like to give something back to the community in the form of lecturing. Lecturing positions can be full- or part-time and aren't confined to universities. You may need a postgraduate degree to lecture at university, but at TAFE you're required to undertake a short training session.

TAFE

No matter where your skills lie, whether as a nurse, an accountant or a gardener, your expertise can be used at TAFE. Lecturer positions at TAFE can be full- or part-time, casual or sessional. To qualify as a lecturer at TAFE you need to be competent in your field and to have successfully completed a Certificate IV in Training and Assessment. You can gain this qualification over a five-day period or a couple of weekends. For some subject areas at TAFE you may be able to get Recognition of Prior Learning.

University

University lecturers need to have postgraduate qualifications. Lecturers are expected to set exams and grade papers. If you've been a leader in your field, you'll be welcomed as a guest lecturer, which means you won't have any of the other arduous tasks to perform.

Certificate IV in Training and Assessment

If you want to take on a training and assessment role in a TAFE college, at a private education provider or in the workplace, you need a Certificate IV in Training and Assessment. This certificate gives you the skills and qualifications required to train others in a structured environment like a college, give on-the-job instruction and conduct one-to-one training of apprentices. You are also trained to mentor and coach staff and conduct workplace assessments.

You can complete this qualification through a five-day short course at a TAFE college or private education provider. If you're planning to teach at TAFE, check whether you can get Recognition of Prior Learning. This means you don't need to undertake a training course.

Consultant

Do you have a specialised set of skills? You may like to set up as a consultant. You can work in your area of expertise or apply your skills to other areas. You may have to think outside the square, but your organisational and other skills are transferable.

If you're still at work and plan to take on a consultancy role when you retire, now is the time to begin your campaign. When your employer tells you that she'll miss your skills, mention the fact that you're planning to do some consulting work.

If your retirement is a result of taking a redundancy package, you may find that you're unable to work for your former employer as a consultant for a specified amount of time. Check your severance package for information.

Consultants need to possess several important qualities:

- ✔ A strong technical knowledge of their field
- ✔ The ability to set their own fees
- ✔ The expertise to understand and negotiate a contract
- ✔ The knowledge of how to withdraw from a difficult situation

Do you want to set up as a consultant but lack, say, program management or interpersonal and marketing skills? Search out organisations that help consultants. For example, the Consultants' Consultant at www. consultantsconsultant.com.au offers a number of resources for those who want to brush up on their skills. The site offers reading material, workshops, courses, free tools and checklists.

In addition, some professional groups, like the Association of Consulting Engineers Australia (ACEA), have their own training programs. ACEA advises and trains its members on issues such as risk management, contracts, insurance, occupational health and safety, industrial and client relations, marketing and how to get paid. See www.acea.com.au for more information.

Check what services your own professional association offers for consultants.

For further information on setting yourself up as a freelancer, consultant or contractor, see *Freelancing for Australians For Dummies*, by Monica Davidson (Wiley Publishing Australia Pty Ltd).

Tour guide

If you like people and enjoy gathering and imparting information, becoming a tour guide may be the job for you. You can work as a volunteer or as a paid guide.

Paid tour guides

As a tour guide you can work for several hours per week or for days at a time. Some forms of tour guiding can be hard work. For example, if you're taking a busload of people on a week-long tour, you may be expected to help with the heavy work of loading and unloading the bus.

If you have expertise in a particular area, you can conduct short specialist tours for the customers on tour buses. You can even create your own tours for the city where you live, such as the chocolate lover's guide, the book lover's guide or the cheap shopping guide.

Universities and colleges offer certificates and degrees in tourism. They cover a diverse range of topics, from eco tourism to attractions and theme parks. You don't necessarily need a tour guide qualification if you have the required knowledge.

Volunteer tour guides

Libraries, zoos, museums, art galleries and city councils all need volunteers to help show tourists around. You can apply directly to the facility where you wish to volunteer or you can apply via a general Web site such as the Centre for Volunteering at www.volunteering.com.au. Chapter 15 has more information about volunteering.

Making a Lifestyle Change

Having worked in the same field for many years, you may have the urge to make a total change in your lifestyle and what you do for a living. If you watch television, you may be aware of the many programs devoted to people seeking a lifestyle change and a different work environment. Some of these changes are undertaken with the flimsiest of research and finances and result in disaster. However, those who take the time to plan and think things through have a better chance of making a successful transition.

Before you jump in and make such a change in your work environment, you need to consider whether you're more suited to working inside or outside. Weigh the considerations in Table 14-1.

Table 14-1	Considering Your Work Environment
Working Inside	**Working Outside**
Clean and dry	Dirty and wet
Air-conditioned/heated	Hot in summer and cold in winter
Sedentary	Active
Recirculated air	Fresh air
More likely to be working with others	More likely to be working alone

Knitting a new career

My friend Leonie made the transition from teacher to successful businesswoman. She decided to change direction and use her skills to set up a wool shop, The Wool Baa, in a local shopping strip. Her organisational skills help her to manage the business, but her people skills are what turned her business into a success. Leonie encourages all her customers to complete their knitting projects in her shop. She provides them with tea and coffee, and her mother gives instruction and any help the customers may need. Customers are also encouraged to share their skills with each other. The shop always looks busy and inviting, and customers are greeted with a warm welcome and an invitation to join in.

Swapping your white collar for a blue one

The idea of white-collar and blue-collar workers is becoming dated: These days, workers need high levels of training, and workplaces are becoming increasingly more computerised. However, for the purpose of this discussion I take *white collar* to mean someone who works inside at a desk and *blue collar* to mean someone whose work includes more hands-on physical work. Some may argue that this means a surgeon is a blue-collar worker, but I think you get my general drift.

If you worked in an office, a doctor's surgery, a classroom or any position where you didn't do much physical exercise, you may now feel the need to change direction to a more active and hands-on lifestyle.

Many people who decide to make a lifestyle change take up an artisan activity. Often, such activities start as a hobby and grow into something bigger. Some of the most popular activities include

✔ Cheese making

✔ Converting your property to permaculture

✔ General gardening and handyman work

✔ Grape growing and wine making

✔ Making and selling homemade products such as muesli or biscuits

✔ Wood turning and furniture making

If you're interested in taking up an artisan activity with the idea of turning it into a business, follow these tips to help ensure that your venture has the best chance of success.

✔ Research your hobby and area of expertise. If you want your new lifestyle to bring in some money, you need to know what's happening in the field. For example, find out how much your product can sell for, who your competition is and what the competition is doing.

✔ Make a business plan. You can find out how to do this from the Australian government's business Web site at www.business.gov.au or you can contact your local Business Enterprise Centre for free advice and support. Visit www.beca.org.au to locate your nearest Business Enterprise Centre.

- ✔ Update your skills by taking a course at TAFE or with someone who is well known and successful in the field.

- ✔ Consider buying a franchise instead of setting up on your own. The advantage of being a franchisee is that you get information and help running your business, but you have to pay fees to the franchisor. Visit the Web site of the Franchise Council of Australia at www.franchise. org.au for more information.

See Chapter 16 for more details about cultivating a hobby.

Changing your blue collar to a white one

If you've worked in blue-collar positions for your entire working life to date, now that you're older you may be ready to change direction and use your skills in a capacity that doesn't involve hard physical work. Or you may be looking for a more highly skilled, better-paid job. Either way, the best approach to changing direction is to undertake some retraining.

Here are some options to consider:

- ✔ If you'd like a desk job or an administrative position, you may need to take a TAFE course to enhance your computer skills, such as a design, desktop publishing or MYOB course. Check your local TAFE college for course details.

- ✔ If you'd like a teaching role and are skilled in a topic that is taught at TAFE, such as plumbing, electrical work, electronics or building, by completing a Certificate IV in Training and Assessment you'll be eligible to lecture at TAFE colleges. See the Sidebar 'Certificate IV in Training and Assessment' earlier in the chapter for more information on this course.

- ✔ If you like helping people and are looking for a more flexible job, perhaps as a business you can run from home, you may like to retrain as a natural medical practitioner and become a massage therapist, naturopath or reflexologist. Again, contact your local TAFE for course details.

If you're worried about participating in further study because you don't have the necessary qualifications, don't despair — you can easily get your skills up to speed with a bridging course. See Chapter 13 for more information.

Vintage skills

My friend Mary had a variety of unskilled, low-paid jobs while she was raising her children. Once her children had grown up and left home, however, Mary decided that she wanted a more highly skilled, better-paid job in administration. Mary sat down to write her resume, but couldn't think of any skills that she possessed from her work history. Instead, I suggested that she write about a time when she had done something well. This is her story.

Mary was a member of a vintage car club. She came up with the idea of holding a get-together for all the club's members from around Australia. The club's committee liked her idea and put Mary in charge of organising the event. First, Mary contacted the members, to assess whether they were interested in the event. Finding that the members were very much in favour of the idea, Mary set to work. She picked the date, booked the venue, arranged the catering and organised insurance cover. Then she investigated accommodation options and gave the members several choices of travel and stay packages.

During this exercise Mary demonstrated her high-level organisational and communication skills. She also used research and budgeting skills. Based on this evidence, Mary was able to land the administrative job she wanted.

Chapter 15

Giving Something Back by Volunteering

Do you feel a desire to give something back to the community in your retirement? Countless organisations require volunteer workers. You can help out in your local community or travel around the world as a humanitarian or ecological volunteer.

In this chapter, I look at some of the advantages and pitfalls of volunteering and outline some of the many great opportunities available for volunteer work.

Making the Commitment

When you put up your hand to volunteer, you need to make a commitment to the organisation you're working for. You may find it easier to be more committed if you choose to volunteer in an area that you're enthusiastic and passionate about.

Don't rush into the first volunteering opportunity that comes to hand. Take your time to think about what field you'd like to work in. If you've always loved animals, you may like to try volunteering at an animal shelter. If you want to travel or are interested in ecology and the environment, check out the many opportunities available with Greenpeace and similar organisations.

You can simply transpose your work skills to a volunteer situation, or you can do something entirely different. This is the beauty of volunteering: You don't have to remain in the same field in which you spent your working life.

Work out how much time you can dedicate to your volunteering duties. Any time you can give will be appreciated. Some organisations are happy with a few hours per week or per fortnight, but others require you to be there on a more regular basis. Of course, if you're volunteering overseas you probably need to block out several weeks or months on your calendar.

Knowing your rights

Make sure you're clear about your rights as a volunteer worker. Your voluntary labour shouldn't replace that of a paid worker. However, you should be covered by the same health and safety and discrimination legislation as a paid worker. Check out www.volunteeringaustralia.org to read the Universal Declaration on Volunteering.

Make sure you understand how or if your out-of-pocket expenses will be reimbursed *before* you start volunteering for an organisation.

Training

When you've settled on a volunteering position, your job should be adequately explained to you and any necessary training given. You should also be given background information about the wider organisation you're working for so you have an understanding how it operates and what its goals are.

If you're volunteering in another country, find out what housing arrangements have been made for you during your training phase.

Code of practice

The organisation you're working for should explain your rights and responsibilities as a volunteer. The Australian government has posted a model code of practice for organisations using volunteers on the Australian Volunteer Search Web site at http://volunteersearch.gov.au. The code covers areas such as providing a safe workplace, training, insurance, out-of-pocket expenses and support for volunteers. The code aims to protect the rights of volunteers and ensure that organisations taking on volunteers comply with legislation and duty of care.

Background checks

As a volunteer you probably have to undergo a police check, and/or a Working With Children check if relevant. The objective of these checks is to safeguard vulnerable sections of society and to make sure that you're responsible enough to handle money or drive a vehicle.

Police check

The organisation you're volunteering for may initiate your police check and ask you to sign a consent form. Your information won't be released to the organisation without your written consent. The police check includes only current convictions and doesn't take account of matters pending before a court.

At the present time, a police check isn't transportable between states or between organisations, but this may change in the future.

If the organisation you're volunteering for doesn't supply you with the relevant forms for a police check, you can find out how to apply by logging onto the police Web site or Department of Justice Web site in your state or territory, or by visiting your local police station. The procedure for applying for a police check varies from state to state.

If you're volunteering in the ACT or overseas, you need an Australian Federal Police check. You can find out more about this check on the Australian Federal Police Web site at www.afp.gov.au/business/national_police_checks.

Working With Children check

Volunteers who want to work with children usually have to undergo a Working With Children check (known as a Blue Card in Queensland). The Working With Children check looks for serious sexual, violent and/or drug-related offences. The enquiry includes spent convictions and findings of guilt from when you were under 18. The check is valid for five years.

The organisation you're volunteering for may supply you with the relevant forms, but if not you can find out how to apply by logging onto the police Web site or Department of Justice Web site in your state or territory, or by visiting your local police station. Application processes vary from state to state.

The Give and Take of Volunteering

Volunteering isn't just about giving. As a volunteer you also receive many different benefits — none of them are monetary but they're important to your health and wellbeing.

What you give

By the time you retire you've acquired a huge repertoire of skills and knowledge. Even if you don't want to use the specific skills you've acquired in your working life, you'll have a store of general skills to draw on. Here are just some of the many skills you may be able to offer as a volunteer:

- **Communication skills:** You have finetuned the art of communicating, whether you're talking to supervisors, work colleagues or your family. You're a skilled communicator.

- **Decision-making skills:** These are part of your daily life, from deciding where to take the family for a holiday to when to sign a contract.

- **Organisational skills:** You may not have organised large-scale events but you've probably organised complex events, like getting the whole family dressed, fed and out the door on time ready for school and work in the mornings.

- **Problem-solving skills:** You're constantly solving problems, like how to make the new microwave fit into the old microwave's smaller space.

What you get

In return for your time and commitment to your volunteering role, you benefit in numerous ways:

- **You acquire new skills.** You can make your volunteer experience work for you as you learn new things, even if that means catering for 100 hungry people.

- **You feel satisfaction in helping others.** Enjoy giving others hope.

- **You have an incentive to get going in the mornings.** It's great to have something positive to do every day.

- **You can increase your social contacts.** You're going to be spending plenty of time talking and mixing with others.

- **You keep your body and mind active.** This is particularly important as you get older.

Volunteering Opportunities

If you've already acted as a volunteer, you have some idea about what's involved and the many opportunities available. You may even know exactly what you'd like to do, but if not, how do you sort your way through the thousands of opportunities to pick the one that's right for you?

The first decision you need to make is whether you want to volunteer at home or abroad. This decision may be easy to make if you don't have a travel budget. From here, your search is *slightly* narrower and you can start sorting through the options. Remember, you may be happier and more likely to stick with something if you enjoy it. If you need help working out what you'd like to do, go back to Chapter 2 and work your way through the exercises on your values and what makes you tick.

Volunteering at home

Probably the best place to start your research is on the Web. You can find thousands of Web sites dedicated to volunteering, but you may find it useful to begin with those that explain volunteering and what you need to know about getting involved. Here's a sample of sites specifically related to Australia:

- ✔ Australian Volunteer Search at `http://volunteersearch.gov.au`, which covers volunteering opportunities in every state and territory
- ✔ Community.gov.au at `www.community.gov.au`. Click on 'Get Involved'
- ✔ Volunteering Australia at `www.volunteeringaustralia.org`

Then you can find out more about specific categories of interest to you. The following sections should give you a taste of what's available.

Working with children

If you want to work with children in *any* capacity, you need to pass a police check and a Working With Children check (see the section 'Background checks' earlier in the chapter). You may also need to undertake some training. You can volunteer in a number of areas. Here are some ideas you may like to research:

- ✔ **Becoming a cuddle granny or granddad:** You can provide help in special-care nurseries such as the Mater Maternity Hospital in Brisbane. See `www.mater.org.au/Home/Support/Volunteers.aspx` for details.
- ✔ **Fundraising:** Many organisations need volunteers to help with fundraising. Contact your local council or church for ideas.

✔ **Helping children with illnesses or special needs:** Vicnet Directory has a list of Australian associations that help children with special needs. Visit www.vicnet.net.au/family/famspecial for more information.

✔ **Supporting parents and families:** You can help parents whose children have special needs through your local hospital.

✔ **Visiting sick children in hospital:** Help keep children comfortable by providing companionship and activities.

✔ **Working with homeless children:** To find out more contact your church or council, or a charity like Barnardos at www.barnardos.org.au.

In addition, look around your local community to find a council, school or church program in need of volunteers. Or contact your local hospital: Some children need temporary respite care in a home to help them deal with a crisis situation; others need to be distracted from the problems of serious illness or difficult family situations.

Back to school

A number of organisations provide mentoring programs in schools. These programs aim not only to support young people but also to involve the community in schools. To become a mentor you need to undertake some training and have patience, empathy and life experience. You also need to have an encouraging and positive attitude towards students.

Check out the following programs:

✔ Mentoring Australia at www.dsf.org.au/mentor has the threefold aim of assisting vulnerable children, enhancing the lives of seniors and retired people, and providing community involvement in schools.

✔ School Volunteer Program at www.svp.org.au provides opportunities for volunteers to mentor school children. The program aims to support children and young people to achieve their potential.

Once again, to take part in any of these programs you need to pass a police check and a Working With Children check (see the section 'Background checks' earlier in the chapter).

If you don't want to work with children directly, you can support your local school by taking part in fundraising projects and working bees.

Going green: Conservation and the environment

You don't have to go overseas to get involved in conservation volunteering. Your local council will have a number of environmental and conservation programs you can join, including programs that help people to manage their household waste, conserve water or clean up local beaches and parks.

On a broader front you can get involved in causes like animal liberation, echidna care, frog census, and marine and reef watch.

Check out these Web sites for more ideas:

- ✔ Australian Wildlife Conservancy at www.australianwildlife.org.au. This site lists various opportunities such as seed collection, planting, fencing, weeding and fauna surveys.
- ✔ Department of Environment and Conservation Nature Base at www.naturebase.net. The Department offers a number of volunteer projects in areas such as scientific research, community education and manual labour.
- ✔ Earthwatch Institute of Australia at www.earthwatch.org/australia. Earthwatch organises various volunteering projects in Australia: You can help to conserve all sorts of creatures from echidnas to turtles. Expeditions may cost from $300 to $5,000 and usually last 10–14 days. You probably need to arrange your own flights, insurance etc. You don't need any special skills and will get all the instruction you need on-site.

  The Earthwatch Web site has a comprehensive list of questions with answers that will help you to decide if wildlife conservation is for you.

Fundraising

Fundraising is an essential part of any charitable venture. You'll be welcomed with open arms if you offer to raise funds for an organisation. There are the obvious ideas such as selling raffle tickets, chocolates, wrist bands or sausages. You may have your own unique ideas or you can access Web sites for fundraising ideas: You'll be amazed at the number of ideas available.

If you're interested in fundraising for a specific charity, try these suggestions:

- ✔ Australian Cancer Research Foundation at www.acrf.com.au
- ✔ Juvenile Diabetes Research Foundation at www.jdrf.org.au

If you're looking for more fundraising ideas, check out the following Web sites:

- ✔ Australian School and Club Fundraising Specialists at www.australianfundraising.com.au
- ✔ Fundraising Ideas at www.fundraisingideas.com.au

Helping the homeless

There's a great need for volunteers to help the homeless by undertaking activities such as counselling, providing food, offering companionship, helping with activities and community projects, and mentoring. You need to complete a training program if you choose to work in this field.

You can volunteer to help at your local church or community centre, or you can contact a national organisation that provides services to the homeless. Start with these two organisations:

- ✔ Mission Australia (www.missionaustralia.com.au) helps those in need to find a pathway to a better life.
- ✔ The Salvation Army's Oasis Youth Support Network (http://salvos.org.au/appeal-campaigns/the-oasis) provides food, accommodation, counselling and important training programs for homeless youths. The organisation also runs a 12-week training course for volunteers.

Margaret rekindles her love of horses through volunteering

My sister Margaret has always been keen on horses. So too is Margaret's granddaughter, Lily, and it was through Lily that Margaret became involved with Riding for the Disabled.

Margaret says: 'Riding for the Disabled is a not-for-profit organisation that enables children and young adults with physical and mental disabilities to enjoy the experience of horse riding. The organisation partially funds its expenses by charging able-bodied people for lessons. Lily took lessons at her local branch of Riding for the Disabled and this was how I discovered that volunteers were needed to help with riders who have disabilities.

'Depending on your skill you can lead the horses or be a side walker, which means you walk beside the horse to see that the person stays upright in the saddle. Either way, you get a couple of hours exercise out of doors each week.

'It's amazing how much pleasure kids and young adults with disabilities get from the experience of riding a horse. Children with physical disabilities use muscles they wouldn't normally use, and children with mental disabilities become more communicative and in some cases less angry and more relaxed.

'I'm overwhelmed by the optimism and cheerful nature of the kids in spite of their (sometimes severe) disabilities. They're always cheerful and tell great jokes. They make me realise that the things I think I have to complain about are very insignificant and that I should be very grateful for the good health of my own children and grandchildren.'

Helping people with disabilities

To volunteer to help with activities for people with disabilities, you need to complete a training program and a police check. You can volunteer on a number of fronts, from helping with Riding for the Disabled to reading to the blind. Or you can contact your local council about becoming a companion to a person with a disability. You'll receive genuine joy and reward for your efforts.

Hospital helper

Private and public hospitals need volunteers to help in many ways, both front of house and behind the scenes. Some of the tasks hospital volunteers take on include

- **Carer support:** You may like to provide a listening ear and a warm atmosphere to help family and friends of patients. Small things like a cheery face and a cup of tea are most welcome when you're supporting a sick friend or relative in hospital.

- **Flower stalls and kiosks:** You can sell at the kiosks or generally help out.

- **Fundraising:** This position is a much-needed support role, from selling raffle tickets to organising and supporting events.

- **Meet-and-greet patients and visitors:** Many people feel confused and wary when they enter a large hospital. You can help them with a friendly smile and information.

- **Office and administration support:** You can help in a variety of tasks, like retrieving files, answering requests and supporting other volunteers.

- **Patient support:** You can help patients by visiting them, delivering books, newspapers and magazines, and listening to their needs.

- **Patient transport:** If you have your own car, you can drive people to and from appointments

- **Therapy support:** You can support the therapists by helping out with games, discussions and music therapy.

For some roles you may require training.

If you volunteer in a children's hospital, you may find yourself working in the education centre, or reading stories and playing with the children. Contact your local hospital to find out more about its volunteer programs.

Animal-assisted therapy

Many hospitals, nursing homes and children's facilities use visiting animals for pet therapy. Animals such as dogs and cats can provide companionship to those who are lonely, and help physically rehabilitate patients who learn to groom or train an animal. Pets and handlers must undertake training. Check out Lead the Way at www.ltw.com.au for more information about animal-assisted therapy.

Zoo friends

Volunteers are welcome in zoos for a number of roles: You can take tours, work in the office, collect data on the animals or run touch tables where skins, skulls and other parts of animals are displayed. You need to undertake a training course before you begin your duties. Contact your local zoo for more information.

Volunteering abroad

Volunteering abroad is a great opportunity to help out those in need and at the same time experience a different culture up close. You need to set aside a block of time, like a month or two, and you also need to undergo a federal police check (see the section 'Background checks' earlier in the chapter).

Ask yourself this ...

Before you commit to volunteering abroad, think about the conditions you may work in and the conditions you want to work in, and then ask yourself the following questions:

- ✔ Am I flexible? Can I take on different work chores or a strange situation without much preparation?

- ✔ Am I self-reliant? Can I work on my own without any language support?

- ✔ Am I medically fit? (You may have to undergo a medical before you leave, and you may be working in an area that has no medical aid.)

- ✔ Am I prepared to give myself wholeheartedly?

- ✔ Can I adapt to a different culture?

- ✔ Can I eat anything — literally?

- ✔ Can I survive without a hot shower and a flushing toilet? Can I handle a communal toilet facility?

✔ Can I work in extremes of climate without the benefit of air-
conditioning or central heating?

✔ Do I genuinely care for people and my work?

Be honest with yourself when you answer these questions. Volunteering
abroad requires you to be flexible in your approach to others and adaptable
in your living conditions. If you don't think you can tolerate extremely hot
or cold weather or you're not able to eat unfamiliar food, for example, you
should consider volunteering closer to home.

If you genuinely want to volunteer abroad, you may be more comfortable
joining a highly organised group that can help you to ease into the new
situation. Talk to the organisation you wish to volunteer with and make sure
you understand what's expected of you and what support you receive. The
more you prepare yourself, the better you can cope in the field.

Ask about this ...

Some well-funded agencies pay for their volunteers' air fares and cover out-
of-pocket expenses, whereas others expect you to cover all your expenses
plus pay a fee for the experience.

You can find volunteer projects that are packaged as volunteer holidays, so
while you're helping others you're also free to do your own exploring. You
have to pay your own way and perhaps pay an extra fee to participate in
these projects.

Here are some questions you may like to ask a volunteer organisation:

✔ Can I take my spouse or partner?

✔ How much will the experience cost me financially?

✔ What sort of accommodation will I have and who will arrange it?

✔ Who arranges the necessary paperwork such as visas and permits?

✔ Who books and pays for my air fares and transport to and from the
airport?

✔ Who pays for any medical expenses like vaccinations?

✔ Will there be medical and security back-up?

✔ Will I be reimbursed for out-of-pocket expenses?

✔ Will I have the opportunity to travel and learn the language while I'm working?

✔ Will I work in a group or individually?

✔ Will there be other English-speaking volunteers?

✔ Will my insurance be paid by the organisation? (Check with the organisation to see whether you need more insurance than a normal travel insurance policy provides.)

The answers to these questions should help you decide how comfortable you are taking on the volunteer position. They also help you to

✔ arrange any necessary travel insurance, have appropriate vaccinations and put in place a back-up plan in case of an emergency

✔ plan side trips to expand your own knowledge and enjoyment of the region

✔ set a budget, so that you know how much you have to pay for travel, accommodation and out-of-pocket expenses

Some volunteer programs cost in excess of $3,000. Make sure that you thoroughly check out the terms and conditions before you set off.

What you get in return

You gain huge benefits from volunteering overseas. For example, you:

✔ Bring back knowledge and understanding of other cultures to your community

✔ Broaden your outlook by meeting people from different cultures with different standards of living

✔ Gain satisfaction from helping others

✔ Learn a new language — even if you're in a country for only a few months, you'll pick up the basics of the language and pronunciation

✔ See a side of the country no tourist sees from an air-conditioned bus

Volunteer opportunities

The list of overseas volunteer projects is seemingly endless. It's really a matter of deciding where your interests lie and which countries you'd like to visit. For instance, you can be a:

✔ **Carer at an orphanage:** Help out in any of the thousands of orphanages around the world where care and resources are in short supply.

- **Medical helper:** Your skills will be appreciated by many organisations around the world.

- **Sports coach:** Use your football, surfing or netball skills to teach children self-confidence as well as the English language.

- **Teacher of English:** Help children in a foreign country to learn the English language. If you don't have a suitable teaching qualification, you can attain one online or in a class.

- **Wildlife conservationist:** Go to the desert, the ocean, the forest or the ice to rescue, observe or feed the animals.

If you participate in a language project, you may spend some time in a language class and the remainder of your time volunteering. You may be billeted with a local family so you become involved in the local culture. You will also have time off to experience what the area has to offer. Some of your expenses may be paid for but you may have to pay for your own air fares, visas, insurance and out-of-pocket expenses.

Do your research. Know what you're getting into and talk to people who've volunteered. Here are a few Web sites to get you started:

- Australian Business Volunteers at www.abv.org.au. This organisation recruits volunteers who have at least five years professional experience in their field. Volunteers are needed to share their skills in many areas, including business and accounting, trade and technology, health, marketing, shipping, forestry and fisheries. Australian Business Volunteers covers all the costs its volunteers incur such as flights, visas and accommodation, and provides a daily living allowance for basic living costs.

- Australian Volunteers International at www.australianvolunteers.com. Working in partnership with organisations from other countries, volunteers are sent to train local workers in areas of skill shortage. Volunteers receive the cost of their air fares and are paid a living allowance.

Some projects advertise themselves as 'senior-friendly'. They don't define the term, but I assume they're saying that they value the wisdom and experience of age!

- Transitions Abroad at www.transitionsabroad.com lists senior-friendly volunteer projects, such as helping to preserve orang-utans and their habitat in Sumatra and Borneo, taking part in archaeological excursions and volunteering to work in HIV/AIDS prevention in Thailand.

✔ Volunteer Abroad at www.volunteerabroad.com.au lists nearly 200 programs suitable for 'senior volunteers' in countries from Argentina to Thailand.

Chapter 16

Cultivating a Hobby

A hobby can transport you to another world. When you're immersed in your hobby, enjoying what you're doing, time flies. The list of hobbies available is as long as your arm — way longer, in fact.

And by attending shows, swap meets and other activities your hobby can turn into a social affair, and your circle of friends will widen. You may even decide to expand your hobby into a money-making venture.

In this chapter, I discuss a few popular hobbies. I also take you through the basics you need to know if you decide to set up a small business based around your hobby.

Developing a Hobby

When you were working, you probably didn't have time to do anything more than dabble in your hobby — if you had one — unless you're one of the lucky few who turned their hobby into their job. In retirement, however, you have the time to really get stuck into a hobby. You need a few basics to enable you to cultivate your hobby:

- ✔ **An understanding spouse or partner:** This area could be tricky. However, the plus side to having a hobby is that it gives you both some time apart — unless you share the same hobby.

- ✔ **Enough money to indulge your habit:** Money is really just a matter of prioritising. You can always unload items you no longer need at swap meets or exchange them for things you now want. Anyway, what's wrong with eating baked beans five nights a week?

✔ **Somewhere to work and store your stuff:** This also may be a bit tricky, especially if you've made the decision to downsize. You may need to think creatively, or work out what you can live without in order to accommodate your hobby.

Finding a hobby

If you've never had a hobby, you may wonder what sort of hobby will suit you. This is obviously a very individual choice, but you can try the following exercise to help you to narrow down your choice.

1. **Imagine yourself spending time engrossed in a hobby.**

   What are you looking for from this hobby? Does it

   - Allow you to express yourself?
   - Get you out of the house?
   - Create social situations?
   - Give you opportunities for physical exercise?
   - Occupy enough of your time?
   - Provide mental stimulation?
   - Tap into your creativity?

2. **Think about the types of activities that may interest you.**

   You may find that one hobby alone won't fulfil all of your requirements. If you want something that helps you to keep physically active and that taps into your creativity, you may need to look at two hobbies, such as cycling and photography. Of course, you can combine the two — there are no hard and fast rules where hobbies are concerned!

Popular hobbies

The following section provides a sample of some of the most popular hobbies. Follow up on any that are of interest to you — you never know where they may lead you!

Sometimes you won't know whether a hobby will suit you until you've tried it. Don't be afraid to sample a number of different activities before you settle on one or two.

Book worms

If you're an avid reader and would like to share your insights and enjoyment with other readers, consider joining a book group. The Centre for Adult Education (CAE) runs book groups throughout Australia. You can join an existing group or start a new one. Visit www.cae.edu.au for more information.

Book groups are also springing up in book stores, so check out your local shop. You may receive a discount on the books you buy. Some stores provide members with a glass of wine or a cup of tea or coffee to enjoy at their meetings.

Bushwalking

To enjoy all that nature has to offer you can join a bushwalking club. Bushwalkers are a very friendly and inclusive bunch of people who enjoy socialising. Walks are well planned and rated from beginners to more experienced.

You can make some wonderful discoveries about your environment. You can even join in walks on overseas trips, which usually provide a cheap way to travel with a group of like-minded people. And you may have a close encounter with an echidna or a leech — or perhaps a bear if you go walking in Canada.

You may like to get involved in other outdoor pursuits such as bird-watching or orienteering.

Visit www.bushwalkingaustralia.org to find a bushwalking club in your area.

Collecting, from art to zoology

There are collectors, and then there are *serious collectors*. Collectors may have half a dozen or so items scattered around the house. Serious collectors have an entire house and several sheds full of their collection, and all items are rigorously researched and catalogued.

Collecting usually begins as a fascination for an item or a knick-knack — a teapot or motorbike, say, or whatever takes your fancy. If you watch the television show *The Collectors*, you have some idea of how your passion can dominate your life. You find collectors who're obsessed with just about anything you can imagine — snow cones, tractors, the colour orange ...

As your interest in a particular item grows, you start to amass more, perhaps without realising just how many items you have. When you find yourself having more than enough items to wear or use — or, more tellingly perhaps, you can't bear to wear or use *any* of the items — you can start to think of yourself as a true collector. Now you're getting *serious*. You need to make sure that the items are kept in good condition. You have to find out about their provenance and start cataloguing your collection.

A good place to start researching your collection is your local library. You can find reference books on a wide variety of subjects. Also try to get involved in relevant clubs, attend lectures and go to auctions and swap meets.

If your collection starts to get really large, you need to think about what to do with it when you're finished with it, or it's finished with you. For example, you can will it to your heirs, donate it to a museum or sell it (as a complete collection or split up).

If your collection becomes an investment, you have to pay capital gains tax if you sell the items. Likewise, if you will your collection to your heirs, they may be liable for capital gains tax if the collection is sold. Visit the Australian Taxation Office Web site at www.ato.gov.au for more advice on capital gains tax.

Games: Online and off

Games have entered a new era. You can play computer games on your own or join other gamers online. You can download free games and trial games in a few seconds. Computer games can be as simple as Solitaire and Free Cell or you can take hours to set up villages, towns and whole countries where you fight wars, build an environmentally sustainable environment or disappear into the world of mythology.

Simply type 'games' into your search engine and you get a million or more game Web sites to choose from. To play it safe stick to well-known sites like Nine MSN (http://arcade.ninemsn.com.au) and the Australian Broadcasting Commission (www.abc.net.au).

If you download games from unknown Web sites, make sure that you have all the requisite virus protection software on your computer. You can download virus protection software from the Web (type 'virus protection' into your search engine) or talk to a sales rep at your local computer store.

For face-to-face interaction with real humans, you can play bridge, poker, mah jong or any number of board or card games. Your local neighbourhood house and U3A will have facilities for card game enthusiasts to get together and play. They also offer bridge lessons if you need to brush up your skills. If you'd like to know more about bridge clubs and competitions, visit the Australian Bridge Federation at www.abf.com.au.

You can also play Scrabble at competition level. Scrabble Australia's Web site at www.scrabble.org.au has lists of clubs to join, online games and competitions around Australia.

Green thumbs

Gardeners are a hardy lot. They don't retire, they just grow into the landscape. If you love gardening, retirement is the time when you can really get stuck into your hobby. If you join your local gardening club, you can meet plenty of like-minded green thumbs and get the chance to swap or buy plants and seedlings for minimal cost. Ask your local council for details of clubs in your area.

Young children love to garden — well, they like to get wet and muddy and sometimes eat snails. Encourage your grandchildren to sow some vegetable seeds or seedlings and help them to look after their crop. Then you can have fun together cooking the resulting produce.

Think hard before you make the commitment to move to an apartment if gardening is important to you. But if you simply have to downsize and say goodbye to your garden, all is not lost. Having your own garden is not the only way you can enjoy your hobby. Here are some other options you can try:

- **Join your local community garden scheme and work your own allotment.** You meet new people who share your passion and with whom you can swap tips. Ask your local council how to access an allotment or visit the Web site of the Australian City Farms & Community Gardens Network at www.communitygarden.org.au.

- **Do some garden maintenance for an elderly gardener.** Many older people would treasure your help in their garden. You can bring pleasure to yourself and someone else by helping in this way. Ask friends and neighbours if they know anyone who'd like some help.

- **Take part in an overseas garden tour.** These tours are usually hosted by knowledgeable gardeners and take you to the beautiful gardens of the world. To find out more simply type 'garden tours' into your search engine or talk to your local travel agent.

Genealogy

Don't underestimate how easy it is to get hooked on tracking down your family history. Begin your search by talking to relatives and asking whether they have any old birth, death or marriage certificates. You may even find that someone has already had a stab at the family tree. Your elderly relatives will have lots of family stories that can also point you in the right direction.

Frank's quest

My involvement in family history began with a simple request from a relative for some dates for my great uncles, who were killed in the First World War. This led to contact with my cousin, Frank, in England. Frank had started on his own family history when he retired and needed some more information about the Australian side of the family. After nearly 10 years, Frank is almost at the end of his quest. The finished work will be magnificent, with photos of four generations. It will take a whole wall to display it.

'Initially, I came rather reluctantly to begin research into the Kennedy family history', Frank says. 'Despite going back to 1795, I had run out of leads after some lengthy research into my father's English family (Ellis). I knew that the Kennedys originated in Northern Ireland. My experiences in the Ellis investigation helped to get me started with the Kennedys. I also found Family Historian Version 3 by Calico Pie, which enables me to attach photos to individual entries. This made things come alive!

'Little did I realise that my quest would take me to Ireland, Australia, Brazil, the US, South Africa and the Isle of Man. I've found 260 individuals to be added to the tree. By far the greatest number are in Australia; they are the descendants of Elizabeth Kennedy, who emigrated to Australia. When family members are spread far and wide, it's vital to have helpful contacts in each country.'

Most local libraries now have dedicated genealogy sections with access to various online databases. Your state library will also have a large genealogy section. Besides atlases, biographies and histories of surnames, you can find information such as

- Australian cemetery and immigration records
- Ancestry library edition, which gives you access to more than a billion names
- Australian indigenous family history
- Civil registrations in England and Wales
- Church of Jesus Christ and Latter Day Saints' files
- Electoral roles and directories
- Indexes to civil registrations of births, deaths and marriages
- Lists of convicts
- Military/service records

The Internet has a wealth of Web sites dedicated to genealogy and family history. For instance, the National Library of Australia Web site at `www.nla.gov.au/oz/genelist.html` has numerous links to both national and international Web sites that may help you in your search.

See *Tracing Your Family History Online For Dummies*, Australian Edition, by Matthew Helm (Wiley Publishing Australia Pty Ltd) for more advice and information.

Golf

Essentially, the game of golf is a never-ending contest between you and the golf course — regardless of who you're playing against. The maddening thing is, no matter how infuriated you get when you play, the game hooks you in so that you *always* come back for more.

Golf has a reputation of being a wealthy person's sport, but that's not the case. Some clubs do have annual fees in the thousands, but others have fees in the hundred-dollar range. Don't forget, if you're a member of a golf club you can play as many times per week as you like — in effect, the more you play, the less you pay.

Have a couple of lessons if you're serious about the game. This will prevent you from developing too many bad habits. The handicapping system of golf means that everyone has an equal chance to win a competition.

Log onto the Golf Australia Web site at `www.golfaustralia.org.au` for more information.

Lawn bowls

Lawn bowls has a new face in the 21st century. Once the domain of oldies dressed in white with very sensible shoes, the sport has opened its doors to younger people, more flamboyant dress and even bare feet.

Try bowls out at a club near you. Pop in and play a few ends. Or visit the Bowls Australia Web site at `www.bowls-aust.com.au` to discover what the game's all about and how to contact your local club.

Patchwork and quilting

Patchwork is traditionally practised in a community setting. Before the advent of television, women would gather together to create warm quilted clothing and bed covers from fabric scraps. Patchwork is now as much a work of art as it is a craft. If you like to sew, find a group of like-minded people near you. They may gather in a patchwork shop, at your local community hall or in the adult education centre.

Use the following Web sites to start you on your quest:

- ✔ Australian Patchwork and Quilting at www.apqmagazine.com.au
- ✔ Australian Quilters Association at http://home.vicnet.net.au/~ausquilt/welcome.htm
- ✔ National Quilt Register at http://discover.collectionsaustralia.net/nqr/

If you're a quilter you'll be bowled over by the Amish town of Intercourse, Lancaster, in the US: You can visit the many quilting shops and the quilt museum and see the magnificent quilts displayed there.

Pets

If you've always wanted a pet but have been too busy, you may decide that now's the time to find your new furry companion. Choose your pet carefully. Don't choose an active dog because you're going to start an exercise regime: Start the exercise program first, *before* you get the dog — or there might be two of you sitting on the couch watching day-time television. If you want to know more about choosing a pet, go to Chapter 18.

If you're thinking of showing your pet, the Dogs4Sale Web site at www.dogs4sale.com.au has some good tips for getting started, whatever your pet may be. You find information on going to shows, talking to owners and generally finding out how showing works. You should also talk to breeders of the animal you want to purchase to find out what standard of animal you should buy.

Water sports

Have you thought about water sports? Like many Australians, you probably live on or near the coast, or near a lake or river. More and more retirees are taking to the water in one form or another.

Were you a surfer in your youth? Take down that Malibu, dust off your wetsuit and ride the waves again. You may find many of your old compatriots ready to greet you. If you're a novice, sign up for lessons. Try a paddle board so that you can stand up and surf the smaller inshore waves.

Surfing isn't the only water sport available, of course. If you're like me and prefer to enter the water without a board you can don your flippers and take to the waves for the ultimate thrill of body surfing. Those who don't mind getting wet and blown about can have a go at windsurfing or kite surfing.

Perhaps you prefer to stay above the water rather than in it? You can go fishing, paddle a kayak, canoe or outrigger, or sail a yacht.

You'll find details of tour companies that provide kayaking adventures around the coast or on inland rivers in the travel section of your weekend paper or on the Internet — just search under 'kayaking'.

Woodwork

Many Australians enjoy retiring to their sheds and making objects out of wood. At any country market you can find someone selling handmade bowls, benches, knitting needles and other beautifully crafted objects. You can use simple carving and shaping tools or get the whole shebang of lathes and saws.

The Woodworking Australia Web site at www.ubeaut.com.au has information on events, products, suppliers, woodworkers and much more.

Financing your hobby

Hobbies can be expensive, and unless you have unlimited resources you may need to raise some funds to finance your hobby from time to time.

Try these ideas:

✔ Set up an online account to sell your excess items or any double-ups you may have

✔ Sell what you make or produce at local markets

✔ Teach your hobby at your local community centre or neighbourhood house

✔ Visit swap meets and trade with other hobbyists

Turning Your Hobby into a Small Business

After you have the time to devote to your hobby, you may find that it expands so much you want to start selling your products or services. Before you know it you're running a small business. Before you head too far down this track, take some time to think about what running a small business requires in terms of your time and business know-how.

Most hobbies grow organically rather than in a structured way. If this happens to you, you may find that you're committing more time, energy and money to your hobby than you anticipated. A successful business needs planning — and not just business planning. You're the mainstay of your business: You need to assess the amount of time you're prepared to put in and the skills you do — or don't — possess.

On the plus side, a well-run small business gives you immense satisfaction. You're your own boss: You can run your business however you choose. Having your own business will give structure to your day and a reason for you to get up in the morning and it will keep you mentally active.

Do you have the time to commit to a business venture?

How much time do you want to devote to your hobby business? Retirement brings with it the promise of freedom from time constraints. You've just begun to enjoy the occasional sleep-in, long lunch or overseas trip. Now that you've thrown off the shackles of full-time work you have some balance in your life and can devote more time to friends and family and activities that are important to you.

Think carefully about how much time you want to tie up in a business venture. Calculate how much time and energy you want to give to the following (and not necessarily in this order):

- Entertainment
- Friends and family
- Health and fitness
- Travel
- Your partner or spouse

After you've worked this out, you know how much you can commit to your business. Alternatively, if you've taken early retirement you may enjoy devoting yourself to building your business while your partner is still working. Or you may decide to make the business a family affair.

What are your strengths and weaknesses?

Even if you decide that you have the time to commit to a small business, you need to assess whether you have the skills to run that business successfully. You also need to look at the opportunities that are available to you and the threats that may be in your way. One of the best ways to do this is to complete a strengths, weaknesses, opportunities and threats (SWOT) analysis. A SWOT analysis is a visual representation of the things you need to consider before you start any venture (see Figure 16-1).

SWOT stands for

- **Strengths:** What are your strengths? For example, if you want to sell your patchwork quilts, are your products of exceptional quality? Do you have a good eye for colour and pattern?

- **Weaknesses:** What are your weaknesses? Do you struggle with figures? Can you keep organised records?

- **Opportunities:** What opportunities are out there for your business? Is there a niche area in the market, perhaps, that you can fill?

- **Threats:** What are the threats that may impact on your business? Is anyone else targeting the same market? If so, what are these competitors charging for their products and is there enough business to support you all?

Strengths	Weaknesses
Opportunities	Threats

Figure 16-1:
A SWOT
analysis.

Running a business requires some very necessary interpersonal skills:

- **Communication skills:** You must have good communication skills. At a minimum you have to communicate with suppliers and customers. Be clear and concise in all your dealings. Make sure you use the right communication medium: Sometimes a phone call or personal meeting conveys your message more clearly than an email or text. Understand what you want to get out of each encounter. Are you trying to sell, explain your method or get paid? Map out an agenda for each meeting so that you cover all your points.

- **Negotiation skills:** Are you a good negotiator? Be careful to work out your bottom line — this is the price you will not go below otherwise you'll lose money. Try to think about all the angles, and if something comes up that takes you off guard, get back to the other person — don't make rash decisions on the spot.

- **Organisational skills:** Can you keep organised records? You need to know what's happening in your business: How much you're making and how much you're spending. You need a good filing system. Get some computer training if you don't already have this knowledge so that you can track your business efficiently.

In addition, you need to be physically and mentally strong. The success of your business depends on you, at least in its initial stages. If you become unwell, you have to keep working and running your business.

Last, but not least, you need the support of your family, especially your partner or spouse. Developing a small business usually requires you to put the business first, before anything or anyone else.

Developing a business plan

Planning is the *essential ingredient* for a successful business. You need a *business plan* not only to apply for a business loan but also to know where your business is heading. Making a plan allows you to focus on:

- Where you're going (your business goals)

- How you'll get there (the steps you'll take to achieve those goals)

Here's what you need to do:

1. **Begin by writing your vision.**

   This need be only a couple of short sentences. Maybe you want to create the best educational toys for children? Or make the best gluten-free pickles and chutneys?

2. **Decide how, when and where your business will operate and be organised.**

   Are you going to work from home, rent premises, share premises or invest in a freehold property?

3. **Analyse the market.**

   What competitors are out there? What do they charge? Does your product or service fill a niche in the market? How can you market your product or service? How can you sell your product or service?

4. **Develop a financial plan.**

   What are your start-up expenses? What are your ongoing expenses? How much can you charge for your product or service? How long will it take for you to *break even* (have your income exceed your expenses)? Note that you probably won't start to break even for *at least* 12 months, so you need to factor in the capital to sustain yourself until then.

Applying for an ABN

When your hobby moves into a money-making venture you can apply for an Australian Business Number (ABN). You don't have to apply for an ABN if your business turns over *less than* $75,000 a year. However, if you trade without an ABN, other businesses that deal with you have to deduct tax of 48.5 per cent from all payments made to you.

To find out whether you satisfy the criteria for applying for an ABN go to the ATO's Web site at www.ato.gov.au. To register for an ABN go to the business.gov.au Web site at www.business.gov.au. If you think you may already have an ABN, you can look it up on this site.

Registering for GST

If your business turns over *more than* $75,000 per year, you must register for Goods and Services Tax (GST). You can't register for GST if you don't have an ABN (see preceding section), but note that you don't have to register for GST if you have an ABN.

You may find that you want to register for GST anyway, because by registering you can claim back the 10 per cent GST that your suppliers charge you.

After you've registered for GST, you need to add GST to all your tax invoices, collect this money, offset the amount against the GST you've already paid and send the difference to the ATO via quarterly Activity Statements.

You can't charge for GST unless you're registered for GST.

Talk to your accountant or financial adviser for more help in sorting out the financial side of your new business, especially how to handle GST.

To find out more about GST and to register for GST go to www.business. gov.au.

Help is at hand

Heaps of information is available to help you to set up and run your small business.

✔ Download a business plan template from www.business.gov.au.

✔ Get help from the government's small business Web site at www. business.gov.au. You can find information on a wealth of topics, including:

- E-business

- Employing people

- Home-based businesses

- Importing and exporting

- Marketing research

- Licences and regulation

- Occupational health and safety.

✔ Read the following:

- *Business Plans For Dummies*, Australian Edition, by Paul Tiffany, Steven Peterson and Veechi Curtis (Wiley Publishing Australia Pty Ltd)

- *Small Business For Dummies*, Second Australian Edition, by Veechi Curtis (Wiley Publishing Australia Pty Ltd).

✔ Visit your nearest Business Enterprise Centre for assistance and advice in running your business. To find you nearest centre check out `www.beca.org.au`.

Home-based businesses

If your business isn't essential to your financial survival, you can limit your venture. Instead of opening a shop to sell your goods, you can sell them from home, from a stall at local markets or online.

To set up a home business you may need to get a licence and permit. Each state and territory has its own regulations, as does each local council. If you're working from home, use only a small area of your house and don't impinge on your neighbours with noise or traffic, you may not need a permit. Visit `www.business.gov.au` or the Business Licence Information Service at `www.bli.net.au` to find out the requirements in your state or territory. You must comply with any state or local council regulations to work from home.

Business Victoria at `www.business.vic.gov.au` publishes a guide to setting up a home business. Much of the information on this Web site is pertinent to home-based businesses in any state or territory. You'll find advice on:

✔ Basic requirements for home-based businesses

✔ Tax issues for home-based businesses

✔ Setting up your work area and insuring your business

From teaching to rearing goats

Fred James was a teacher and head of school until school closures gave him the opportunity to retire early and do what he'd always dreamt about — raising animals and growing his own vegetables.

Fred had kept a few animals while he was working, but with the long hours he spent at school he had little time for his livestock. Retirement allowed Fred to have a more disciplined approach to his livestock and gardening. Money was not his motivator. As Fred says, 'My real motivation was to keep physically active, to have a structured day and to decide my daily destiny.'

Fred made some money by selling his goat's milk and plants from his property. But his plan to raise turkeys didn't work out, because the installation costs of cold storage units was too expensive.

'Now, 21 years down the line from early retirement I can look back with pleasure on my retirement hobbies and the pleasure and occasional pain they gave me', he says. 'I can look at my garden and see the impact that I've had on it. I thank my wife, Nora, for her contribution to those hobbies and for her patience when garden and animals came first. My tip for retirement is to develop your interests. Look for challenges, don't just vegetate.'

Part V
Relationships: Now and in the Future

Glenn Lumsden

'The kids are long gone, we're retired,
we can finally start doing all those things
we used to do when we first met.
Can you remember what they were?'

In this part ...

During your working life you built successful relationships with your work colleagues, but now the structure of your life and friendships are about to change. In this part, I discuss strategies for retaining existing friendships and building new relationships with family and friends. Retirement is a time of adjustment within the family: Suddenly, you're sharing a space with someone else 24/7. I provide tips on maintaining relationships and sharing the family home. Finally, I give you some ideas for sharing the care of elderly parents.

Chapter 17

Adjusting to Changes on the Home Front

Retirement brings with it changes in many familiar routines. You no longer have your day ready planned — usually, you don't need to be anywhere or do anything at any particular time. Not having a set place to go to each weekday means that your home is probably your centre of activity. One of the biggest changes you may face is sharing this space 24 hours a day, seven days a week with the person you live with.

In this chapter, I give you some tips on how to share your life with your spouse, partner or house mate on a 24/7 basis. It's amazing how chores and normal routines, like using your computer, suddenly take on a whole new meaning when there are two of you wanting to use the same items, perhaps at the same time. I also tackle the subject of inviting an elderly relative to share your home.

Adjusting to Home Life

Deciding how to spend your new-found freedom in retirement will be more difficult for some than others. If you've always worked part-time you'll have developed other activities to keep you busy, such as gardening, working on your fitness, some type of craft activity or volunteering to help others.

However, if you go from working full-time 10+ hours per day to zero, you may feel a bit lost for the first few months of your retirement.

Don't get into the habit of hanging around the house in your tracksuit or you may encounter problems with your partner, and if you live alone this isn't very conducive to starting the next phase of your life. The best antidote is to get up, get dressed and take some action. You'll find heaps of suggestions for keeping active in Chapters 11 to 16.

Get moving. The more inactive you are, the greater the likelihood that your health and wellbeing will deteriorate.

Sharing the same space, 24/7

In your former life you and your spouse, partner or house mate got up, got dressed, ate breakfast, stacked the dishwasher and left for work — or perhaps just one of you did the chores before leaving for work. Either way, you were occupied somewhere else for at least eight hours a day on work days and didn't see each other during that time. Now you may both be in the same space for 24 hours a day, seven days a week.

If you're not in a partnered relationship but have joined forces with a good friend to share living expenses, you probably live a more independent existence than a married or de facto couple, but you still have to negotiate the chores and living space.

This new experience in living arrangements can be a recipe for disaster, or it can be wonderful. You may find yourselves getting under each other's feet at the beginning, but as you adjust to the new situation it should all run quite smoothly.

Try these 10 popular tips to help you navigate your living space in retirement:

- ✔ **Avoid asking, 'What's for lunch?'** 'What do you want for lunch?' is slightly more likely to get a positive response. Even better still, make the lunch.

- ✔ **Find out how to cook.** Get a recipe book and work your way through it. This means shopping for the ingredients as well.

- ✔ **Give each other time to do your own thing.** It may be a bit confronting at first to see your partner going off to language lessons or lunch with friends, but you'll soon have your own activities.

- ✔ **Initiate some meal planning.** Don't greet the question, 'What'll we have for dinner?' with the answer, 'We just had breakfast!' It may be true, but unless you decide to eat out for every meal (which you can do, if you want to) you need to do some basic food planning. You can even devise a menu roster for each week if you're well organised.

- ✔ **Let go of the reins regarding cooking, cleaning and home maintenance (if you hold them).** Your partner may not do things to your strict standards, but the house will no doubt remain standing.

- ✔ **Notice what needs to be done around the house.** Don't suffer from domestic blindness. If you're planning a day out together, recognise that you have to do a bit more than get dressed and hop in the car.

- ✔ **Plan some activities you can do each week to take you out of the house.** It's important to expand your circle of friends.

- ✔ **Respect each other's way of adjusting to your new lifestyle.** Give each other space and respect each other's routines.

- ✔ **Share some relaxing time together during the week.** You can get very busy in your retirement, but remember you're not at work, so you can take time off to be together.

- ✔ **Take a trip together when you first retire, if possible.** This will ease you both into each other's company again before you tackle the new living arrangements.

Respecting each other's territory

It's easy to tread on each other's toes when you're adjusting to a new lifestyle. However you decide to approach the first few weeks of your retirement, it's a time of adjustment for both of you.

If you and your partner decide to retire at the same time, you need to take a fresh look at how you interact with each other and how you handle the chores (see the sections 'Making Time to be Together' and 'Negotiating the Housework (What a Chore!)' later in the chapter).

On the other hand, if your partner has been holding the fort at home while you worked, he or she will have developed set routines covering everyday domestic arrangements such as how much soap powder to put in the washing machine and which cleaners to use in the bathroom. Your partner may also have a lifestyle routine, like going to French classes on Mondays, helping his or her parents on Tuesdays, meeting friends for lunch on Wednesdays, looking after the grandchildren on Thursdays and volunteering at the hospital on Fridays.

Where does this leave you? What do you do while your partner's out? Suddenly, unless you've already organised your own activities, you're faced with many empty hours each day. You can do any of the following:

- ✔ Investigate volunteering opportunities to help others

- ✔ Join your partner in his or her activities

- ✔ Sit on the couch and watch television (but the thrill of that may not last long or make your partner happy)

- ✔ Take up your own hobbies

If you volunteer to do the washing and cleaning, ask your partner to walk you around the house and explain how things work and what needs to be done, just as you would induct a new worker to your workplace.

Giving each other room to breathe

Realistically, if you've been dedicated to work for the last 30 years you probably won't have much territory in the home. And your partner may find the same thing. Every corner of the house has already been put to good use. And if you've downsized, you may have even less space than you did before. You may yearn for a shed or a study, somewhere to work on your hobby.

When your hobby starts to flow over into limited living space, this can be a real problem and a bone of contention. Similarly, if you have only one spare room and you both want to use it for your hobbies, you may encroach on each other's space — and get on each other's nerves. One answer is for you to join a Men's Shed (see Chapter 19) or enrol in a course at your local community centre or University of the Third Age (see Chapter 13). This will give you space to work on your hobby and an opportunity to get out of the house and make some friends. Or you could look around your area for an unused garage or shed to rent for a small fee and make this your hobby headquarters.

In addition, you may have to share the same computer and printer. You're probably used to having a workplace computer with all the latest software and technical support. Now, if one of you wants to research your family tree and the other wants to write a book, your one desktop computer may no longer be adequate. You either have to work out a roster system or invest in more hardware. If you have two computers, consider networking them so that you can share your Internet connection, files and software.

You need to retain some independence and friendships after retirement. Keep in contact with old colleagues with whom you can reminisce occasionally.

Avoiding the hero or martyr role

To avoid conflict it's easy to fall into the hero or martyr role, especially when one of you has retired and the other continues to work. You may find yourself taking on all the domestic chores and in so doing limit your opportunities for getting on with your retirement plans.

Be aware that doing jobs around the house can become an excuse for not getting involved in other activities.

Negotiating the Housework (What a Chore!)

Although these days men in paid work are taking on more household chores, typically women do the majority of the work around the house, whether they're working full-time or not. Men spend more time on home maintenance. Now that you've retired, you can totally switch roles, keep the status quo or do the chores together — it's entirely up to you. The following sections include some things to think about when you're negotiating the chores.

Meals and menus

Meal planning and preparation are never-ending activities. When you both worked you may have taken sandwiches to work every day or eaten at cafes or restaurants. Now that you're home, do you keep to your old routine and make sandwiches? Do you wait for your partner so that you can eat together? Do you both eat the same type of meal? Who'd have thought lunch could be so fraught — and yet it can be a big point of contention for newly retired couples.

In addition, your partner may ask you what you'd like for dinner — or you may ask your partner. Unfortunately, this question probably comes straight after breakfast as the day's plans are made. You or your partner may not be used to thinking about what to eat for dinner until you arrive home and smell what's cooking. The question may seem annoying, but if no-one plans ahead you'll end up having takeaway or cheese on toast. This is okay once in a while, but if you eat fatty foods regularly your toes will soon disappear from view under your expanding stomach.

You can discuss the lunch question or agree to just roll with the punches. It'll probably settle itself as the days unfold, but the evening meal can be more difficult to negotiate. Preparing healthy meals is time-consuming and at this stage of your life takeaways and rushed lunches come home to roost, especially on the waistline.

You can decide to stop cooking completely and eat only raw foods, or you can make cooking an enjoyable pursuit. Follow these suggestions to take the chore out of mealtimes:

- **Become food savvy and ecologically minded.** Find out what ingredients are in the foodstuffs you eat and how many kilometres they've travelled to your table.

- **Challenge yourselves with new foods and dishes.** Cook foods from around the globe.

- **Concentrate on getting your five serves of vegetables and two serves of fruit every day.** And make them tasty as well as nutritious.

- **Enrol in a cooking class to learn how to cook something you don't usually eat.**

- **Grow your own food.** You need only a small plot of land — or even just a few tubs — to grow your own herbs, lettuce, cherry tomatoes, snow peas and dwarf beans. Most vegetables have a dwarf variety that crops heavily and tastes so much better than food you buy from the supermarket.

- **Join a community garden scheme.** As well as having some space to grow your own veggies, you meet like-minded gardeners and get lots of hints and advice on growing produce.

- **Pick your own produce from farms.** Make jams and bottle or freeze the excess.

- **Shop at farmers' markets.** Soak up the atmosphere and choose the freshest seasonal produce — the food has so much taste.

Who does the cooking?

Before Jim retired he didn't think much about mealtimes. His wife, Lyn, produced an evening meal most nights — and if not, they had takeaway or ate out. When Jim retired, Lyn began asking him what he wanted to eat for dinner. He really didn't care. As the weeks turned into months he found he was presented with a blank shopping list with the word 'dinner' in bold print scrawled across it.

He eventually got the hint and decided to sit down and talk to Lyn about the cooking routine. Lyn explained that she'd cooked thousands of meals over the last 30 years and wanted a break. They had friends who ate out for every meal except breakfast. They could do this too because they lived in an inner-city suburb with a lot of restaurants, but they decided there were days when they just wanted to kick back and not have to go out to eat. Also, unless they chose carefully it wouldn't do their fat intake much good either, and they'd both gained weight already since Jim had retired.

They both agreed to take responsibility for their diet, with each cooking two or three meals per week. Jim found this difficult at first, but the more he practised the better his cooking became, and he began to enjoy the process and take pride in the outcome.

Cleaning and home maintenance

Some people's standards of clean are more strict than others, but most people feel better in clean and reasonably tidy surroundings. Cleaning is another constant. Your may feel that your house is a bit like the Sydney Harbour Bridge — you never finish maintaining it, inside or out: No sooner have you completed one cleaning cycle than you have to start at the beginning again.

Traditionally, women cook and clean, and men paint and mow the lawns, but you may share the roles differently in your home. What happens if the person who's cooked and cleaned for 30 years decides to retire from that particular job? Or the one who's fixed leaking taps and mown the lawn wants to do other things?

Unless you decide to outsource all the chores, at some stage you have to face the inevitable and negotiate who does what. Follow these tips to make the process as smooth as possible:

- ✔ Sit down together with a glass of wine or cup of coffee and talk about what has to be done.

- ✔ List all the regular jobs in and around the house each week. Work out how often you need to clean the toilets, iron clothes, shop, mow the lawn, sweep the paths, trim the hedges, vacuum, wash the dishes and so on. Then add the special tasks like major painting jobs, pruning and rubbish removal.

- ✔ Decide who'll do each job and how many jobs you can afford or want to outsource. If you've always hated mowing the lawn, perhaps your partner can take this on in exchange for cleaning the toilets? Or perhaps you can pay someone to do these chores.

- ✔ Make cleaning and home maintenance a team event. Set aside a regular time when you both blitz the house and garden. If your partner loves vacuuming and you love gardening, let your partner take on the vacuuming while you fix the garden.

- ✔ Make sure that you can both take on some of the maintenance roles. If you or your partner lack the skills required, go along to some DIY lessons at your local hardware store or neighbourhood house.

By working together, you find that the chores are done in no time and you're both a lot happier.

Making Time to be Together

I've talked about how to come to terms with the nitty-gritty of everyday life together. You also need to think about how you and your partner can spend some *enjoyable* time together. It may seem strange having to address this issue, but as you get used to retirement and your activities take over, you may find that you're busier than ever. Many retirees really do wonder how they ever had time to work. If you're both involved in different hobbies or volunteer jobs, you may find that you're spending less and less time together.

One way to catch up is to set aside time each week for a special lunch or dinner. You don't have to eat out, but you can make the effort to spruce up a bit, perhaps have some friends over and cook a special meal.

Having lunch out somewhere is a good way to enjoy some relaxing time together. Better still, make a day of it:

✔ Find somewhere you haven't been before and explore the region or area before or after you eat.

✔ Take a picnic and ride your bikes to a river or other scenic spot. Or load your bikes onto your car or the train and explore one of the local cycle ways.

✔ Take public transport to a spot, say, 10 kilometres away, have lunch then walk back home, stopping for afternoon tea or coffee along the way.

Here are some further suggestions to get you thinking of ways you can spend more time together:

✔ Do something neither of you have done before, like hang-gliding or learning to dance the salsa.

✔ Make a list of art galleries, museums, nature reserves, wineries or other places you want to see and visit a different one each week or fortnight.

✔ Take some long trips or short breaks, exploring a different part of the country and staying away overnight.

✔ Visit a spa, enjoy the mineral baths and have a massage: You'll both feel revitalised.

And this may sound a little indelicate, but don't forget to keep the romance in your life. What's that old saying about snow on the roof but fire in the hearth?

The Second Car: Independence Versus Expense

Most working families have two cars these days. However, in the retirement rationalisation process, you may decide that you now need only one car. This makes good sense economically and environmentally. But, before you actually take the step and sell one of your cars, consider how you may manage sharing the one car. Perhaps you can cope perfectly well, especially if you live near regular public transport routes. However, if you don't have access to public transport you may find that sharing the one car can curtail your or your partner's activities.

If you suggest selling your partner's car and keeping yours to share, you may be met with unexpected resistance. Be aware that a car can mean more than just a way to get around. It can also represent independence and a sense of freedom. Many older people report that having to stop driving is the most limiting factor on their independent living. While you're not at this stage yet, of course, losing your car can still have a negative psychological effect.

Sharing the Care of Aged Parents

One of the fastest growing clubs these days is the 100 years and over club. Australia has the second-longest life expectancy after Japan.

One great example of a long-living Australian is Emily Beatrice 'Bea' Riley, who celebrated her 112th birthday on 13 October 2008 with a tipple of champagne surrounded by friends and relatives. Bea lived in her own home until she was 99.

Unfortunately, not all elderly people are able to live independently when they're in their 80s and 90s, let alone their 100s. There may come a time when one of your elderly parents or relatives has to either go into aged-care accommodation or move in with you. If you opt for aged-care accommodation, you'll need to understand how the aged-care system works. Chapter 9 explains the aged-care system and also discusses finding suitable accommodation for your relative.

Handling the emotional and time commitment

Although you may be able to deal with the practical aspects of getting your parent assessed for aged care and either finding suitable accommodation and settling your parent in or helping your parent to stay in his or her own home, you may not be prepared for the physical and emotional commitment required of you or your partner.

To help you cope, you need to be able to share the process with those closest to you. Talk things through and apportion tasks to each person according to their strengths. One of you may be better able to understand the financial side of the process, while another is better at sorting out the finer details of the living conditions in an aged-care home.

If you're lucky, you have time to plan ahead so that you can sort things out without the process taking too much of a toll on you. However, the reality is that one of your parents will die sooner than you're ready for (even if your parents live to be 100, you're never really ready when they die) and your remaining parent may need help managing at home or moving into aged-care accommodation. Or your seemingly healthy and indestructible parent may suddenly become ill and need care. If this happens soon after you retire, you have to factor in a whole new set of variables while adjusting to your new life.

You need to rely on all your skills at this time, including

- **Communicating:** It's important to be able to communicate your feelings to your partner and family and to enlist their help. You also have to talk to a wide range of people, from assessment team leaders to aged-care managers, doctors and nursing staff.

- **Planning:** The more you can plan ahead, the easier the process of placing your relative in care will be. Ensure your relative has been assessed by the Aged Care Assessment Team (ACAT) and keep the assessment up-to-date. That way, you can more easily swing into action when the time comes. See Chapter 10 for more detail on ACAT assessments.

- **Time management:** Be prepared to devote a number of weeks to sourcing appropriate care for your parent. You may have to put other plans on hold, and your partner's or family's help in holding the fort and listening to your worries is invaluable.

Don't forget to share some down time with your partner or family — go to a movie, have a laugh.

Inviting your elderly relative to move in with you

Asking your elderly relative to move in with you may come as a perfectly natural progression for you. If you grew up in an extended family, taking care of your parents will be part of the life process. On the other hand, caring for an elderly relative in your own home may be a huge commitment and can really change the dynamic of your household.

The change in your household structure will cause a change in your relationship with your partner too. Before you make the commitment to accommodate your relative in your home, you need to sit down together and discuss all the pros and cons of doing so. And, more importantly, you must reach a united decision. The option won't work if one of you harbours resentment about the situation — and this can ultimately lead to problems in your relationship.

You can accommodate your relative in your home in several ways:

✔ In a separate bedroom, but sharing the communal rooms in your home

✔ In a separate section of your home, so that your relative has private use of a bedroom and bathroom and perhaps a living room

✔ In a granny flat attached to your home or within your property grounds

The size of your home and your financial constraints may well dictate which option you choose.

And don't forget that help is available if you decide to care for your relative in your own home: You're not on your own.

✔ Access all the council and government services available to help you look after your relative. See Chapter 9 for more information.

✔ Join a carer's group. See the Department of Health and Ageing's Aged Care Web site at www.agedcareaustralia.gov.au to find a group near you, or contact your local council for information on carer support networks.

✔ Organise respite care for your relative for a short time each year, so that you and your partner can get away and spend time together alone.

Chapter 18

Maintaining Relationships with Your Nearest and Dearest

*W*hen you retire you move from a structured work environment to a complete absence of structure. And it's not only your work that changes — so do your relationships.

When I was working, I had my day planned out even before I arrived at work. My long 'to-do' list was waiting for me, but so were my colleagues, some of whom over the years had become my friends. I loved being able to have a cup of coffee and a quick chat, or to catch up after work.

After I retired I moved to a different part of the city and spent a lot of time out of town. The structure of my day changed and so too did my friendships. When you embark on a new phase of your life maintaining friendships can be hard — especially if you move a long distance away from your friends.

In this chapter, I help you to explore the changing nature of your relationships with your family and friends after retirement. I outline action plans you can use to actively maintain old friendships and establish new ones. I give you some activities to use to build stronger relationships with your family. I also cover the benefits and requirements of pet ownership.

Understanding Your Relationships and Roles

In order to understand your relationships with others, you need to understand your own behaviour. Retirement offers you a great opportunity to reflect on your workplace behaviour and consider how this may translate from the cut and thrust of the work environment to the more laid-back social setting of retirement.

You take on different roles during different times in your life. In the workplace you may be the person everyone consults for an expert opinion or the one who's relied on to spot the flaws in new proposals. Because you often spend more waking hours at work than at home, you can easily get stuck in your workplace role and behave the same way at home. In retirement, though, you need to let go and adopt a new persona.

Realising that professional role-playing has its place

Begin by thinking about some of the roles you play at work. It's easy to slot into a particular role or persona in the work environment. Here's a list of workplace roles:

- **Clarifier:** Wants the issues explained
- **Devil's advocate:** Examines the negative side of any proposal
- **Expert:** The knowledge giver
- **Implementer:** Gets the project underway
- **Initiator:** Comes up with new ideas
- **Judge:** Delivers the decision
- **Peacemaker:** Wants peace at any price

Do you recognise yourself in this list?

All these roles have both positive and negative aspects. For example, the devil's advocate may help people to see the other side to a proposal or she may simply point out the problems associated with it. The peacemaker may diffuse tense situations or he may stop useful discussion because it makes him feel uneasy.

Roles are important, but when people apply their workplace personas to other areas of their lives, it can cause problems.

Consider the expert. The expert has developed knowledge and expertise in his workplace over many years. He's used to people seeking him out for consultations and looking to him for answers. This is a valued role in the workplace, but the expert needs to know where his expertise ends and not get trapped into the behaviour of offering his advice on all subjects.

As an ex-teacher, I'm used to giving directions — usually in a very loud voice, as my family likes to remind me. How many times have I heard: 'You're not at work now, Mum!'

Sometimes, it's hard to let go of the role you play at work and drop your mask. However, if you're considering retirement, your children are probably grown up and capable of making their own good decisions — without your input.

Changing hats

Now is a good time to really assess the roles you play both at work and at home and to begin making some changes, if they're needed. Here are some tips to get you started:

- ✔ **Clarifier:** If it weren't for you, the initiator would have everyone climbing Mount Everest without an oxygen mask. As the clarifier, you know all the *I*'s must be dotted and the *T*'s crossed. Be aware that this can stifle spontaneous behaviour, however. You're not playing for sheep stations now, so try to go with the flow.

- ✔ **Devil's advocate:** This is a very important role in the business world. As the devil's advocate, you're relied on to put forward the opposite point of view so that people can think the project through. However, now's the time for some spontaneity. Try saying 'yes' to a family member's proposal and allow her to think about the pitfalls by herself.

- ✔ **Expert:** You're an essential part of the workforce — everyone wants to consult you for your expert knowledge on the subject. However, you need to leave the role at work and make a conscious decision to find out what your family and friends are expert in. Ask *their* opinions and defer to their decisions.

- ✔ **Implementer:** Tasks have to be done and you know how to get them going — without you, the clarifier and the devil's advocate would be debating the project for the next year. At home, be careful not to steamroll your family and friends into taking on something new before they're ready.

- ✔ **Initiator:** You're full of bright ideas — everyone at work expects you to be the brainstormer who gets the ball rolling. At home, try to hold back and let someone else come up with some ideas as well.

- ✔ **Judge:** Someone has to make a decision and the role has most often fallen to you. Unfortunately, at home this behaviour is likely to give rise to mutiny. Try getting involved in more discussion and leave the decision making to others from time to time.

- ✔ **Peacemaker:** You dislike argument and feel the world would work more efficiently if everyone made an attempt to agree. Try to recognise that discussion has its place — even if things do become a little heated.

Spending Time with Your Family

As you age, you probably feel more drawn to your family, just like the people documented in the television show, *Can We Help?* Each week, the show follows men and women in their 50s and 60s who suddenly feel the need to reconnect with brothers and sisters they haven't seen for 40 years or more.

Retirement also offers you a chance to get to know your parents, if they're still alive. Busy lives and the concept of the nuclear family have led to Baby Boomers being separated from their parents during their working lives. Families are unlikely to have more than two generations living together under the one roof. Your parents are more likely to be living on their own or in aged-care accommodation than with you in an extended family.

Spending time with grandchildren gives you the opportunity to impart family values and strengthen family ties — as well as have a great time doing so. As your grandchild grows you'll be able to look at the world through the eyes of a new generation. Your grandchild will gain stability and a sense of family history from you.

Grandparenting (and loving it)

Most grandparents enjoy spending time with their grandchildren enormously. Usually they say, with a smile, that the best part is being able to hand the grandchildren back at the end of the day — they can have all the joy without the angst.

Grandchildren connect you to the world in a new way. Whereas you may remember caring for your own babies as a blur, with your grandchildren you're able to experience the joy of caring for babies or young children without the exhaustion. You can bring a fresh perspective to their day, and they to yours. It's wonderful to be useful to your own children while enjoying baby cuddles and walks.

Sometimes you may disagree with your children's parenting styles and decisions. However, where your grandchildren are concerned it's important you respect their parents' decisions on parenting. Always check with the children's parents before giving gifts, and respect the parents' attitudes to food and other activities — no matter what your views may be.

Grandparenting activities

Grandparenting is a natural part of life. After your grandchildren arrive, you wonder how you ever got by without them. Here are some tips you can use to strengthen your bond with your grandchildren and keep them occupied when you do those necessary childminding stints.

- ✔ **Be a role model for the future generation.** Provide love, care and understanding. Both men and women have a strong sense of wanting to provide care for those they're close to.

- ✔ **Become the family historian.** Keep photo albums up-to-date. You can do this on the Internet or in the traditional way. Keep family traditions alive or create some if you don't have any. You may be surprised how much children appreciate a regular Sunday lunch with their cousins.

- ✔ **Create a memory album dedicated to each grandchild.** This album can contain snaps of each grandchild from birth to the present time. You can also include pictures of grandparents and great grandparents.

- ✔ **Exchange knowledge — don't just impart it.** Get involved with football cards or other fads that your grandchildren are interested in. Take your grandchildren to the zoo and let them tell you about the frogs and reptiles.

✔ **Get involved in your grandchildren's hobbies and get them involved in yours.** Your grandchildren are born understanding the Internet and all the related technology. With their help you can set up your own Web page when you're travelling, so they can keep in touch with you. Most children are interested in learning to knit or cook, or to play cricket or bowls if you're willing to teach them. And they love working in the vegetable patch with you — especially if you give them their own section to look after.

✔ **Go on walks with your grandchildren and gather leaves.** Young children really like pasting things on paper, so gather supplies on nature walks or have lots of magazine pictures on hand. A favourite activity of mine as a child was making doll's furniture from matchboxes.

✔ **Join in with your grandchildren's activities.** Take them to the local pool for swimming lessons or, if you're super fit, take them jogging with you. Get involved in their sport activities as a team manager or coach.

✔ **Listen to your grandchildren and keep their confidence.** One of the most valued aspects of grandparents is their ability to listen and not judge.

✔ **Provide continuity in a society where a child's life might be fragmented.** Many children spend their time divided between crèche, school, after-school care, home and sometimes parents.

✔ **Take your grandchildren to museums and galleries.** Older children enjoy museums and may even be able to teach you about all sorts of things. Try taking them to art galleries and concerts too.

Do some reading on child development so that you're ready for the different stages in your grandchildren's lives. I know your own children went through these stages too, but ideas change — and I know I'd handle some stages in my children's lives differently if I had my time again.

A little knowledge doesn't hurt, but don't use it to give your own children a lesson on parenting: I can guarantee it won't be appreciated.

Avoiding over-involvement

You need to set boundaries as far as looking after your grandchildren is concerned. Many grandparents feel pressured to take on more childminding than they can cope with. Set limits. Outline how much time you're prepared to babysit, and set aside time for your own activities — perhaps a golf or craft day that's sacred. This may sound tough, but you have to look after your own health and wellbeing.

Remember the oxygen mask principle: When the plane is going down and the oxygen masks fall from the overhead console, you must put on your own mask before putting one on your child. You're no good to anyone if you're unconscious.

Becoming the full-time carer of your grandchildren

Being a grandparent is a natural step, but when people had longer working lives and died younger, they had little time to devote to the younger generation. Now, some grandparents take on the role of the five-days-a-week carer while their own children work full-time.

Another growing trend is for grandparents to have sole responsibility for their grandchildren as full-time carers. If an adult with children dies, is ill, has an addiction or for some other reason can no longer care for their children, a grandparent is often the most obvious choice of carer for the children. Becoming a full-time grandparent carer isn't easy. A number of government agencies recognise this and are setting aside funds for sole-carer grandparents.

If you care for a grandchild full-time, check out the groups that can provide you with support. For instance, the Grandparents and Grandchildren Society Australia Inc (GAGS) provides emotional, social and physical support for grandparents raising grandchildren. The society has a newsletter, and organises meetings and social outings. Call 02 6652 5545 or email deanneokeefe@hotmail.com for more details.

The Seniors.gov.au Web site at www.seniors.gov.au has information on the grandparenting program run by the Council of the Ageing and on family assistance payments. The Web site also has information on legal services you may need, as well as a list of grandparent support organisations.

Becoming a volunteer grandparent

If you don't have grandchildren but would like to become involved with the younger generation, you can become a volunteer grandparent.

Local schools and kindergartens often want older people to come to grandparent and special friend's day. Also, some local councils, such as Hobsons Bay City Council, advertise for volunteer grandparents to give support and companionship to disabled children and their families. Contact your local council to see whether such programs operate in your area.

Extended Families Australia at www.extendedfamilies.org.au is an organisation that pairs older people in a grandparenting role with children with disabilities.

You need a Working With Children check before you can work with children in a paid or voluntary capacity. You can obtain the forms to apply for this check from the justice commission in your state or from your prospective workplace.

Ageing parents: Bridging the gap

It's easy to get caught up in a hectic lifestyle. Time flies and suddenly you realise that you don't *really* know your parents. Many parents of Baby Boomers lived through the Depression and World War II. Often, these people experienced events they were reluctant to talk about at the time, but that obviously had a huge impact on their lives. It can be fascinating to sit down with your parents and talk to them about their early lives. And more often than not, they appreciate your interest and the time you spend with them.

Delving into your family history

It's natural at this stage in your life to begin wondering where your family came from. You have generations following you and now you have the time to investigate who you are and where you fit in the scheme of things. You're aware that your family's story may become lost if you don't track it down and share it with other members of the family. Finding out more about where your family came from is endlessly fascinating. If you're interested in working on your family's history, here are some suggestions to help you get started.

✔ Make time to interview your parents and elderly relatives and record your conversations. Or give your parents a dictaphone or an iPod with a voice-recording function and ask them to talk into it, relating stories and family history. You can then transcribe the tape using speech-recognition software, such as Dragon NaturallySpeaking (www.voicerecognition.com.au).

Think about your own life and ask your parents questions so that you can draw a comparison between your life and theirs. Ask your parents about shopping, entertainment, growing up and other ordinary life events.

✔ You can print out this record for other family members. Or you can add the information to your grandchild's album (see the section 'Grandparenting (and loving it)' earlier in this chapter). This record provides a wonderful keepsake and insight into another generation.

Memories

To publish my mother's and father's memoirs, I contacted Seaview Press, a small South Australian company that specialises in helping people who want to self-publish. Before the stories could be printed, I had to put them into Word documents and edit them (as the editing service costs more). I supplied numerous photographs, some of which were incorporated into the text while others were used as centreplates.

When my father saw the proofs of his book he was amazed at how much material he'd produced. And there was more to tell, because we took his story only to the end of World War II.

The press produced 50 copies of a very professional looking soft-cover book for each story. Self-publishing costs money, but the company advertises the books for sale on its Web site and also in a brochure.

My mother's book has sold out. This was not a money-making exercise: It was done so that my extended family could have an understanding of where they came from.

My mother's book included a family tree, and this has since sent other members of the family off on their own genealogy searches.

The process of recording and publishing my parents' stories gave me an insight into their lives that I would not have ordinarily gained.

Alternatively, if you have plenty of material, say, enough for an 80-plus page book, you may like to have your story published by one of the many small publishing houses around. You need to have your story typed up and edited before you hand it over for printing. Or you can send your story to a copy centre and have it photocopied, bound and covered: This option is heaps cheaper than publishing, but still satisfying.

✔ After you've found out a little of your family history, you may well be hooked and wish to delve further, beyond the memories of living relatives. See *Tracing Your Family History Online For Dummies*, Australian Edition, by Matthew Helm (Wiley Publishing Australia Pty Ltd) for more information.

Avoiding carer burnout

If you're responsible for caring for an elderly parent or relative, you can easily fall into the trap of feeling guilty about your caring role. Other relatives and friends may say that you're not doing enough for your relative — or you may feel that you do too much and begin to feel resentful of the person you're caring for.

If you suspect that you're suffering carer burnout, take some steps to prevent it.

- ✔ **Have fun.** Don't fall into the habit of doing only dutiful activities with your elderly relative, such as cleaning and shopping. Once a month at least, make a point of doing something fun. Go somewhere special for lunch — or drive to a local beauty spot and have a picnic. Even if the weather's not perfect and you end up eating in the car, you feel better when you change your surroundings. The trip may even give you something to laugh about together later.

- ✔ **Set limits.** Give yourself some time off. This may sound harsh, but you have only a certain amount of energy to give to others. You have to be kind to yourself as well and renew your own energy supplies — or you may very likely be useless to yourself and your relative. Remember the oxygen mask principle — refer to the section 'Grandparenting (and loving it)' earlier in this chapter.

Making time for brothers, sisters and cousins

As time goes by, you can lose contact with brothers, sisters or other relatives. Perhaps you've moved interstate or overseas, or travel a lot. Or maybe your cousins, who you were close to as a young child, are busy with families of their own. Now you have the opportunity to rekindle family ties.

Hold regular get-togethers

When everyone's busy, family get-togethers don't just happen: Often, the only way to get the ball rolling is to start it yourself. If you'd like to keep in regular contact with your siblings and other relatives, try these suggestions.

- ✔ If your relations live nearby, make regular times to see each other and note the dates in your diary, so that you remember.

- ✔ If your family live interstate, arrange occasional weekend trips to see each other. With cheap air fares, you can probably book ahead to fly interstate every two months or so to meet up for the weekend. Or put aside time regularly to catch up with phone calls or emails.

✔ Host a family barbecue. If you'd like everyone to bring a dish, make up a menu list to refer to when guests ask what you'd like them to bring. Divide the meal into nibbles, salads, meat and desserts. Alternatively, ask each family group to bring their own meat, or supply the meat yourself and ask guests to bring the salads and desserts. If you go with the latter option, you'll also have something to serve if someone's running late.

✔ Do something fun together. Play golf, go ballooning. Meet up for early morning water aerobics, or a bike ride and breakfast. Go to a chic flick with your sister, or to a cricket match with your brother.

Set boundaries

Don't be the one who always organises the activities or pays every time — after a while, you won't enjoy your get-togethers and will end up being resentful. Ask your siblings to participate in organising the events too — most times, they just need a little encouragement.

Hold a family reunion

Family reunions are an enormous amount of work, but heaps of fun. You can go about arranging a family get-together in a number of ways. For example, you can host an event for all the family, or for females only or males only.

Most importantly, when you're dealing with a large number of people you need to plan well ahead. Here are some ideas to help make your task easier:

✔ **Decide on the venue well in advance.** The venue could be your house, or perhaps everyone could put in some money to hire a local hall. Bowling clubs make great venues. An added advantage of such a venue is that playing a game together such as bowls (or mini golf) helps prevent cliques forming and gets people mixing with those they don't know well and may not otherwise have much in common with.

✔ **Research accommodation options for family members who need somewhere to stay.** Make a list, and ensure that you cover a wide price range, from caravan parks to hotels.

✔ **Research your catering options.** For example:

• Ask everyone to provide a plate of food. Plan the menu beforehand and make a list so that allocating dishes is easy.

• Ask everyone to chip in to pay for professional caterers. Check out all the options, and don't forget to approach your friendly local cafes and delicatessens — they're often into catering for parties too.

Moving house to be closer to family

When you retire you may decide to sell up and move closer to your family. Such a move, whether between suburbs, interstate or overseas, has a number of benefits. For example:

- ✔ You can spend time with your elderly parents. It's a great opportunity to really get to know your parents and help them out in times of need.

- ✔ You can get to know your brothers and sisters again, enjoying shared memories and investigating new experiences.

- ✔ You can share in the joys of grandchildren and help your own children when they need you around.

However, you need to take some precautions before selling up and moving. First and foremost, you need to check that family members won't be moving on any time soon — you don't want to be chasing them around the country. You also need to check out the social scene and medical facilities in the new location. Chapter 10 has more tips on moving house.

Maintaining and Building Friendships

Leaving work means leaving a community — a place where you know people, and where you're able to interact, listen to others' problems and discuss your own. You share the same aims and general outlook as your colleagues. You can meet your workmates for lunch or coffee and you may even meet socially after work. At work, you're expected to be at a certain place at a certain time, and if you're not, someone will find out why.

When you wake up on the first morning after your retirement, you realise that you don't *have* to be anywhere! Nor do you have anyone to share the morning's problems with over a coffee. There's no-one to care where you are. This can be a frightening prospect, but you'll soon get into the swing of creating new networks.

Staying in touch

When changes occur in your life, you can easily let friendships slide. But keeping in touch with friends is crucial to maintaining a healthy outlook on life. Retirement is a time when the days can slide by ... months later you may look back and wonder what happened to your life — and your friends.

Perhaps you don't think of friendship as something you need to work at? However, maintaining friendships requires some groundwork.

Being organised and proactive are keys to maintaining your friendships:

- ✔ Keep an appointment diary and set aside regular time for catching up with your friends.
- ✔ Make time to exercise with a friend. A walk in the park or along the esplanade, followed by coffee, is a companionable way to spend some time together.
- ✔ Organise a shopping trip into the city and meet work friends for lunch.
- ✔ Send emails to your friends. Or better still, write letters or postcards: After all, finding a personal letter among the bills in the letterbox is a lot more special than receiving an email.

Going it alone

My friend Andrea retired from her job after the death of her mother. Andrea had been very close to her mother and found she needed time to come to terms with her grief. After years working in finance, Andrea wanted to take some time to find herself. She described her working life as getting up, going to work, visiting her mother and going home to bed. Weekends were usually reserved for recovering from the working week. Andrea was accustomed to dressing in the full work regalia of pantyhose, suit and full make-up.

Andrea didn't take the safe road to retirement. Although she had lived in Sydney for many years and owned property in Brisbane, where she also had many friends, she decided to retire to Melbourne where she knew no-one. This took Andrea way out of her safety zone. She had been secure in her work identity. Now, not only was she out of her work routine, she had also lost friends because she was no longer a well-paid executive.

Andrea describes those first few weeks in Melbourne as a time of living in tracksuits and watching Dr Phil on television. So she decided she needed to become organised. She began to keep an appointment diary again and made lists of activities for the day ahead. This helped her put some structure into her day.

Six months on, Andrea knew that she would return to Brisbane and resume a previous relationship, but she stayed on in her rented house in Melbourne until the end of the year: She was enjoying her new lifestyle. Having worked briefly in fashion design in San Francisco, she was attracted to the idea of handcrafts and had joined a knitting group. She took Pilates classes and volunteered at the Sacred Heart Mission in St Kilda.

Andrea has now set up house in Brisbane and says that, being an 'at home' type of person, she loves to do things around the house, like gardening, and prefers having a sense of being 'fixed, secure and belonging'. She feels more at peace with herself now and is better able to live the life she wants.

Cultivate the art of communicating outside the workplace.

- ✔ Become a good listener.
- ✔ Listen just to listen, not to solve problems or to give advice.
- ✔ Relax while you're listening. You don't have to score a point or win an argument.
- ✔ Show that you're listening with a nod of the head or a verbal cue.
- ✔ Forgive small slights. Everyone makes mistakes or has an attack of 'foot in mouth' from time to time. Don't dwell on these moments. Let them pass.
- ✔ Praise your friends. Look for the positive elements in your friendships and pass over the negatives.

Widening your circle of friends

Social isolation can be debilitating — and life-threatening. Isolation and its companion, depression, can lead to poor eating habits and the over-consumption of alcohol. The Better Health Channel Web site (www.better health.vic.gov.au) lists depression and isolation as two of the risk factors for heart attack. If you'd like to know more about this, check out the Better Health Victoria Web site.

Isolation can contribute to your feeling that retirement is an unsatisfactory state of affairs. To ensure that you don't become isolated in your retirement, put in some groundwork, preferably before you retire. Investigate a few groups to join so that you're in contact with others — say, a hobby group or an exercise group.

Men's Sheds is designed to counteract the growing problems that retired men can experience with isolation, loneliness and depression. At the 150 Men's Sheds across Australia, men can drop in, use equipment to make projects and hang out. Visit www.mensshed.org for more information and see Chapter 19.

Many community and church groups run activities and offer great opportunities for meeting new people. To find out what's happening in your area, check your local paper or try your local council's Web site.

Here's a random list of 10 of the hundreds of activities available in my area (they're probably available in your area too):

✔ **Aqua aerobics:** A wonderful exercise for those who prefer to keep their joints intact.

✔ **Belly dancing:** Hey, have a laugh as you exercise!

✔ **Bike-riding group:** For the hell riders or the more genteel.

✔ **Book club:** For improving your mind and meeting people.

✔ **Camera club:** Discover how to use your camera for your travels.

✔ **Computer classes:** You may know your way around a word processor or spreadsheet program, but how are you on Facebook?

✔ **Informative walks around the area:** Discover the history and secrets of your own suburb.

✔ **Knitting group:** Surprisingly, a variety of people join these groups.

✔ **Volunteer group:** Visit people who for whatever reason are afraid or unable to leave their homes — take them to the pool, teach them English or serve meals. See Chapter 15 for more information on volunteering.

✔ **Woodworking group:** An opportunity to make friends and work with wood under the guidance of an instructor.

Going bush

Bushwalking is an experience for the mind and the body: Not only do you exercise your muscles, you also acquire a deeper understanding of nature.

Bushwalking clubs can be a great way to meet new people. Clubs grade their walks from easy to difficult, so don't be daunted if you've never tried bushwalking before. An added bonus is that bushwalking groups often organise Australian and overseas travel on a budget.

When I joined a bushwalking club a few years ago, I was instantly welcomed by the group. I looked around me and saw that most members were retirees: I wondered how they'd keep up. Needless to say, I was the one who staggered out of the bush at Powelltown, Victoria, eight hours later followed only by the *whip* (the person who takes up the rear to make sure no-one is left behind). The rest of the group were sitting on logs having hot tea and cakes that they'd prepared earlier. We had crawled up muddy banks and slithered down them, crossed over old trestle bridges and disturbed an echidna — and I'd had an intimate encounter with a leech. I was hooked.

Visit the Bushwalking Australia Web site at www.bushwalkingaustralia.org.au for more information on bushwalking clubs in your local area.

When I retired I joined a local knitting group. The group often welcomes visitors from Europe, Asia and the United States, who drop by to knit and have a chat. After initially feeling a bit daggy about joining a knitting club, I'm now a proficient sock knitter. No sooner have I finished one pair than someone clamours for another.

Looking for more resources for retirees? Check out these Web sites:

✔ Life Activities at www.life.org.au, where you can find links to activities run by Life Activities Clubs. Life Activities Clubs operate in local areas and offer leisure, educational and social activities such as walks, cinema outings, picnics and lectures.

✔ Probus at www.probus.com.au is a system of clubs where semi-retired and retired people can meet to enjoy each other's company and participate in activities.

✔ The Council on the Ageing at www.cota.org.au, where you'll find heaps of information on retirement activities, as well as links to local COTA branches.

You don't need to be isolated. If your working life has been very structured, you may find it difficult at first to break into a new group, but you soon discover that everyone else is like you — looking for company and mental stimulation. Plus you find that your contribution is valued by the other members of the group.

Furry Friends

Animals: Most people consider themselves to be either a pet person or not. And pet lovers may consider themselves dog people or cat people, or even fish, snake and rat people. Pet ownership can have a number of benefits for retirees. For a start, if you own a pet you never have to come home to an empty house.

Of course, you need to exercise the utmost care when choosing your pet, because this creature will be totally dependent on you for a number of years. A big dog, like a Great Dane, may live for 8–10 years, but a smaller dog or cat can provide you with 15–20 years of love and affection.

Some pets, such as parrots, cockatoos, tortoises and donkeys, can live for 30–50 years or more, so if you're thinking about one of these pets you need to consider its future when you're no longer able to care for it.

Choosing a pet

Selecting your pet is a serious business, mainly because most pets — with the exception of butterflies and other insects — will be reliant on you for some years. I know those fluffy little bundles in that pet shop window look very tempting, but you need to do some preparation before you go pet shopping.

If you're considering getting a pet, ask yourself these questions:

- ✔ Are you able to spend a lot of time with your pet?

- ✔ Are you active or sedentary?

- ✔ Do you live in a house or an apartment?

- ✔ Do you have a garden? What size is your garden?

- ✔ Do you want a pure-bred animal, or are you happy to choose one from the pound?

- ✔ Do you want your animal for companionship, or for showing or breeding purposes?

- ✔ Do you want a young animal or one that's already trained?

- ✔ How much money do you want to spend on your pet, now and in the future?

On the Internet you can find several great Web sites to help you select the right pet for you. One example is PetNet at www.petnet.com.au. Simply enter your details and requirements, and PetNet provides you with a recommendation for the type of cat or dog that suits you and your lifestyle. For example, if you live in a townhouse or unit with a small but secure backyard and want a moderately active dog that you're willing to walk for 30 minutes a day, but do not want to spend more than one hour a week grooming, PetNet suggests a Boston terrier, whippet, beagle or short-haired dachshund.

Don't choose an active dog because you want to start exercising. If you don't already exercise now, having a pet is not likely to change this. Be careful about choosing a high-maintenance animal if you're not prepared to put in the hours and money required to keep your animal comfortable.

Rather than furry friends, perhaps you want to keep snakes or other reptiles as pets. If so, you probably need some specialist advice. Snakes can live for a long time. You also need to understand the legal requirements for keeping reptiles in Australia. Each state issues its own licences. Check your state's or territory's Web site for the necessary permits:

- ✔ **Australian Capital Territory:** Department of Territory and Municipal Services at www.tams.act.gov.au
- ✔ **New South Wales:** NSW National Parks at www.environment.nsw.gov.au/nationalparks
- ✔ **Northern Territory:** Parks and Wildlife Commission of the Northern Territory at www.nt.gov.au
- ✔ **Queensland:** Environmental Protection Agency at www.epa.qld.gov.au
- ✔ **South Australia:** Department for Environment and Heritage at www.environment.sa.gov.au/parks
- ✔ **Tasmania:** Department of Primary Industries and Water at www.dpiw.tas.gov.au
- ✔ **Victoria:** Department of Sustainability and Environment at www.dse.vic.gov.au
- ✔ **Western Australia:** Department of Environment and Conservation at www.calm.wa.gov.au

Maintaining a healthy partnership

You may have heard that pet owners are often healthier than other members of the community. They're reported to have lower blood pressure and pulse rates and to pay fewer visits to the doctor than people who don't own pets.

Stroking and patting a pet can reduce the physiological indicators of stress, including high blood pressure. Pet owners enjoy unconditional love from their animals. No matter what may happen during your day, your pet is always there, ready to listen to you and greet you with affection and delight.

Pets are used as companion animals in hospitals and nursing homes. The presence of a pet therapy dog in a hospital has the potential to decrease medication doses for patients. So keeping your pet healthy has the added bonus of keeping *you* healthy.

Try these suggestions for maintaining your pet's health:

- ✔ **Feed your pet a healthy diet.** Think about the food you and your pet eat. Ask your vet for advice, if you're not sure.

- ✔ **Groom your animal regularly.** The act of spending time looking after your animal's coat is also 'time out' for you.

- ✔ **Walk your dog regularly, preferably twice a day.** Check out how much walking your dog needs. Border collies, for example, need lots of exercise and stimulation. (I'm not sure you can walk your pet tarantula — and if it were me, the running away would be exercise enough.)

Finally, enjoy your pet's companionship. Take time to relax and talk to your animal.

Building friendships through pets

People who walk their dogs gain more than physical health benefits: They're seen as friendly and approachable. Walking your puppy makes you instantly popular — people want to stop and admire your cutie. Dog owners usually become part of a community group when they take their dog for exercise at off-leash parks. They're also more likely to greet each other than walkers without dogs.

You can join a club associated with your pet. For example, about 5,000 dog shows are conducted in Australia every year. Whereas in the United States owners can make money from dog shows, in Australia it's more a case of love than money — although if you win best of breed, your animal progeny could be worth big bucks (a show-quality kitten was recently sold for $1,500). Showing your animal can become a way of life. Many competitors make several interstate trips each year to show their animals. For them, the show circuit is their social life.

Part VI
The Part of Tens

Glenn Lumsden

'After all that exercise, what say we unclog those arteries?'

In this part ...

1 explore 10 secrets to a happy and healthy retirement. I also include 10 really useful Australian government Internet sites that you may find yourself accessing again and again as you plan and live your retirement dream.

Chapter 19

Ten Secrets to Happy Retirement

The best thing about retirement is the lack of deadlines and work responsibilities. You can operate to your own schedule. You can even totally reinvent yourself if you so wish. On the downside, as wonderful as it sounds, too much sitting in the sun — or in front of the television — idling away the hours isn't the best plan for a happy and healthy body and mind. You need to strike a balance.

This chapter gives you 10 easy ways to keep active and maintain good health in your retirement.

Keeping Fit

To get the most out of your retirement, good health is essential — and regular exercise will help you to maximise your health. If this is the first time you've thought about exercising since you were at school, don't worry — you're not alone. It's never too late to get active, just make sure that you start your exercise routine gradually and build up slowly. The most important thing is to find something you enjoy doing. Here are two great exercises that provide fun and fitness — and the chance to make new friends into the bargain.

Aqua exercise

Working out in water can be as easy or as strenuous as you make it. Because water supports you, it doesn't cause wear and tear on your muscles, joints and tendons, so you won't have the bone-jarring aches and pains that come with high-impact exercise like jogging or aerobics. Aqua exercise is a great way to begin an exercise regime — especially if you're carrying a bit of excess weight.

You can make up your own routine, swimming or walking up and down the pool for example, or you can join an aqua class such as aqua aerobics. Set to music, these classes are fun and challenging. They're also a great way to make new friends as you connect with the regulars.

Since aqua exercise isn't weight-bearing, you'll need to combine it with some other form of exercise such as walking or weight training to increase your bone density. Perhaps you can walk to the pool?

Don't forget to stay hydrated. You won't notice yourself sweating while you're in the pool, but you must remember to drink plenty of water during and after exercise.

Contact your local pool for details of classes, and see Chapter 7 to find out more about keeping fit and well in retirement.

Cycling

Cycling is another exercise that's easy on the joints because it's not weight-bearing. Start off slowly and work your way up to a higher level of fitness. You may experience some back strain to start with — and some pain in your rear. Buy a nice comfy gel seat unless you're a serious road rider.

You can spend thousands of dollars on your bike and clothes, but you'll be just as fine with the basics. Padded pants, gloves and a helmet are essentials. Make sure you get advice on getting your bike properly fitted so that the handlebars and seat position are right for you.

If you don't have very good balance and don't feel secure on a two-wheeler, investigate buying a recumbent bike or even an adult three-wheeler — all the rage in some suburbs for doing the shopping.

You can ride on your own or join a cycling group. And you don't have to cycle on the road: Most suburbs have some form of cycleway available. If you want a long ride in the country, you can find trails along disused railways and logging tramways in almost every state. You can find out more about these and cycling in general in Chapter 7.

You always ride into a headwind on the way home!

Staying Healthy

Having a healthy mind and body, and therefore an overall sense of wellbeing, means you not only need to stay fit but also to eat well, connect with others and take charge of your finances. Here are some quick tips for doing just that.

Eating your way to good health

Have you noticed already that as you age, you need to eat less to maintain the same body weight? It's a fact of life for many Australians that with the more mature years comes the inevitable middle-aged spread. I swear I went to sleep happily on the eve of my 54th birthday and woke up five kilos heavier the next day!

Good nutrition helps maintain a healthy body and may even reduce the ageing process, and combined with regular physical activity it may prevent disease and improve your quality of life. So, rather than dieting to lose your excess weight (and so risk missing out on valuable nutrients) you're better off eating a nutritiously adequate diet, keeping physically active and maintaining muscle mass.

Here are some tips to help develop healthy eating habits:

- Choose foods low in salt.
- Consume only moderate amounts of sugar and foods containing added sugar.
- Eat smaller portions. Have three main meals per day and limit snacks to twice a day.
- Eat plenty of cereals (including breads, rice, pasta and noodles), preferably wholegrain.

- ✔ Eat plenty of vegetables, legumes and fruits.

- ✔ Have more oily fish.

- ✔ Restrict your meat intake. Eat lean meat, fish, poultry and/or alternatives.

- ✔ Include milk, yoghurt, cheese and/or alternatives. Choose reduced-fat varieties where possible.

- ✔ Limit saturated fat and moderate total fat intake.

- ✔ Limit your alcohol intake if you choose to drink.

Enjoying time out with others

Check out these two great organisations where you can get together with like-minded others and have fun: One for the boys and one for the girls.

Men's Sheds

If you want a shed but have nowhere to put it, or just want to spend some time with men who share your interests, then a Men's Shed may be for you. The Australian Men's Sheds Association (AMSA) is a not-for-profit organisation that helps men to link up with or start Men's Sheds in their own local community. The sheds offer a place where you can catch up with your mates, work on projects, swap tips and help others. Besides doing your own projects, you can help make toys, furniture and items for charities and hospitals. You can also access information and services on topics such as health and wellbeing.

Visit AMSA's Web site at www.mensshed.org to find a shed in your local area. If you don't have a local shed, you can start one yourself with help from AMSA. The association will give you advice on issues such as:

- ✔ Administration

- ✔ Discussions with local community groups

- ✔ Finding sponsors and other funding

- ✔ Initial planning

- ✔ Insurance

Red Hats

The Red Hat Society started in the United States when Sue Ellen Cooper bought her friend a red hat for her 55th birthday. Since then Red Hat Societies have sprung up around the world. The order of the day is for women to get together and have fun. There aren't many rules to follow, except if you're over 50 you must wear a red hat and purple attire to official functions, and if you're under 50 you must wear a pink hat and lavender attire.

To join these happy women go to www.annabella.net/redhat/queens.html or www.matildarose2.com/index.htm and find your local Red Hat chapter.

Staying in touch

After you leave work and no longer see your work colleagues and friends on a regular basis, you can easily slip into a solitary existence. You may need to make a little effort to keep connected with your family and friends, but doing so can make a big contribution to your health and feelings of wellbeing. Make time to see old friends and go out and make new ones.

If you have grandchildren, make sure that you spend some quality time with them. You may find that you're more relaxed with your grandchildren than you were with your own children. You can give your grandchildren the gift of your time, which is always really appreciated, especially when they're little.

Flip back to Chapter 18 for more tips on staying connected.

Money matters

Money *does* matter, especially when you realise you're going to spend the next 30 years or more without earning an income. You have to make your money work hard for you. Before you retire, try to make sure that you're in the best possible financial situation to leave work. Find out exactly how much superannuation you have and in which funds. Get some good financial advice and take the time to learn as much as you possibly can about your finances.

After you've retired, it's up to you to make the most of the finances you have. Check out what government pensions or concessions you may be eligible for to make your budget stretch further. You may not be able to travel around the world first class, but you can still enjoy your local community.

Find out more on how to make the most of your retirement dollars in Chapters 3, 4 and 5.

Think very carefully before you act as guarantor for someone such as your son or daughter. If that person is unable to pay back his or her loan and you have guaranteed the money with your house, the bank can — and will — sell your house to recoup its money. This would be absolutely devastating for you and can cause trauma within your family unit.

Fun Things to do With Your Time

Retirement should be all about having fun, doing things you enjoy. What have you always wanted to do but never had the time? Learn a new language? Travel through Tuscany? See more of Australia? Finally finish all those UFOs (unfinished objects) you started when you took up your hobby 20 years ago? Here are some great ideas to keep you active and enjoying your retirement.

Heading back to class

Your brain needs exercise to keep it working efficiently. You can help keep it supple and functioning well by setting it some challenges, like learning another language.

You may like to begin your journey back to study in the relaxed atmosphere of a neighbourhood house or University of the Third Age class, where you'll learn something new and make friends as well. Everyone's in the same boat, and you don't have to pass exams.

If you haven't been to school for a long time, or weren't particularly adept at your lessons, taking up study again can be daunting. Remember, however, that you're a completely different person from the one who sat in the back row and gazed out of the window. As a mature-aged student you bring so much life experience and understanding to your learning that concepts which were once difficult to master will now fall into place.

Check out Chapter 13 if you want to hit the books again.

Making stuff and collecting things

Finding the right hobby adds another dimension to your retirement. Your hobby may be something you've always wanted to do or it can be a whole new venture. The important thing is that it enhances your life. If you don't already have an interest, don't be afraid to try lots of different hobbies until you find one or two that really grab you.

You can turn your hobby into a social affair by joining a group of like-minded people. By being involved in a group you'll not only keep in contact with others but also gain useful information and be able to swap and trade items.

You may even decide to turn your hobby into a money-making venture. Chapter 16 has lots of ideas for hobbies and advice if you're thinking of turning your hobby into a small business.

On the road again

Like many Australians you may get the travel bug and want to head off around Australia. But before you rush off and dispose of your house, pack up your van and get going, you need to do some research. If you plan ahead before you go, sorting out the big issues like finances, where to look for work if you need to and what to do with your house, as well as things like how to look after your vehicle, tow your caravan, find somewhere to stay and survive in the outback, you should have a safe and enjoyable trip.

One place where you can find much of the information you need, as well as stories of those who've travelled before you, is the Internet. A number of Web sites are dedicated to Grey Nomads. A good one to start with is ExploreOz at www.exploroz.com, which offers a comprehensive guide to travelling around Australia and is easy to navigate. Make sure you're prepared for your trip and you'll find some great adventures on the Grey Nomad trail and meet many new friends.

You can get more information on joining the Grey Nomad brigade from Chapter 12.

Volunteering

Helping others not only takes your mind off your troubles but also gives you a sense of satisfaction as you see how others can benefit from your actions. When you put your hand up to volunteer, your days take on a definite shape and your mind stays active as you plan how to go about your job.

Thousands of organisations are crying out for volunteers, both at home and overseas. Often, you won't need any formal qualifications to help out, just life experience and a genuine willingness to help make a difference. You can volunteer at your local community centre, raise funds for a national charity, mentor schoolchildren, look after injured animals, or do your bit to help save the environment or an endangered species — no matter what your interests, you'll find a volunteer role to suit you. You'll also have the chance to connect with many people and perhaps acquire new skills.

See Chapter 15 for the lowdown on volunteering.

Chapter 20

Ten Useful Internet Sites for Retirees

In This Chapter

▶ Finding reliable information online

▶ Linking to Australian government Web sites

*T*his chapter covers my suggestions for 10 useful Australian government Web sites to help keep you up-to-date and informed concerning your finances, health and wellbeing in your retirement. You need to visit these sites to discover the full range of topics. Of course, with the millions of Web sites around, as you're surfing online you may discover other sites that you think are equally useful or interesting.

Bookmark your favourite sites by clicking on 'Add to Favorites' so you can easily find them again.

Online Resources and Tools

The Internet can be a valuable tool when you're seeking information and advice. However, not all Web sites are created equal in terms of providing reliable, quality and up-to-date information, and some sites are easier to navigate than others. The sites listed here are a safe starting point in your online research.

The Australian government's Web sites are easy to navigate and give you the right information every time.

Australia.gov.au

The Australian Government site at www.australia.gov.au is a portal to the Web sites of all government departments. If you're not sure which department you need, you can search this site for more than 300 categories. The user-friendly site has a list of government quick links and government initiatives, helpful topics like National Nutrition week, a weather report and a place to have your say.

For example, if you click on 'Family, Home & Community' you find links to numerous Web sites on various topics, including aged care, community organisations, finding a missing friend or relative, messages from the prime minister, and the national public toilet map — so you can plan your trip from Sydney to Brisbane and know every public toilet stop along the way!

Australian Biography

Australian Biography at www.australianbiography.gov.au contains interviews with some very interesting and remarkable Australians, including the following:

- Faith Bandler, a civil rights activist
- Franco Belgiorno Nettis, an industrialist
- HC 'Nugget' Coombs, an economist
- Lily Ah Toy, a Northern Territory pioneer

Compiled from the *Australian Biography* TV series, the site has an easy-to-access index as well as full interview transcripts. This site is great for catching up with Australian personalities and history.

Australian Department of Foreign Affairs and Trade

The Australian Department of Foreign Affairs and Trade (DFAT) Web site at www.dfat.gov.au offers an advisory service for Australians travelling overseas. The site lists the destinations that the Department advises against travelling to and those you should reconsider travelling to. Take note of these travel advisories — if you ignore them and travel to one of these destinations, then have to be evacuated because of civil or military unrest, you may jeopardise your insurance.

The site also has information about road safety overseas, passport applications, health alerts, international scams, severe weather, and airport security regulations. In addition, the site explains how Australia's consular services can assist you when you're travelling overseas. Consular officials can provide assistance and advice if you become seriously injured or ill and can liaise with your relatives. Consular officials can also visit you if you've been imprisoned overseas, but they can't get you out of prison or pay your hotel or medical bills.

Australian Government Attorney-General's Department

The Attorney-General's Department aims to achieve a just and secure society. At the Department's Web site at www.ag.gov.au you find an easy-to-use directory that lists the areas the Department covers. These range from crime prevention and information law (which covers topics like copyright and privacy) to human rights and anti-discrimination.

By clicking on these topics, you're linked to relevant Web sites. For example, if you click on 'All Commonwealth legislation' you're taken to the Attorney-General's Department's ComLaw Web site. This site is part of Australian Law Online, which aims to give the community easy and low- or no-cost access to the law. Here you can check out new or commonly viewed legislation on topics such as air navigation, bankruptcy, crime, customs and tax.

Australian Taxation Office

The Australian Taxation Office (ATO) Web site at www.ato.gov.au provides all the information you need to know about taxation. You can complete your tax returns online, find answers to frequently asked tax questions, determine what you can and can't claim, and calculate how much tax you're likely to pay.

The site also links to the ATO Superannuation Web site. The super site has information concerning how to access and manage your superannuation benefits. The downloadable pamphlet 'Super and Your Retirement' covers accessing your super, starting a TRIP and how tax applies to your super and other entitlements. You can also find information on choosing a super fund, employer contributions, growing your super, super and tax, and termination benefits.

If you think you may have some lost super, try searching using the online tool, SuperSeeker, on the ATO's site.

Centrelink

Centrelink is an Australian Government statutory agency that assists people to become self-sufficient and supports those in need. At Centrelink's Web site at www.centrelink.gov.au you can use the handy A–Z directory to help you find information on the site. For example, under 'A' you'll find links to information about the age pension and age pension claim forms, as well as an assets fact sheet, which explains what's considered an asset for assessable purposes.

This site has heaps of information if you've retired or are planning to retire. For example, you find information about

- ✔ Concession and healthcare cards
- ✔ Payments for retirees, such as the age pension
- ✔ Pension loans scheme
- ✔ Pension bonus scheme and allowances

You can find out about the Financial Information Service's financial and lifestyle seminars, which are held for people who want to know how to prepare for retirement and to explain pension options.

You can also download useful publications, such as the booklet 'Are You Planning for or Needing Help in Retirement?', the 'Retirement Payment Rates' fact sheet and *News for Seniors* magazine.

Department of Health and Ageing

The Department of Health and Ageing's Web site at www.health.gov.au is a valuable resource for information about ageing and caring for the aged. For example, you can access aged-care forms, aged-care advocacy and aged-care assessment teams. See Chapter 9 to find out how valuable this information is if you need help caring for an older relative.

The site also contains information on hearing services, mental health, and nutrition and healthy eating, as well as an events calendar that covers events such as beyondblue Anxiety and Depression Awareness month and Pink Ribbon day.

For example, if you click on 'Nutrition and Healthy Eating' you find out how many serves of cereal, dairy, fruit, protein and vegetables you should eat for your age and how much exercise you should do. You can also view a day's diet plan, get tips on the important vitamins and minerals you need for your age group and use the calculator to calculate your body mass index (BMI) to find out whether you're the correct weight or heading for obesity.

FIDO

FIDO at www.fido.gov.au is the consumer Web site of the Australian Securities & Investments Commission. The site covers various topics, including

- ✔ **About you:** The site lists organisations that can help you to plan your retirement and a radio program you can listen to on planning your retirement. You can also find out whether your money will last as long as you hope to.
- ✔ **Financial products:** The site has tips on super funds, retirement income products, insurance, how to safeguard your money in the bank and the share market.
- ✔ **Money tips:** As well as key tips about money management, the site has information on budgeting, dealing with debt, finding out how much money you need in retirement and how to get the most out of your super.

You also find out more about scams such as fake bank emails, superannuation scams, Nigerian letter and lottery scams, and pyramid and Ponzi schemes, and you can download publications and booklets on various topics.

Medicare

The Medicare Web site at www.medicareaustralia.gov.au does more than just provide claim forms and duplicate Medicare cards. It also has information about Medicare's full range of services, including how to enrol for Medicare, what Medicare covers and the Medicare Safety Net, as well as:

- ✔ Australian Organ Donation Register
- ✔ External Breast Prostheses Reimbursement Program
- ✔ National Bowel Cancer Screening Program
- ✔ Pharmaceutical Benefits Scheme

In addition, if you're planning to travel overseas, you can check the site to see in which countries you can be treated under the Medicare scheme. Note, however, that Medicare stresses that you should still take out travel insurance, because Medicare won't cover the cost of private doctors or hospitals, or medical evacuations (which can cost up to $300,000).

Office of the Public Trustee

For information about making a will, administering a deceased estate, applying for probate, granting an enduring power of attorney or setting up trusts, check the Web site for the Office of the Public Trustee in your state or territory:

- ✔ **Australian Capital Territory:** Public Advocate of the ACT at www.publicadvocate.act.gov.au
- ✔ **New South Wales:** The Public Trustee of New South Wales at www.pt.nsw.gov.au
- ✔ **Northern Territory:** The Office of the Public Trustee of the Northern Territory at www.nt.gov.au/justice/pubtrust
- ✔ **Queensland:** The Public Trustee of Queensland at www.pt.qld.gov.au
- ✔ **South Australia:** The Public Trustee of South Australia at www.publictrustee.sa.on.net
- ✔ **Tasmania:** The Public Trustee for Tasmania at www.publictrustee.tas.gov.au
- ✔ **Victoria:** State Trustees of Victoria at www.statetrustees.com.au
- ✔ **Western Australia:** The Public Trustee for Western Australia at www.justice.wa.gov.au

Index

Notes

Notes

Notes

FOR DUMMIES®

Business & Investment

1-74031-109-4
$39.95

1-74031-124-8
$39.95

0-7314-0838-1
$54.95

0-7314-0715-6
$39.95

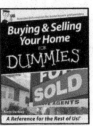

1-74031-166-3
$39.95

0-7314-0724-5
$39.95

1-74031-146-9
$39.95

0-7314-0710-5
$39.95

0-7314-0787-3
$39.95

0-7314-0762-8
$39.95

1-74031-091-8
$39.95

0-7314-0746-6
$29.95

FOR DUMMIES®

Reference

Work / Life Balance FOR DUMMIES

0-7314-0723-7
$34.95

World Poverty FOR DUMMIES

0-7314-0699-0
$34.95

Sustainable Living FOR DUMMIES

1-74031-157-4
$39.95

Wedding Planning FOR DUMMIES

0-7314-0721-0
$34.95

Gardening FOR DUMMIES

1-74031-007-1
$39.95

Australia's Dangerous Creatures FOR DUMMIES

0-7314-0722-9
$29.95

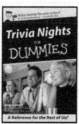

Trivia Nights FOR DUMMIES

0-7314-0594-3
$24.95

English Grammar FOR DUMMIES

0-7314-0752-0
$34.95

Technology

The Internet FOR DUMMIES

0-7314-0985-X
$39.95

QuickBooks QB FOR DUMMIES

0-7314-0761-X
$39.95

MYOB Software FOR DUMMIES

0-7314-0941-8
$39.95

eBay FOR DUMMIES

1-74031-159-0
$39.95

FOR DUMMIES®

Health & Fitness

1-74031-143-4
$39.95

1-74031-140-X
$39.95

0-7314-0596-X
$34.95

1-74031-094-2
$39.95

1-74031-009-8
$39.95

1-74031-044-6
$39.95

1-74031-059-4
$39.95

1-74031-074-8
$39.95

1-74031-011-X
$39.95

1-74031-173-6
$39.95

0-7314-0595-1
$34.95

0-7314-0644-3
$39.95

Printed in Australia
20 Nov 2024
LP037329